THE MEMORIES THAT DO NOT FADE . . .

The polished black marble of the Vietnam Memorial in Washington is mirrorlike in appearance. As I looked into it, I saw my reflection as well as the names. As I read and touched the inscriptions, the wall became a screen, and images I thought I did not recall, or had done my best not to, were vivid and clear. The sights, sounds, and emotions of every day my fellow soldiers died were as intense as if happening yesterday—or today.

At each panel, I paused and stared at the names in my own reflection. Why them and not me? I looked for my own name and was relieved and perhaps a bit ashamed that it was not etched alongside my comrades' names. . . .

Also by Michael Lee Lanning
Published by Ivy Books:

THE ONLY WAR WE HAD

VIETNAM
1969-1970:

A COMPANY
COMMANDER'S JOURNAL

Michael Lee Lanning

IVY BOOKS • NEW YORK

Ivy Books
Published by Ballantine Books
Copyright © 1988 by Michael Lee Lanning

Grateful acknowledgement is made to the following for permission to
reprint previously published material:

Army Times Publishing Company: text excerpt from a cartoon by Michael T. Hodgson which appeared in *Army Times*. Used by permission.

Henry Holt and Company, Inc.: excerpt from the poem ''Stopping by
Woods on a Snowy Evening'' by Robert Frost. Copyright 1923 by Holt,
Rinehart and Winston and renewed 1951 by Robert Frost. Reprinted by
permission of Henry Holt and Company, Inc.

Harold Matson Company, Inc.: excerpts from CASTLE KEEP by William Eastlake. Copyright © 1965 by William Eastlake. Used by permission.

Newsweek, Inc.: excerpts from the November 10, 1969 and November
24, 1969 issues of *Newsweek*. Copyright © 1969 by Newsweek, Inc. All
rights reserved. Reprinted by permission.

Harold Ober Associates, Inc.: excerpt from COMPANY K by William
March. Used by permission.

Library of Congress Catalog Card Number: 87-91054

ISBN - 0-8041-0187-6

Manufactured in the United States of America

First Edition: March 1988

ACKNOWLEDGEMENT OF QUOTED MATERIAL

p. 28 Simon & Schuster, © 1952, used by permission.

pps. 38–40 NEWSWEEK. © 1969, by NEWSWEEK, Inc. All rights reserved. Used by permission.

pps. 85–86 NEWSWEEK, © 1969, by NEWSWEEK, Inc. All rights reserved. Used by permission.

p. 126 Robert Frost, "Stopping by Woods on a Snowy Evening," © 1966. Henry Holt and Company, Inc. Used by permission.

pps. 259–260 CASTLE KEEP, © 1965, William Eastlake. Used by permission.

p. 261 Michael T. Hodgson and ARMY TIMES, © 1970. Used by permission.

p. 270 William March, COMPANY K., © 1984, Arbor House. Used by permission.

for . . .
Reveilee Ann
and
Meridith Moore

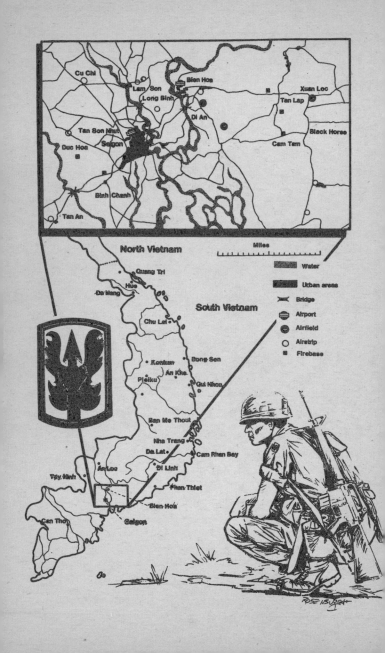

INTRODUCTION

It has often been said that every man who goes to war has the material for at least one book. When I began writing about my time in Vietnam nearly fifteen years after my return from the conflict, I initially thought my "one book" would be an extremely thin volume. Long months and many worn typewriter ribbons later, I discovered that the memories were so vivid and the happenings so intensely recalled that one book was not sufficient to relate what a year in combat with an infantry company was really like.

The title of the first volume was easy to formulate. With all the negative attitudes toward our Vietnam involvement, GIs learned to shrug and say, "It wasn't much of a war, but it was the only war we had." That statement, however, did not mean that we had not done our job as well as, and perhaps better than, those sent to far off battlefields before us.

THE ONLY WAR WE HAD (Ivy Books, 1987) relates my first six months in Vietnam with the 199th Light Infantry Brigade in the booby-trap-plagued rice paddies of the Delta region and later in the rubber plantations and thick jungles south of War Zone D near Xuan Luc. The half-year includes five months as an infantry platoon leader with C Company of the 2nd Batalion, 3rd Infantry, followed by a month as the leader of the Batalion's E Company Reconnaissance Platoon.

The combination of terror and hardship, generously mixed with extended periods of boredom, had transformed my initial naivety about war from movie-theater glory into harsh reality. I had aged in time beyond years. All that mattered any longer was the survival of my men and myself. I no longer thought in terms of patriotism nor was I concerned about the validity of the war itself. Killing the enemy and destroying anything that belonged to him was merely a way to insure our own longevity.

After six months in the field, officers normally rotated to relatively safe staff jobs in rear areas. When my time came, I had no desire to leave the field, for command of a company had become my objective. Despite the fact that I had been in the Army for less than 17 months and was still more than half a year from meeting minimum requirements of time in grade for captain, I felt I was ready for command. It was where I firmly believed my experience and abilities would best contribute.

Fortunately the batalion commander, Bernard O. Loeffke, agreed. At the conclusion of my time as a platoon leader, I was given a week of Rest and Relaxation (R&R) in Hawaii. Shortly before my departure for the leave, Loeffke informed me that on my return I would assume command of Bravo Company and, if at 23 I was not to be the youngest infantry company commander in Vietnam, it would be likely that I would have the least amount of time in uniform.

Although I had learned and experienced much as a platoon leader, company command would not change the way I felt about Vietnam. I feel now as I did then. As recorded in the Introduction to THE ONLY WAR WE HAD, ''I am proud to have served in Vietnam. I feel no guilt, have no regrets, harbor no memories that I cannot cope with, and—except for a few terrifying moments and the many young men resting for an eternity under neat rows of military headstones—would change nothing. What I do feel is satisfaction and pride in doing what had to be done, in standing up when called upon by my country and being prepared to die if necessary.''

As with the first volume, this book is based on my journal entries recorded inVietnam; the letters I wrote to my wife, brother, and parents; and the memories that do not fade. In my efforts to explain what the war was like on a day-to-day basis, I have included my actual journal notations followed by more detailed explanations of the daily occurrences. Quotations are included as they were recorded in my journals. Their sequence is incidental except that they meant something at the time.

Although the second half-year remarks are not as idealistic as the earlier journal notations, they are reproduced here as they were written nearly two decades ago. The thoughts that follow the daily entries are as I remember them today—older, hopefully more mature, and yet with a full realization that what I was then is the single most important influence on what I am today. For I am still proud and have no regrets.

This book opens with my journal entry written in flight from Hawaii back to Vietnam after a week of R&R with my beautiful, understanding, and very pregnant wife, Linda. Six months prior I had left her in San Francisco with a feeling of great confidence that I would survive the war. Although I was returning to where I wanted to be and to the command I had so desired, I was no longer so confident.

Vietnam changed not at all during my week's absence. A new company and different men awaited me, but individuals who were an important part of the first six months would continue to cross my path. My former commander and fellow platoon leaders in C Company, CPT Jim McGinnis, LT Bill Little and LT Norm Sassner would still offer advice and friendship. CPT Jim Lewis, SP4 Larry Morford, SP4 Roger DeForrest and a host of others would continue to play roles of tragedy and comedy in an ongoing play that varied from real to unbelievable and always unforgettable.

🛩 20 OCTOBER 1969

> Guess most of today was lost in flight—One hour on Guam—then into Tan Son Nhut and Camp Alpha around 1630
>
> Tonight I learned that I do command B Co—Signed assumption of command orders, etc.—Feels good—Later tonight got very sick—Fever, vomiting, etc.—Little sleep

At the Bravo Company rear orderly room I signed a simple paper that stated, "In accordance with Army Regulation 600–20, paragraph 3–4a, the undersigned assumes command of Bravo Company, 2nd Battalion, 3rd Infantry, 199th Light Infantry Brigade effective 20 October 1969."

I had no idea what the referenced regulation had to say, nor did I check. All I knew was that I had reached my goal: company command. With seventeen months in the Army, and at only 23, I was quite proud of myself. Signing for the company was the easy part; the hard part would come as soon as I joined the company in the jungle.

Later that night my fever and chills came back, accompanied by continuous vomiting. At the time, I assumed my illness was a combination of the recurrence of malaria, symptoms which I had suffered as a platoon leader, and my readjustment to Nam. Not until I reread my journals sixteen years later did it occur to me that perhaps I was simply scared.

Took my jeep to Black Horse from BMB—Strange, my jeep—Saw LT Sassner—Old C Co plt ldr—Just back from emergency leave

Bad news—learned this morning C Co had 2 KIA—SGT Ross and PFC Jackson—Knew Ross well—Damn fine man

LOH ride to join my company near Cam Tam—Brought out temporary FO—LT Jim Blevens—34 days left in country—Hope I can get an FO soon

Moved south for night position

We are moving to a BDA (Bomb Damage Assessment) for a B-52 strike

Norm Sassner had returned a few days before from attending his father's funeral in the States. Immediately after his arrival, he had to go to the Long Binh morgue to officially identify two of Charlie Company's dead.

Death of a parent was important enough to allow a son to leave the war zone to pay last respects. But the fathers of Ross and Jackson would bury their sons, who would never reach twenty. I was beginning to understand a major difference between war and peace: in peace sons bury their fathers—in war fathers bury their sons.

Sassner said he hated to be the one to tell me because he knew SGT Ross and I had been close. As a member of SGT Breeckner's squad in the third platoon, Ross had been one of the men who found me and my recon team back on 7 August. I never had the chance to tell him thanks.

As a platoon leader, my transportation to and from BMB (Brigade Main Base) at Long Binh had been accompanying the platoon or hitching a ride with whatever convoy was available. As a company commander, I had my own jeep, complete with driver. I was anxious to get to the field, but I was careful enough to wait for the protection of the daily mid-morning convoy before starting out.

Upon arrival of Black Horse, I met Loeffke and the new Operations Officer, MAJ Richard Humphrey. Without a welcome back or congratulations on my new job, both began briefing me as though I had never been gone or had never been anything but the Bravo Company Commander. Humphrey showed me on his map where a B-52 strike had gone in the night before. My first mission was to follow the bomb path for an assessment of the damage.

As we walked to the helipad, Loeffke asked if I had any questions. I told him my only concern was an approaching annual general inspection of the company administrative procedures in the rear at BMB. When I asked what I should do about the inspection, the battalion commander gave me my first guidance as a rifle company commander. He said, "Lee, don't worry about anything except getting bodies."

At the helipad I was joined by 1LT Jim Blevens who told me that Bravo had not had an officer artillery forward observer (FO) for a while and that the scrgcant who had been filling in was going on R&R. Blevens nonchalantly added, "I volunteered for the job. I know you by reputation and thought you might be needing an FO."

It was not until later that I found out Blevens had only thirty-four days left on his tour when he met me at the helipad. Over the next week I was so busy I did not get to know Blevens well. I did not need to. Anyone with a month left in-country who would volunteer to leave his safe rear job and return to the jungle with a new company commander had to be a damn good man.

Minutes after I met Blevens, we were in the air. A bulging rucksack and bandoleers of ammo stooped my shoulders. The damn steel pot was back on my head. My ever-present M-16 was in my hands and, as I sat in the chopper, the days ahead seemed to reach to forever. I cursed myself for looking forward to command and for being so damn happy over the whole situation.

Yellow smoke drifted up from a small clearing. As we landed, Blevens and I jumped from the skids and ran to the GIs at the edge of the smoke. 1LT Steve Beig, the XO, handed me his code book, shouted, "Good to see you," over the rotor noise, and raced to the waiting bird. Bravo was mine.

In minutes I had met the platoon leaders and radio-telephone operators (RTOs) and given instructions to move out on our new mission. The sweat-soaked fatigues and the silence of the boonies came back with all too much familiarity.

I spent as much time watching my new command as I did looking for the enemy. The company moved fairly well, but then we set up our night defensive position: every man used an air mattress; soldiers continued to smoke after dark; only one man in ten was on alert; radio volume was loud enough to be heard across our perimeter.

My air mattress remained in my rucksack. Except to turn down my command post (CP) radios and pull the plugs on the mattresses nearest me, all I could do was wait nervously for the sun to rise.

> Moved into bomb area to the southwest—Found 33 destroyed bunkers in bomb area—Also possibly one body B Co has field strength of 100–110—Have 3 plts—1 plt is OPCONed to Bn for ARVN training—Hope to get them back soon

Early in the morning I called the two platoon leaders, 2LT Brian Schmalz and 2LT Bill Bolenske, to my CP. The third platoon leader, 2LT Jack Kidalowski, whose unit was at Xuan Luc on a two-week mission helping the ARVNs, would receive his instructions upon his return.

The platoon leaders were about my age. Both had been in the Army slightly longer than I had, each having gone through basic training after being drafted and through Officers' Candidate School. They had been in-country for less than two months.

I was thoroughly pissed at the lack of security and apparent complacence during the night, though I did my best not to convey my anger to the lieutenants. I told them that I expected immediate changes in the company's operating procedures: air mattresses would be used only in base camps; there would be no smoking after dark; and never would less than twenty-five percent of the troops be awake and alert at all times.

I emphasized that our well-being, as well as our mission to destroy the enemy, depended upon our being quiet, alert, and aggressively fighting the gooks on our terms rather than theirs. My philosophy was that if all of us were diligent, no matter how difficult the times, the results would be worth the effort. If we could get all of us through a year in the jungle, we could fuck off the next fifty or so years of our normal life-expectancy.

Another of my changes was to disband a group of five soldiers called the Company Tiger Team, which had guarded the Company CP and occasionally pulled a reconnaissance. Apparently, its primary job had been to guard the old commander.

Both lieutenants listened closely; I could tell that they were experiencing the trepidation that always goes with meeting a new commander, but their nods seemed to indicate that they concurred.

Bolenske broke in once and said, "You're not saying anything that everybody doesn't already know. It's just that no one made us do it right before. The men are good, and it won't take long to get things squared away."

Schmalz again nodded in agreement. As I dismissed the officers, Brian turned and asked, "We've always had a captain as commander. Since we're all lieutenants, what do we call you?"

I smiled and answered, "We're in the Army. When the troops are around, my call sign or sir is appropriate. When it's just us, call me Lee. As long as you do as told, I really don't give a damn."

Soon we were moving through the jungle. The Tiger Team troops had returned to their old squads, and while I could tell that they did not particularly like that, the reactions of the other soldiers convinced me that my decision had been a good one.

After a couple of transmissions back and forth to Battalion and the platoons, I could see that my RTOs, SP4 Ronnie Coleman and SP4 Bill Nesmith, knew their jobs well. RTOs always have a strong allegiance and bond with the man for whom they carry the radios. Often they are the last in a unit to thoroughly accept a new boss. This was not the case with Coleman and Nesmith, as they greeted me that first morning with a cup of coffee. While I had been talking to the officers, they had repacked my poncho liner into my rucksack. Like the platoon leaders, they seemed to welcome a change in leadership.

The bomb strike area was easy to find. Bombs weighing 500 or 750 pounds each had left a line of destruction several hundred meters wide and over three klicks (kilometers) long. Craters eight feet deep, huge trees snapped like matchsticks, and uprooted stumps—all interspersed with occasional strips of vegetation—offered a maze that was more difficult to penetrate than the jungle.

Our count of bunkers destroyed by the ARC LIGHT, as the B-52 missions were called, was strictly an estimate. At the edge of the destruction were depressions and cut logs that could be identified as former bunkers. In the middle of the slash of carnage, we could only guess at what had been destroyed.

Our report of one body was also a guesstimate. We found small pieces of skin, bone, and guts. The stench of human dead—a smell like nothing else—filled the air. I told the lieutenants that if they could find three hands, legs, ears, or balls, then we would report more than one. However, with bombs so big, nothing was left large enough to count.

Continue BDA to the west—Sixteen more bunkers destroyed—One bloody bandage—One trail, fresh with water buffalo footprints

Moved northwest for night position—Supposed to air-mobile tomorrow to Tan Lap

B Co definitely needs some upgrading and strong leadership—However they do have what seems to be outstanding personnel—NCOs are about average—2 plt ldrs I have with me are at least average

Have one PFC who has a live lizard—6–8 inches long on a dog tag chain on his helmet—PFC feeds him bugs etc.

Now that I was a company commander, I decided that my journal entries should be more detailed. My new procedure was to make notes immediately after occupying a night position. The few minutes I spent alone with my journal gave the platoon leaders time to get their sectors organized before my inspections.

The RTOs found it interesting that I kept a daily journal. Ron Coleman remarked that he had thought about starting a diary but had never gotten around to it. I had never thought my keeping a journal was unusual, but Ron's statement reminded me that I had now been in three companies and had never seen another man writing a daily log.

My late-day routine of journal writing spawned another daily event. Bill Nesmith patiently watched my scribbling every afternoon as he monitored the Company radio net. As I returned my book to its plastic-bag wrapper, Bill asked when he was getting a job in the rear.

Nesmith, a former railroad worker from Florida, had been drafted a year out of high school. Now, after nine months in the field, he persistently lobbied for a safer job. Initially his daily badgering was irritating, but the young soldier had such a good sense of humor that our daily debate became more fun than bother. My usual answer to him was that he was going nowhere until I did, and I planned to stay in the field forever.

After climbing through the bomb damage area all day, we were glad to reach the end of the air strike. The bloody bandage, along with more decaying body parts, was evidence that the bombs had done more than put holes in the ground. Water buffalo hoof prints indicated that a unit large enough to require the beast of burden to move supplies was in the area.

Although I had only been with Bravo two days, I could tell that the individual soldiers were every bit as good as those in Charlie Company and recon. The sergeants were particularly strong but were typically young and inexperienced. They followed orders well and seemed to welcome the increased demands.

🚁 24 OCTOBER 1969

Moved to west for airmobile—As usual it was late AM to FB Maureen—Is very new—Has three 105s and a plt of tracks for security

I have one plt here—Third plt—Second plt at Tan Lap
and my first plt at Xuan Luc as an honor guard
Bn is really pushing—Missions are changed very frequently
One of my new lts—2LT Brian Schmalz from N.J.—
has a rather interesting background—BS in chemistry, almost has Master's—Very intelligent and looks to be good
with experience—A good plt ldr

I was confident I could do the job as company commander. Yet I was very aware that Bravo's performance
would be under close scrutiny by Brigade and higher headquarters. Loeffke had taken a risk by placing a junior lieutenant in command when several captains were waiting for
the opportunity.

Shortly after our arrival at Maureen, the first platoon was
airmobiled to Xuan Luc to guard the forward brigade headquarters. Although it would be a good break for Bolenske
and his men, the fragmentation of the company was frus-
trating. Kidalowski, whom I had not yet met, was in Tan Lap
with his platoon training ARVNs. As the company commander, I was, of course, responsible for the platoons wherever
they were. Yet Schmalz's platoon was the only one I could
directly influence. I recalled that CPT Jim McGinnis, my old
C Company commander, had experienced the same frustrations when Battalion had pulled out platoons for other missions.

My concerns were tempered with the realization that
Loeffke was orchestrating my assumption of command
with the same rationale he had used in making me the
recon platoon leader as a stepping stone to that command.

Schmalz and his platoon sergeant, SSG English, were
an unusual pair. English had a college degree in biology
and had earned his stripes in NCO Candidate School. Although called a "shake and bake" sergeant because of his
school-produced stripes, he, like Schmalz, was highly re-

spected by the men. Both Schmalz and English had done work toward master's degrees before their draft notices arrived. I doubt if there was a platoon in Nam with a better educated leadership.

Maureen, a bleak base located in a large clearing between the rubber plantations and the jungle, was twelve klicks southeast of Black Horse. Our maps showed a village had once stood there, but beyond a few foundation stones, nothing remained. Maureen was not much better than the destroyed town it stood on. Established only as a temporary base for the artillery, its protection was limited to a four-foot dirt berm encircled by a single row of concertina wire. A platoon of armored personnel carriers from the Brigade's D Troop, 17th Cavalry, was the primary defense.

Maureen was not much, but as I was the senior commander on the ground, she was mine. The tracks and artillery were under my operational control, and I spent much of my time coordinating the defenses of the diverse units.

Securing a too-large fire base with too few men was only one of my problems. While SSG English was training several of his men in the use of the M-79 grenade launcher, LT Blevens's radio operator joined the group without permission.

The RTO's first shot exploded too close to the berm. Because the soldier had fired from the top of the berm rather than from behind it as instructed, a small piece of shrapnel lodged in his leg. English explained the man's failure to follow instructions while I examined the wound. I could see the small piece of metal just under the skin. It was time for a lesson to my new command.

I explained to the RTO that he could be dusted off and face a court-martial for not following orders, or he could stay and be treated in the field. My estimation of the soldier went up when he said, "Shit, sir, I fucked up. Cut the damn thing out here."

SP5 Crowe, the company chief medic, cleaned the wound and, using tweezers, quickly extracted the shrapnel. Doc frequently changed the bandage over the next few days as he checked for infection. The RTO was soon healed and paid much closer attention to what he was told.

🚁 25 OCTOBER 1969

Continue operations at FB Maureen—Sent third plt on a 3k RIF today—Neg results

Saw LT Jong—old C Co FO—Good swapping stories and news—He is one of the most outstanding men I've met in RVN—Is in for Silver Star for work with ARVNs in War Zone D recently

I believe reason we are pushing so hard at present is that we will be leaving the area soon

Today had mail and first hot meal in 5 days

Is getting hot as hell again

Often I sit and think of last 6 months—It has been the best and worst of memories of my lifetime—Once you are a combat Infantryman you see many things differently

A fire base could not be properly defended by just sitting on the berm behind a machine gun or by stacking sandbags. By sending Schmalz's platoon out on a recon, we could monitor any movement of the gooks in our area. The patrol also helped to instill offensive spirit in the troops.

I was surprised when Don Jong flew in to visit the artillery. Now the XO of the battery but still getting to the field often, he brought me up-to-date on his last few months, including telling me about his volunteering as FO for a large ARVN operation. He did not go into any detail about the Silver Star except to say that things had gotten so bad that he had had to become an Infantryman for a while.

Jong was somewhat subdued during our conversation. When I asked him why he was not his usual jovial self, he replied, "One-six, don't get to liking the war too much. You've been in the boonies a long time."

When I responded with a puzzled frown, Don smiled and said, "Hey, don't forget, even you can get killed."

With a laugh, I said, "Bullshit."

My talk with Don caused me to reflect about the last half year. I no longer sweated the small stuff. My basic philosophy had become that if no one was dead or dying—or doing something that would lead to that—I was not going to worry about it. I did not dwell on my own safety. Too many other men's lives were my responsibility to allow for that. If I took care of them, I reasoned, they would take care of me.

Another day at fire base—Easier than humping the boonies but someone always coming in to look things over—Visits today by BN CO and Dep Bde Cdr Col Ripley—All have many questions—Actually little sweat if you don't worry about it

Sent third plt on mission with tracks—D/17 Cav—Rather a calm day

We are in a fire support base—However no bunkers to speak of—Made hooches out of ponchos—At least we have air mattresses

Everyone doing a lot of experimenting with C-rations—Main objective: to make them taste less like C-rations

We do have shower facilities—Put water in a plastic container at midday—Set it in sun—Soon have very warm water

My call sign Bitter Super Bravo 15—Co, just Six

We had done the best we could to secure Maureen, but I was not proud to show the results. My request to Loeffke for additional defense materials for more concertina wire and bunker-building materials was met with the response that the fire base would be closed down in a few days.

Loeffke was interested in my initial impression of Bravo Company. He agreed with my assessment that the men and leaders were good but that the company was lacking in confidence and aggressiveness. I pointed out that with the platoons so spread out it was difficult to square away the unit. He said that I would soon have them back—which was exactly what I wanted to hear.

The battalion commander also briefed me on the latest intelligence reports and our future operations. Since the rains were finally letting up, we anticipated that the enemy would be moving back into our area of operations (AO) in greater numbers. Loeffke said that logically they would come from the north and northeast out of Cambodia. We were to concentrate north of Highway 1 to intercept their movement.

The plan sounded good. I had no desire to command from a fire base, and I looked forward to increased contact. Maybe Jong was right about the damn war becoming likable.

My excitement at the news of our AO did not make the days at Maureen go any faster. While no one was unhappy to see the monsoon season over, we found it hard to be enthusiastic about the dry season when the only shade we could find was under our ponchos hooches. Mosquitoes swarmed under the roofs, sharing our shade. Insect repellent seemed ineffective, and I could tell how tired I was by whether I slapped at the bloated bodies or just let them feast undisturbed.

Although we got an occasional hot meal at Maureen, C-rations were still the basic diet. There were twelve different meals in each case, but each case contained exactly the same meals. Because the contents of each box of rations was stamped on top, we turned them facedown to prevent those with first choice from selecting the more desirable meals. We also rearranged the order of the individual boxes as the old-timers had memorized the exact location of each ration—even upside down. In the end, it really did not make much difference. All the C-rations tasted much the same after a short time anyway.

Several of the Bravo soldiers broke the wires that bound the C-ration cases by twisting them with rifle barrels. I ended that practice immediately, as the pressure on the rifle could damage the sights or the zero of the weapon.

Quite a few cans remained after the troops finished choosing meals and making trades. The leftovers we punctured with can-openers or bayonets, stacked with the cardboard boxes, and burned. We did not want the gooks to have any of our rations, no matter how much *we* hated them. They could carry their own chow from Hanoi.

Occasionally a can, not punctured well enough, would burst its seams, blowing food on everybody who was close. Anyone who has ever been the victim of an exploding can of C-rations understands the comment made to soldiers who bunch up in the field: "Spread out, one peanut butter grenade could get you all."

---

27 OCTOBER 1969

Still at FB Maureen—My plts still spread out—Supposed to airmobile to FB Verna tomorrow—Maybe I can get the Co back together there

Letters from Linda today—Sounds as if she enjoyed R&R as much as I did

She also mentioned Susan and a friend possibly meeting their husbands in Saigon—I think this is so ridiculous—It just reminds me once again of the ease of living in the uncaring attitude of our brave "Saigon warriors"

C Co got another gook today—A couple of days ago they killed the woman VC leader the BN had been after for months

My contempt for those in the rear increased with each day I spent in the boonies. This feeling was shared by the other grunts and at times we hated the REMFs (rear-echelon mother fuckers) more than the enemy. At least we could fight back against the gooks.

We realized that the support troops were a necessity for operations in the field, but we resented their relative security and far better living conditions. It just did not seem right that for every one of us in the field sixteen of them were in the rear; virtually all the wounded and killed came from our ranks rather than from the spit-shined mass of REMFs.

Rarely did anyone express anger toward the draft-dodgers and street protestors back home. We considered them to be so contemptible that they were not worth the breath it took to discuss their lack of patriotism or guts. Besides, they were inaccessible and far removed from our daily lives; the REMFs were much more available for our abuse.

Our resentment of the REMFs was pervasive. Yet, although we did not admit it, we knew that they, too, faced the loneliness of family separation and some threat to their well-being from the occasional rocket attacks and sabotage bombings. I suppose that the REMFs were at times as scared as we were, for danger is relative to one's exposure to it. The fear of being killed by a rocket in an air-conditioned bar in Saigon was probably no less terrifying than that of being killed on a jungle patrol.

It was difficult to sit in Maureen and listen to radio reports of other companies getting body counts when my patrols were producing nothing. The fact that my old platoon in Charlie Company was adding to its count of enemy dead made me feel a little better. Larry Morford, a sensitive, religious man, had increased his personal kill record with the first contact I noted in my journal. A former professional stage dancer, he was the best point man I ever encountered.

Charlie Company had also zapped the local female VC leader and her one-eyed deputy whom we had long doubted existed. They had walked out of the jungle directly into the kill zone. The VC pair, who had escaped pursuit for over a decade, had died without returning a shot. The bodies had been taken into Cam Tam for display in the public square. Before the villagers had filed by the bodies, the woman's black pajama bottom had been pulled down, fully exposing her privates to the viewers. The half-naked corpse had served as a reminder that the VC no longer controlled the surrounding jungle. After a day of exhibit, a hole was blown in the middle of the dirt square with C-4, and the by-then bloated bodies kicked into the makeshift grave.

---

28 OCTOBER 1969

AM by CH-47 to FB Verna—Landed on Highway 1—Working with a joint CP with D Co—CPT Lewis in command—Loeffke came by tonight

Have one plt of B 4/12 OPCONed to me—Have plts employed north of Highway 1 to block enemy supply routes

Verna is nice—Hot meals—Even a movie at night—Hope we can stay here for awhile

Got copy of orders to B Co—Assignment: PDY—Permanent duty as CO—Looks good

"Live by chance, love by choice, kill by profession."
Unknown

Fire Base Verna was co-located with an ARVN (Army of the Republic of Vietnam) pound about halfway between Long Binh and Xuan Luc. Security for the base was provided by the ARVNs so that we could put as many of our men as possible into the jungle.

LT Bolenske and the first platoon were waiting for the third platoon and me as our helicopters set down on Highway 1. A platoon from another battalion arrived by truck a few minutes later with orders placing them under my operational control. Including the attached platoon, Bravo was back up to over 100 field strength.

CPT Jim Lewis met me at the sandbagged stucco hooch serving as Verna's command post and provided me with maps and further instructions from Battalion Operations. My first meeting with Lewis had not been under such pleasant circumstances. On 3 July, we had been in a battle where his Delta Company and McGinnis's Charlie Company had attempted to overrun a heavily fortified bunker complex that resulted in nine GIs dead and twenty wounded.

Our two companies were assigned an AO about twenty klicks long paralleling Highway 1 and extending eight klicks north into the jungle. Delta was to cover the western half while Bravo had the eastern sector.

The entire AO, except for a few villages and small cultivated plots, was thick jungle. I divided the area into three equal sectors and instructed the platoon leaders to recon to the north. Once they had located major trails, they were to establish ambushes in attempts to catch enemy infiltrating back into our area.

I was somewhat apprehensive about the orders for me to co-located my CP with that of Delta Company. Lewis was a senior captain with a long time in command, and I was concerned that, as the ranking officer, he would want to command both companies on the operation. The Delta Commander quickly eased my fears by treating me as an equal. Beyond using our RTOs to spell each other and to keep a map of platoon locations posted, we remained independently in charge of our units.

Over the next few days, I had the opportunity to get to know Lewis well. It occurred to me that our joint operation might be another of Loeffke's techniques to help me learn the ropes of command. If so, I did not mind. Anyone could learn much from the battle-wise Delta CO.

Lewis and I spent much time rehashing the fight of 3 July on what we called Butterfly Hill. Our re-creations of the day's events were in sync with one exception. When I asked what had happened to a lieutenant who was first to get on the dust-off despite his minor wound, Lewis said that he was not aware the officer was on the medevac that pulled them out of the jungle. As I told Lewis about the officer's apparent state of shock and resulting lack of concern for his men, Lewis became angry. The lieutenant was supposed to be in charge of securing the wounded and preparing an LZ for the evacuation. At the hospital the lieutenant had managed to secure a transfer to a safer job based upon what Lewis had presumed to be a serious wound. By the time Lewis was out of the hospital, a replacement for the old platoon leader was already in the field.

Lewis ended the conversation by saying that maybe he would run across the lieutenant again someday. If he did, I am sure the lieutenant got what he deserved.

Continue block of enemy routes

D Co had awards ceremony for some of their personnel today

CPT Lewis and I get time to check things at BH and BMB since we have two companies here

Went to BH today ironing out some Co problems—Am going to have to get the old "red book" (UCMJ) out

Black Horse has about 2500 ARVNs moved in there now

Got a haircut today from a traveling gook barber—Kept an eye on him when he got his razor out

Coachman elements—Railroad security—was out for ambush last night—Had an LTC with them—"Doesn't know there's a war" type

> "You have never lived until you have almost died."
> Unknown

Differences between being a platoon leader and a company commander were becoming more apparent. The keys to a good unit were still fair and equal treatment of everyone, supporting the NCOs, and taking care of the men in every respect. As a platoon leader, I could lead by example and see personally to each of the men's needs. My role as company commander was different in that now my primary means of taking care of the men was to guide and command the platoon leaders properly. Taking care of the soldiers was still top priority—and an occasional kick in the ass to an individual was at times the best technique of seeing to the welfare of the entire unit.

I hated to impose punishment for minor offenses by means of the Uniform Code of Military Justice. However, the ''Red Book'' provided a quick way to get the attention of the men who were slow to follow their sergeants' instructions.

Battalion was still operating its command post from Black Horse. The large complex had been taken over by the 18th ARVN Division and the Old Guard as our Battalion was known, now occupied a small concertina-enclosed sector. No longer was there a PX nor any of the other facilities formerly run by the 11th ACR. The small officers' club was gone, its building ironically serving as a brightly painted Buddhist temple.

Personal services were now mobile. The traveling barber shop consisted of a stool, a fairly clean sheet, scissors, hand clippers, and a straight razor. My RTOs enjoyed watching me hold my M-16 across my lap outside the sheet as the laughing barber finished the trim with his razor.

❧ 30 OCTOBER 1969

> Lost plt of B 4/12—They go to Xuan Luc
> Do much coordination here with ARVNs, etc.
> VR of area in LOH this afternoon

More FB type work—Many problems but at least no humping

Wrote quite a few letters

Received orders yesterday for Bronze Star with Oak Leaf Cluster

Went to nearby village for coordination with ARVN advs—They really have it easy

Recon plt stopped by—Good to see some of the old-timers

> "You'll wonder where the yellow went when you napalm the Orient."
>
> 1st Marine Div saying

The loss of the attached platoon from the 4th Battalion 12th Infantry left me again with only two platoons. Kidalowski and the second platoon were still detached to help train the ARVNs.

I had been pleased with the 4/12, as they were a motivated unit. It was interesting to note that their methods of operation varied little from the Old Guard. Equipment carried, radio procedures, basic loads of ammo, and jargon were pretty much the same. Phrases such as, "It don't mean nothing," "It's a lick on you," "Take two salt tablets and drive on," and the ever-present, "What are they going to do? Send me to Vietnam?" were common remarks of boonie rats regardless of unit.

The statement "It don't mean nothing" was fairly close to the way I felt about my second award of the Bronze Star medal. I had received the first Bronze Star with Valor Device for making the mistake of misjudging the size of the enemy force we went up against on 7 August. The second medal was for "meritorious service" for my six months as a platoon leader. All it meant was that I had survived for half my tour—which I guess did "mean something" after all.

Since Verna was on Highway 1, we got quite a bit of drop-in traffic. Nevertheless, I was surprised to see the recon platoon and its new boss, Bill Little. Bill, a fellow platoon leader in Charlie Company, had been badgering Loeffke for the job since my departure and had finally gotten his chance.

As Bill and the platoon got back on their truck, I reminded him that he owed me a case of beer from the Texas A&M–West Point football game. He smiled and said he would deliver it soon.

🛩 31 OCTOBER 1969

Payday—LT Steve Beig my XO out to pay troops—He didn't have mine—Guess someone will show up and pay me

Case of beer delivered from MAJ Scaggs, BN XO, for loss of bet on Tex A&M–Army game

Get another VR of area in a LOH—mostly to confirm positions of B&D elements moving north

My CP is set up in what appears to be an old school house—Pretty nice—Have cots etc.—We have a jack-o-lantern for Halloween sent to my medic by a friend—I hope we get no "trick or treaters" tonight—Our security is poor here

"I was the ordinary man about whom songs are

never written, stories are never told, legends are
never remembered—To live in the hearts we leave
behind is not to die."

A Stone for Danny Fisher
Harold Robbins

A light helicopter allowed the XO and me to visit the
platoons in the jungle and to get a visual recon of the
entire AO. At Lewis's request, we also overflew Delta's
platoons and confirmed their locations.

Returning to the relative luxuries of Verna, I felt a little
guilty for enjoying the advantages of being a company
commander. At the same time, I realized that the stay at
Verna was temporary and I would spend many more nights
under my poncho liner than in the sandbagged school
house.

In many ways, the jungle was preferable to Verna.
Relying on the ARVNs for security, I never felt safe in
the compound. The small, plastic, snaggletoothed jack-
o-lantern might scare children trick-or-treating back in
the world, but I doubted if it would deter an NVA sapper.

Verna
   Another month begins
   Half (3 guns) of A Bat 40th Arty left our location to
FB Crystal by CH-47
   Visit by DCO Ripley today
   Three-six found Co size VC night position—Pursuing
10–15 gooks
   Today is Saturday—I know only because LT Monty
Meaux B 4/12 XO—'67 A&M—stopped by and said Ags
are at Ark today—One day is much like another over
here
   No mail for a couple of days as of today—Always bad
on morale
   New *Playboy* in today—Always good for morale
   I remember reading my 1st journal in Hawaii—I was
the young LT out to win the war in first months—I am
now "older" and more realistic

Schmalz's discovery of the place the dinks had briefly
stopped was a good sign that activity was picking up. I
directed the platoon to follow the heaviest trail and spent
most of the day waiting beside the radio for their reports.

Monty Meaux had learned about my being at Verna from
his platoon, which had been OPCONed to us the week
before. It did not seem any more unusual to see Monty
along Highway 1 than it would have a couple of years
before to find him in the broad quadrangle between our
dormitories back in Texas. In fact, most of the time Vietnam seemed more real than all the other times before.

   Meaux's reminder that it was Saturday and the day of

the A&M–Arkansas football game was the first time I realized that I was no longer aware of the day of the week. My first journal had the day and date preprinted on each page. The new record book pages were blank. But as long as the medic remembered what day was Monday for the weekly big orange pill, weekdays were not important.

Six months before, I had seen my part in the war as a noble effort in support of a worthy cause. My scope was much smaller now, as I rarely thought nor cared about the overall conflict or philosophy of right or wrong. All I worked for was the one hundred men of Bravo Company and our mutual survival. The enemy had become something subhuman, and whatever means we could take to kill them were fine with me. The troops often voiced my sentiments when they said, "It's not who's right, but who's left."

2 NOVEMBER 1969

Verna
   Big Day—I for once have all my plts back—My pay finally caught up—Got lots of mail
   Also gave 3 Art. 15s—AWOL and failure to obey lawful order—I hate to give ART. 15s but this is to get some weak points ironed out in the company—Am also going to make some personnel changes
   Talked quite a while today with a LT who is an ARVN

advisor—His job is certainly not as hard as a plt ldr—But
does have lots of problems

My observations on ARVNs: Fairly good fighters but
are too lazy to go out and look for a fight

Getting paid and receiving mail were nice, but finally
having my entire company back far overshadowed the other
events. Jack Kidalowski and his platoon seemed equally
happy about their return.

Jack, a little older than myself, had served as an enlisted
man for a year before going to OCS. He outranked
Schmalz and Bolenske by a few months' time in grade.
This, combined with his having been in Nam a few weeks
longer, meant he would be the logical replacement for
Beig when the XO completed his tour in December.

Several inches under six feet, Kidalowski was even thin-
ner and more wiry than the normal grunt. His quiet but
confident manner made it obvious why he had been selected for the independent duty of assisting the ARVNs.

After briefly explaining to Kidalowski the changes I had
been demanding of the other platoons, I assigned him a
sector of our AO. By the next hourly situation reports on
the radio, I happily noted all of Bravo's platoons on my
map.

I spent much of my energy planning the platoons'
movements so they would be near LZs for resupply at least
every third day. If no clearing was available, the supplies
were kicked out of a hovering chopper into the tree canopy
or into a bomb crater. Whenever possible, I planned the
resupply mission at an LZ so replacements and R&R re-
turnees could join their platoons. Also, because Battalion's
SOP did not allow mail to be dropped through the trees,
I tried to schedule the resupplies so the mail could be

delivered directly hand-to-hand. Days without mail were devastating to morale.

I hated to resort to Article 15s—nonjudicial punishment. However, if anyone failed to do his part, it meant more work and possibly increased danger for the others. There was no sympathy for malingerers, and most of the men saw the fines of seven days' pay or loss of stripes as fitting justice.

The monsoon season had passed completely now. No breaks occurred in the tropical heat, and we sweated just sitting in the shade. When our jungle fatigues did dry completely, circles of salt from dried perspiration ringed our underarms and zigzagged down our backs.

Often at Verna I tried to get some sleep during the quiet times so I could stay awake longer at night monitoring the radios and occasionally reassuring a scared RTO. More often than not I just lay on my cot sweating and listening to radio broadcasts of old *Lone Ranger* and *The Shadow* shows on the Armed Forces Network (AFN).

I allowed transistor radios in the fire bases, and one or more were constantly tuned in to AFN. The GIs had long ago discovered how to take an Army PRC-77 radio battery and remove one of its cells to power the civilian sets.

Verna

Changed plts positions around quite a bit today

ARVN 5th Cav arrived this location to begin operations to our south—They had BG and COL ARVN types with them—General was the biggest VN I've seen—About 6 ft 1 in—CPT Lewis and I filled them in on our mission

Bn SGT MAJ Quick visited—Good bullshit session with him—From war in Korea (he was machine gunner) to country living—He is from Missouri (Ozarks)

Pres Nixon makes VN speech tomorrow—Doubt if he will say much

> "Don't think I could make it as a civilian. I wouldn't even know who to salute out there."
>
> CPT J. Lewis
> D 2/3 199 LIB

I continued to move platoons around trying every possible way to find the enemy. Delta Company and the rest of the battalion were experiencing the same negative results. All we seemed to do was coordinate with the ARVNs and each other.

Things were so slow that the physical characteristics of an ARVN ally were the only things I could find interesting enough to record in my journal. The ARVN 5th Cavalry Regiment Commander was an impressive-looking soldier, causing Nesmith to remark, "He's the biggest damn gook I've ever seen." I had to remind him to show a little more respect for a general officer, regardless of his ethnic origin.

It was beginning to look as though, if I stayed at Verna long enough, everyone in the whole damn war zone would stop by for a visit. The high point of this otherwise boring day was the conversation with Sergeant Major Quick, a graying NCO with a deeply lined face that reflected his more than twenty years in uniform. A veteran of two wars, he appeared to be an old man—and one tough son of a bitch.

NCOs of Quick's rank, especially when filling the job of top sergeant in a battalion, rarely acknowledged a lieutenant's existence. Sergeants Major would salute young officers to set the example for the enlisted men, but they would just as readily chew out a "butter bar" second lieutenant as they would the greenest "fucking new guy" (FNG) private. The only difference would be a gruff "Sir" at the end of each statement.

Quick either swallowed his pride or ignored my lieutenant's rank in favor of my position as company commander. Whatever the reason, we conversed as fellow combat Infantrymen rather than as old to young or NCO to officer.

Much of our conversation was about life in rural areas, country cooking, and the excitement of harvest time. I was surprised that, when I asked him about the Korean War, he said, "Except for being cold instead of hot, it was not much different from Nam or any other war. When you're getting shot at and seeing young boys die, it's all the same."

Our talk lasted so long that the Sergeant Major stayed too late to return to Black Horse before nightfall. Borrowing a cot from one of the RTOs on duty, he spent the night. Before leaving he told me it was good to be with real soldiers again. Apparently to the Sergeant Major even those at Black Horse fell into the category of REMFs.

Verna

Busy, not so good day—Still trying to get some reorganization done and getting people back to field

Attended ARVN meeting—Filled them in on what we are doing

1st plt captured 3 VC suspects today—Had 800+ pounds of rice in their possession

VN COL seems very curious as to when I make CPT—Don't think he is used to LT Co CO

Loeffke spent night at our location—Said B Co would move out of here soon

Linda should be having the baby soon—Wow!

Went out with resupply vehicle—Going a little batty

Most of the hamlets along Highway 1 were populated by Catholics from the North who had come south in the 1950s, after Vietnam was divided. Intelligence sources had received indications that one of the villages was providing supplies to the infiltrators, and the word was that the local priest was a VC sympathizer.

I moved Bolenske's platoon back to the highway and went in with the resupply to brief him on the mission. Bill had already found several heavy trails leading from the village into the surrounding farming plots and on into the jungle. One of the largest trails went by the parish church.

I told Bolenske that anyone who entered the tree line beyond the fields was fair game. Bill, with no particular emotion, asked, "Does that include the priest?"

I answered, "I don't give a damn who comes into our

jungle. If they cross the tree line, kill them and we'll sort out their religious preferences later.''

Later in the afternoon, Bill reported that three villagers had made several trips from their hooches to a vegetable plot near the jungle. They were carrying something, but it did not appear to be weapons. I told Bill to check them out on their next trip.

He called back a few minutes later and said he had detained a young woman and two middle-aged men. In a hole covered with woven mats were sacks of rice totaling over eight hundred pounds. A helicopter came in after my report to Battalion and picked up the suspects and their rice. It was a small victory, but we felt good knowing that some communists would miss a few meals.

Bill continued to ambush the approaches to the village. As we expected, the absence of the three villagers had alerted the rest of the hamlet not to venture into the fields. We might have missed getting the priest, but we would settle for the three rice suppliers.

Much later the S-2 (battalion intelligence officer) confirmed the obvious—that the three were VC. They had been sent to a POW compound by the ARVNs but had refused under rather harsh questioning to reveal any other information about the enemy in our AO.

Three POWs were as good as three body count, but no one ever bragged about how many prisoners he took. In fact, except for unarmed civilians whom we detained in non-free-fire zones, I do not recall ever taking a prisoner. Neither NVA nor VC were prone to give up if they had a chance to fight or flee. Those who were wounded and might have preferred to surrender were not given the opportunity. We never approached a downed enemy without continuing to shoot and throw grenades at the body. The

chance to capture a wounded prisoner was not worth the
risk of his trying to take a few of us with him.

Despite everything that was going on, I still had more
than ample time to think about my impending fatherhood.
Linda's doctor had predicted the due date as the second of
December.

🜚 5 NOVEMBER 1969

Verna
    Usual day of coordinating with ARVNs—Moving and
deploying plts
    Got word to depart this area in the morning on an
airmobile—Looks like it's back to the jungle for me

> "They looked determined and reverent at the same
> time. But still they're a bloody good bunch of kill-
> ers."
>
> Gen. George S. Patton III—of soldiers he
> saw at a memorial service in Vietnam

Winning the hearts and minds of the people had long
been the catchphrase for victory in Vietnam. Supposedly
our gaining the trust and confidence of the South Vietnamese would lead to the end of their support of the Viet
Cong as well as develop a staunch resilience to defeat the
NVA. The program may have had some success, but it
was not one that fit in with the traditional Infantry way of

waging war. Most of the grunts figured that if we had them by the balls, their hearts and minds would follow.

By late 1969 our government had finally discovered what we fighting the war had learned long before. US soldiers in the numbers then present could not do the job alone. It was time to get the ARVNs out of their compounds and into the jungle.

The new program's intent was to reequip and retrain the Army of South Vietnam so that it could replace most American troops by the end of 1970. Details of the Old Guard's part of the program appeared in *Newsweek* with a picture of one of Kidalowski's troops teaching ARVNs how to use their new M-16s. The second platoon enjoyed its worldwide publicity, and more than one soldier, including Kidalowski, showed me the article as proof that he had not been screwing off while the rest of us were in the boonies.

Although the article was headlined, "Baby-Sitting With ARVN," it gave a fairly good account of efforts by Kidalowski's platoon and other units in the Brigade.

Newsweek Saigon Bureau Chief Maynard Parker began the report with a quote from Secretary of Defense Melvin Laird who stated, "President Nixon has a program to end the war in Vietnam. The program is Vietnamization."

Parker then outlined the "crash program" in areas across the country to "upgrade" the performance of the ARVNs. He included the training conducted by platoons like mine, joint operations at all levels, pooling of intelligence resources, and recruiting young Vietnamese from the same areas in which they would fight.

Parker also wrote about the earlier poor performance by the 18th ARVN Division which was the principal unit in our shared AO. The 18th, since the arrival of the 199th, had improved its enemy-to-friendly "kill ratio" from five-to-one to twelve-to-one. Parker also admitted that since the 199th moved in, he was now able to drive from Saigon to Xuan Luc, which was something he "would not have dared to do six months ago."

I felt the Saigon bureau chief did a good job of telling a part of our story. In fact, his article clarified for me what we had been doing the last few months better than the sparse official explanations we received. Parker, however, missed the interesting fact that the 18th had previously been designated the 10th ARVN Division. In a war where anything that was Number 10 meant that it was as bad as it could get, changing the name had been a smart move.

Parker concluded his story with opinions that I agreed with fully at the time. He stated, ". . . the true test of Vietnamization—at least for the province of Long Kanh—will come when the 199th is pulled out." In conclusion he quoted a local villager's reporting that the enemy leaders in the area were spreading the word to their men "to lie low until the Americans leave . . . then we will see the 18th's heels."

History proved neither Parker nor me correct in our evaluation of the 18th. During the North's final offensive before the fall of Saigon in 1975, the last major ARVN unit to fold was the 18th. Its stand around Xuan Luc was the ARVN's most heroic effort of the entire war. The 18th never surrendered but fought until virtually the entire division was killed—fighting for a government and a country that were already doomed. Perhaps, just perhaps, we did a better job "baby-sitting ARVN" than we ever gave ourselves credit for.

> Prepare to AM from Verna—Airmobiled to south—
> Moved west for 1k—Then got word Delta was in
> contact—Moved to PZ—Then airmobiled to blocking po-
> sition—I was picked up by C&C ship and received instruc-
> tions from Bn CO
> Delta had contact with squad-size element—We were
> unable to get in any of it

> "We must be willing to continue our bombing until
> we have destroyed every work of man in North
> Vietnam, if this is what it takes to win the war."
> Curtis LeMay
> *Newsweek*, 10 Nov. 1969

Our efforts to interdict the infiltration routes had produced little, so Loeffke decided to move us back to the
south. The helicopters picked us up at Verna, using Highway 1 as the pick-up zone, and carried us to our new AO.
We had not been on the ground long when the battalion
radio buzzed with the news of Delta's contact. This message was followed minutes later with a call from Loeffke
for us to return to the LZ we had just departed.

Bravo recovered the kilometer of the jungle, which had
just taken us well over an hour to traverse, in less than
fifteen minutes, returning to the LZ at a run. Loeffke
picked me up with his command ship as my troops scrambled aboard the other choppers. He briefed me en route,
saying that we would soon be on the ground near Delta's
contact and we were to dig in to catch the fleeing dinks.

I was glad to be out of Verna and back in the field.

Coleman and Nesmith, the radio-telephone operators, seemed in good spirits despite the fact that they were now carrying their radios rather than just listening to them at the fire base. Nesmith continued to inquire daily about a job in the rear, but he was taking measures at the same time to add to his comfort in the field. Tied to his pack was a small three-legged stool he had, in his words, "liberated from the ARVNs." At each halt he untied the stool and regally took his seat as the rest of us sat on the ground.

Nesmith was not really overweight but he did carry a roll of flesh around his waist. Coleman told his fellow RTO that he resembled Buddha more than a soldier.

Coleman, rail thin and well over six feet tall with bright red hair, looked the part of a soldier no better than Nesmith. Looks are deceiving, however, when it comes to Infantrymen. Both RTOs made my job easier as well as offering comic relief. I gave no reassurance to Nesmith that he would ever become a REMF beyond telling him that if he were replaced, it would have to be by someone as tall as Coleman and myself. I was not jesting, for I had no desire to be the tallest GI in a forest of radio antennas for any gook sniper to try his luck on.

7 NOVEMBER 1969

> Moved from holding, blocking position to south—After
> 1st plt moved east into our block—Movement was
> through some of thickest, wettest terrain that I have
> been in—Really Number 10
>
> Delta Co still following blood trails—Found 1 RPG
> launcher—6 B40 rounds—Two 122 rocket launchers,
> etc—One man wounded in Delta by booby trap

We remained all night in ambush/blocking positions but
once again the enemy was able to melt into the jungle and
escape. The brief fire fight had been a success, however,
as the fleeing gooks had left behind their heavy weapons.
Many a REMF in Long Binh would sleep more securely
with the 8-foot long, 122-millimeter diameter rocket
launchers now in American hands.

Despite the increase of activity, I still took time to write
letters home. Linda had sent a proposed birth announcement that she had designed and sketched portraying a stork
delivering a baby to a home designated the "Lanning Recruiting Center." Inside the card were blank spaces for
the "recruit's" name, vital statistics, and "commanders." I was impressed with Linda's efforts as the announcement seemed quite appropriate, but in the rush of
events occurring around me I only had the time to write,
"The card is fine with me."

In a letter to my parents I asked that they pass along
greetings to Marina Babb, their postmistress. The Sylvester, Texas Post Office was a small one and still operated
with a single worker posting letters into pigeonhole boxes

and hand-canceling outgoing mail. Mrs. Babb added her personal touch to my folks' letters by penciling "Hi" or "Take care" along her initials on the backs of the envelopes.

✈ 8 NOVEMBER 1969

Moved from night position to FB Verna—Got word to move Co to Tan Lap—Then changed to stand-by as a reaction force for a contact—Then back to Tan Lap

Have Chieu Hoi with 3rd plt that is supposed to lead them to bunkers and cache sites

Moved CP into old railroad depot at Tan Lap—4.2 mortars are here but are in the process of moving out—We have RF/PFs here at this location

Have got a new 1st SGT—Beckles—Looks and sounds good

Old 1st SGT Broadhead going home—Was damned good

Have a feeling we will have contact tonight

After arriving at Verna, our next mission was changed several times because we were the unit in the best position to react to any contact in the battalion AO. Recon had been working the area I thought to be our most likely destination so I called Bill Little on the radio to ask for his analysis. Bill said that they had made no contact but had found signs of recent activity. We traded a few barbs and anecdotes about our days in Charlie Company before our conversation was cut short by the arrival of recon's airmobile assets. With the incoming chopper noise all but drowning out the radio transmission, Bill signed off by telling me they were going to look for a suspected NVA headquarters complex farther south.

Loeffke called with orders to establish my company CP at Tan Lap and move my platoons into separate areas of the jungle. He added that the S-2 would arrive with our trucks to brief us on an additional mission.

Minutes later the battalion S-2 drove up with our truck convoy. With him was a young man about 17 years old dressed in black pajamas and Ho Chi Minh sandals. The S-2 explained that the man had surrendered to an ARVN detachment near Xuan Luc the day before. He had turned in an AK47 as well as much information about the VC/ NVA in the area and claimed to know where caches of weapons, including a heavy machine gun, and food were hidden.

In accordance with the country-wide Chieu Hoi program, the soldier was not to be treated as a POW: he was eligible for a cash reward for the rifle he had surrendered, and the promise of additional money for any other weapons he could lead us to had resulted in his offer to show us the caches' locations. Many of my soldiers crowded around the Chieu Hoi, as few had seen a live enemy except through the sights of their rifles. The young man was obviously scared and became more so with all the attention. I showed him my map in hopes he could point out where we would find the hidden weapons. He did not seem to know what a map was as he chattered to the S-2's interpreter. The interpreter said that the soldier could not read a map but could lead us to the caches from Tan Lap. He added that the dink was scared that if he wore his black pajama uniform into the jungle that either we or his former compatriots would shoot him. Scrounging around the fire base, we found an extra set of small jungle fatigues and a rucksack for our new guide.

I did not like the idea of sending the Chieu Hoi with only one platoon because the gook might be leading them into an ambush. My objections were overruled by Loeffke.

According to the translator, the caches were in the third platoon's area, so I turned the Chieu Hoi over to Schmalz. He was not enthusiastic over the mission and was even less excited when I told him to be damn sure no one killed the dink.

The S-2 added to our problem by announcing that he could not spare his interpreter to go with us. He was not interested in my question about how in the hell we were going to communicate with our guide except to suggest that we follow him.

As the S 2 got into his jeep to hurry back to Black Horse, we got on our trucks and drove to Tan Lap. While the platoons were unloading in front of the train station, I noticed the Chieu Hoi had gained a few bumps and bruises on his face during the trip. Schmalz explained that they had caught him trying to steal a can of C-rations. I again reminded Brian that I did not want a dead Chieu Hoi on our hands.

I had my medic take a look at our guide to be sure his "fall in the truck" had not broken anything. Doc reported that he was okay but added, "That sure is one skinny, hungry gook."

Schmalz gathered up Cs and soon his entire platoon was smiling at the Chieu Hoi as he ate can after can of the cold chow. Before the platoon moved out, Brian said he had named the man Pee Wee so they would at least have something to call him. Pee Wee seemed to recognize that he had a new name and either the identity or the chow caused him to act a little less terrified.

Near sundown a jeep pulled in carrying mail, supplies, and my new first sergeant. My old top NCO had been a good administrator but had never been farther forward than Black Horse during my weeks of command. I had said nothing because Broadhead was close to going home.

Beckles's first statement was to say that he was staying the night so we could get to know each other. Of medium height and build, Beckles had the blackest skin of any man I had ever seen. Nearing 40, the native of Panama looked and acted like a professional soldier. Over the next few months I was to find that my new first sergeant was even better than first appearances.

Besides talking to Beckles, I was preoccupied with a feeling that the darkness would bring contact. Schmalz was out there with a dink who had been the enemy less than 48 hours before. All the platoons were in new AOs which Bill Little had felt were going to heat up.

✈ 9 NOVEMBER 1969

My feeling of contact last night was nearly right—3rd plt made contact at 1100 with squad size carrying party— One killed—Pursued—Got one more—I had 105 & 155 arty working block—Then got in 2 light fire teams— Moved 1st plt into blocking position—Then airmobiled in

2nd plt to help—I went in with 2nd—Another light contact with neg results after getting there—No casualties—
Did have a radio antenna shot in two by AK47
　　Most of higher came on my net with suggestions etc.
　　My men did a good job—My first contact as a Co CO—I am satisfied
　　Believe we had squad plus in the area
　　Night ambush

Schmalz was reporting to me on the radio that Pee Wee had led them to a stack of empty ammo boxes but had then seemed disoriented and unable to decide in what direction to go next. As Brian was explaining that they were holding in place for the Chieu Hoi to get his bearings, I could hear the sudden exchange of small arms and automatic rifle fire.

Schmalz reported a squad of dinks had approached their position. Several of the enemy had been carrying heavy packs which they dumped in their retreat after their point man fell to the third platoon's bullets. Brian gave the map coordinates of the contact and the direction of the gooks' withdrawal with the coolness of a much more experienced leader.

My CP became an organized madhouse as many events started to happen at the same time. I had SGT Barnes, the acting FO, call a fire mission to block the dinks' retreat. While Coleman reported the engagement to Battalion, I called Bolenske, who was nearest to the fighting, telling him to move toward Schmalz. As soon as he acknowledged, I ordered Kidalowski to move to the Tan Lap soccer field to airmobile in to help. A last transmission on the company net went back to Schmalz with instructions to pursue the enemy. Brian acknowledged and remained on the horn adjusting the artillery that Barnes now had ripping into the jungle.

Loeffke was on the battalion net with approval of my request for choppers to carry my CP and the second platoon into the fight. He also said two light fire teams of Cobras would soon be on station.

My RTOs were packing up as I coordinated the artillery and gunships to keep constant fire going into the jungle around the enemy. Schmalz kept smoke out so the chopper pilots would not shoot at the wrong target. With a radio mike in each hand, I switched from one to the other, orchestrating the battle as we double-timed to the soccer field to meet the helicopters.

Fifteen minutes after the initiation of the contact, Schmalz reported killing another dink who had run into them in his flight from the wall of artillery. Kidalowski called seconds later and reported he would be at the PZ in five minutes.

By the time my CP reached the soccer field, the second platoon was spread out awaiting the birds. When I got to the gap Jack had left in the center of the formation, I received a call over the radio from the lead slick asking me to pop smoke. We popped the smoke, and one man in each group took a wide-legged stance with his rifle held horizontally above his head to guide his group's bird to touchdown.

Everything was clicking along perfectly until my chopper lifted off. I could feel the chopper struggling to gain altitude as the pilots pulled all available power. When we neared the end of the field, the rubber trees were still towering above us. Suddenly the pilots cut their power and we went back to the ground with a jolt, skidding forward several meters.

The pilots turned and smiled as they waited for the other choppers to clear the tree line. They then hovered and made a slow turn back toward the far end of the field. With a longer run at the trees and more shuddering of the aircraft, we lifted off and joined the formation. En route to the LZ, Nesmith hollered above the rotor noise that Bolenske had reached his blocking position.

Our LZ was a small clearing in a banana grove. We were barely out of the birds and running for the tree line when three dinks opened up. Kidalowski's men returned fire as I called for one of the Cobras to assist. The radio transmission seemed awfully weak for the short distance to the gunship. It was not until later that I noticed Coleman's radio antenna had been shot in two a few inches above our heads.

We had been lucky that we had the only fight going on in the area so we could receive all available support. In addition to the two Cobras firing their entire basic loads, the artillery pumped over four hundred rounds into the jungle. It was a lot of money spent, but we had two bodies as well as several blood trails attesting to the possibility of more dead.

For the rest of the day we tried to regain contact to no avail. Loeffke, who had been orbiting the fight in his command ship, radioed congratulations on the body count and signed off with a simple, "Well done."

My first fire fight as a company commander had been absolutely exhilarating with a rush of almost intoxicating adrenaline. A body count and no friendly losses were exactly what Bravo required to gain that bit of needed confidence.

> Search in contact area—2nd plt to Cam Tam on Viet-
> namization mission—3rd plt swept south—1st plt block
> and ambush N–S trails
> I returned to Tan Lap for coordination—Have 2 EMs
> I will put in for Ar Com w V for 9 Nov actions
> Contact search yielded 100 lbs food and other military
> equipment
> Contact is on increase in this area
> The Co is coming on along with rapid progress
> One of favorite foods of all people in VN is mackerel
> canned in Japan—Comes in a red can with tomato sauce—
> I ate some today—Not bad

A detailed search of the contact area produced over one
hundred pounds of food plus several uniforms, cooking
utensils, packs, and a small amount of ammunition.

Everyone was feeling good about the previous day's
contact, but today was a new day. In typical Infantry fash-
ion, our reward for doing well was simply the opportunity
to do it again.

Bolenske's platoon moved back to its AO while
Schmalz's platoon linked up with my CP and the second
platoon. The battalion S-2 wanted the Chieu Hoi back,
and Kidalowski's platoon was needed for another week of
training ARVNs.

Pee Wee seemed even more terrified than before as a
result of being in the middle of the fire fight with his old
comrades. Surprisingly the third platoon no longer displayed any hostility toward the little dink. His rucksack
was full of C-rations they had given him. Schmalz said he

wanted to keep Pee Wee as a Kit Carson scout, but it was evident that the Chieu Hoi was becoming more of a mascot than an asset. The decision concerning the fate of Pee Wee was not ours anyway as there was much more questioning by the intelligence folks in line for him.

By noon Pee Wee, the second platoon, and my CP had walked back to Tan Lap. Later the S-2 reclaimed the Chieu Hoi, insisting that the reluctant Pee Wee surrender his full sack of C-rations.

After coordinating with the local ARVN detachment for our security, I had some time to take a better look at Tan Lap. Typically I was ignored by the old and mobbed by the young begging for candy and cigarettes. The only difference I could tell between the children of Tan Lap and those of the many other villages I had visited was that they had a leader. About three and a half feet tall, the leader was quite muscular, with an abnormally large head. He seemed to bully the kids yet was protective of those picked on by others. It was some time before I realized that he was a dwarf.

The young man became friendlier after I gave him a pack of cigarettes which he shared with the children. He seemed intelligent and spoke enough English to tell me that he was 20 years old. I wondered, but did not ask, why as an adult in all but stature he remained with the children. Perhaps because of his dwarfism he was the only young man of the village not in uniform and as a result was expected to watch over the kids. Maybe the villagers just did not accept a little person as an adult. The whole situation was just another of the perplexities of Nam that I did not understand.

Tan Lap

This AO getting hot again—3 different contacts yesterday—Delta had 5 or 7 WIA—My old recon plt took several WIA

Also understand that LT Bill Little was KIA—Old C Co plt ldr buddy—Understand that a gook was about to open up on them—Little pushed his RTO out of the way—Tried to engage with M-16—Gook was just a little too fast

My 3rd plt still working in 9 Nov contact area—Found 3 small and 3 large bunkers—Also medical, cooking, and sleeping equipment—Also I crossbow

Have 1st plt on joint recon with ARVNs

Schmalz and I were commenting over the radio about the crossbow's being a good souvenir when I overheard reports of recon's contact on the battalion net. Recon's transmissions were coming in weakly, but evidently Battalion was receiving them clearly. Although I did not recognize the voice reporting for recon, I could tell from the terror in the man's speech that the fight was not going well.

The trembling voice said that they had one killed and one wounded. Rather than giving the line number of the KIA, the voice on the radio reported that "Outpost 40" was dead. I grabbed my code book in futile desperation, hoping not to confirm what I already knew. Outpost 40 was the call sign I had used only a few days before to contact Bill Little.

I listened to the subsequent reports the rest of the day

and night. The details were confused as all initial battle reports tend to be, but the one clear fact was that recon had not been able to retrieve Bill's body. Charlie Company was the nearest unit to the contact and was moving to assist recon. McGinnis reported over the radio that they would be in position to support by early morning. Loeffke called and directed me to have Bravo prepared to airmobile to assist at sunup.

About midnight I sat down with my journal in the dimly lit Tan Lap depot to record the day's events. How was I to write of my best friend's death? The answer was simple. The words that went into my journal merely stated the facts as I knew them at the time. I wrote of Bill's death in the same detached, unemotional tone as I recorded other events. I did not, and could not, write of the sense of loss, of the knot in my chest that made it difficult to breathe, or of the burning desire to vent my revenge on every god-damn gook in the jungle.

I could not write the feelings, for if I had done so, I would also have had to record my other thoughts as well. A month before I had been the recon platoon leader. It could have been me as easily as my friend. No matter how hard I tried to avoid thinking about it, Bill's death made me feel all the more alive. Feelings of guilt that I should have remained with recon were coldly set aside; I knew I would not willingly change places with my dead comrade.

Through the long night I felt every emotion a man can experience. I cursed the gooks, the war, the Army, God, and—more than anything else—my absolute helplessness in not being able to change what had already occurred. Frustrations of the night blended with the fear of tomorrow's unknown. The fight was not over. Soon Bravo would join the battle to recover Little's body.

> We airmobiled in—Linked up with D 17th Cav—Block-
> ing positions tonight—We hit base camp tomorrow—Al-
> ways a strange feeling when you know you are going into
> contact
>
> This morning my 3rd plt received 2 AK47 sniper
> rounds—Lucky gook was bad shot—3rd plt hosed down
> area—I put arty in with no luck
>
> Also saw flashlights in rubber last night—Put arty in

At daybreak I ordered Bolenske and Schmalz to return
to the soccer field PZ. The sniper rounds received by the
third platoon would have been more significant on any
other day. Schmalz wanted more time to search the artillery impact area as well as the location where they had
seen flashlights the night before. However, he did not argue further when I told him to double-time to the PZ because we had more important things pending.

As my RTOs packed up our CP, McGinnis's voice came
over the battalion radio reporting that they had linked up
with recon and were assaulting the gooks' positions which
by now had been identified as a bunker complex. Minutes
later, the Charlie CO reported that they had been kicked
back and requested dust-offs for his wounded.

McGinnis was asking Loeffke to send more help when
a Vietnamese-accented voice broke into the transmission
and said in clearly understandable English, "We have your
lieutenant. Come and get him." A long laugh followed.

It was obvious that along with Bill's body the gooks had

his code books containing all the battalion's call signs, frequencies, and ciphers.

The battalion was spread out all over the AO preparing to converge on the contact area. New code books were impossible to deliver to each company, the supporting artillery, engineers, and air assets on short notice. We all knew the enemy did not stand and fight unless they were confident conditions were in their favor. Now they had the added benefit of listening to every move we made.

Loeffke was on the radio with information that choppers would pick us up immediately. He ignored the repeated transmission breaks by the gooks which varied from unintelligible Vietnamese to distinct English threats such as, "GIs, you die." Loeffke's only reference to the enemy's intrusions was to instruct all stations to minimize traffic until further notice.

On the soccer field I briefed my platoon leaders on our mission. My soldiers were wide-eyed and sober with anticipation of the fight, yet they showed far more confidence than fear as they checked their weapons and adjusted their packs.

We soon touched down in an LZ about three klicks from the bunker complex. Every artillery tube within range was pouring steel into the base. The continuous shelling ceased only for seconds as Air Force F-4s streaked in dropping bombs and napalm.

Loeffke met me on the LZ with a diagram showing the battalion's efforts to encircle the enemy position. Little and his recon platoon had stumbled upon the complex from the west. McGinnis and Charlie Company, after linking up with recon, had assaulted the position from the north with no success. We were to attack from the south.

A platoon of armored cavalry was now breaking through the jungle to link up with us. The bombardment of the base camp was to continue until morning when Bravo and the tracks would attack.

Along with giving me temporary frequencies and call signs, Loeffke told me that he was attaching a platoon from A Company to Bravo because he had been unable to recall Kidalowski's platoon from its ARVN support mission.

In the late afternoon the tracks arrived, and together we pushed in several hundred meters closer to the objective where we assumed blocking positions to prevent the gooks' escape. Although our circle around the enemy was now composed of over four hundred men, it was impossible to block all the avenues of escape. Whether the gooks would stay and take the punishment of the artillery and air strikes, which continued to fire into the base camp throughout the night, or retreat to fight another day, no one knew.

During the night I crouched inside one of the personnel carriers devising my plan of attack on the back of a C-ration carton. A small stream ran perpendicular to our direction of advance about five hundred meters in front of the bunkers. Since we still had over a kilometer of jungle to break through before reaching the stream, the tracks would move in file until we hit the banks. At the stream the tracks would move on line with a platoon of Infantry on each flank and one in the center of the formation. With the seven armored carriers, three Sheridans, and over one hundred grunts, we should be able to overrun the gooks— regardless of their defenses or determination.

At 0300 hours I was still tinkering with the plan when exhaustion overcame me. A couple of hours later Coleman woke me up with the word that the sun would soon be rising.

Coordinated plan for taking base camp with tracks
Have a plt of A Co OPCONed to me—LTC Loeffke
came in to go in with us—He thinks I have a good plan
We started in after all types of arty and air strikes—
We have 7 APCs and 3 Sheridan tanks
After trouble crossing a stream we moved in with
tracks firing—Gooks had just pulled out—Only resistance
was one fire bomb booby trap that didn't get anybody
Set up in base camp and began search

> "Too many of us have not learned that freedom is
> not free."
>
> Gen. Omar N. Bradley

At daylight I briefed Loeffke on my plan. He made no
changes except to say that he was going in, too.

The battalion commander made no mention of Bill Little until I asked if he knew more about how Bill had been
killed. Loeffke said that there were several stories, but the
most accurate seemed to be that Bill had died trying to
help his wounded point man. The soldier had been hit in
the legs, and Bill, along with his RTO, had crawled forward to get the man. The two of them had been dragging
the wounded troop when the gooks opened up, hitting Bill
in the chest. Bill had told his RTO to take the point man
back to the platoon while he covered their withdrawal.
Recon had tried to fight their way back to Little, but they
had been badly outnumbered. Loeffke said that some reports said Bill had continued to fire his M-16 for several
minutes before being silenced.

All stories were as accurate as they could be recalled by soldiers in the midst of a fire fight. Time under fire is nearly impossible to calculate, and rarely did two individuals ever see a battle in the same way.

I had hoped that Bill might still be alive and hiding somewhere in the jungle, but I knew better. The gook RTO had already announced that they had him. That meant Bill was dead, as there was no way they could have taken him alive. After two days, I could only dread what retaliation the dinks had taken out on Bill's body.

The artillery and air strikes continued during our move to the bunkers. Our progress was much slower than I had anticipated because of the great difficulty the tracks had in breaking through the jungle. It was afternoon before we reached the stream. We were delayed further when we discovered that the banks were higher and the water deeper than we had expected.

We finally crossed several hundred meters downstream from where we had planned. Dusk was nearing when we reached the edge of the artillery and bomb impact area.

With every gun firing, we began our final assault. Our initial shots were answered by a huge fireball covering an area half the size of a football field. We could feel the searing heat, but we were far enough away that no one was injured. Apparently our tracer rounds had detonated the fire bomb booby trap early.

Minutes later the tracks crunched over the nearest fortifications. My men spread out, throwing grenades into the bunkers. As far as we could see, there were more bunkers and connecting trenches, but no live enemy remained.

Darkness was fast approaching, so our search for Little would have to wait until morning.

Day started with a bang—Track LT Kim (at 0600) yelled "Good morning, Chuck," and had a mad minute of firing—No return fire—Search began

We found LT Little's body fairly soon—Gooks had partially buried him—3 days in sun—I had to identify body—Not much left—However gooks had not muti lated him—Put body in poncho and carried out to LZ

Linked up with C Co and recon plt—Like old home week for me

Findings:

1 AK47
1 RPG launcher
6 pistols
500 lbs rice
20 Chicom grenades
1 remains of military radio
7 RPG B-40 rockets
20 AK magazines
1000 rounds assorted ammo
5 lbs medicine
20 canteens
10 lbs documents

I have one of pistols—German Nazi 9 mm—Beautiful
Documents say this 274 NVA Regiment Hdqs

Our perimeter occupied only a toehold of the large bunker complex. By beginning the morning with a "mad minute" of machine gun fire from the tracks' weapons, we could begin our search reasonably assured that the gooks were not waiting in ambush. LT Kim's tracks fired up a lot of ammo, but since they literally carried it by the case, they had plenty in reserve to support us against any counterattack.

Leaving Kim's platoon in an observation position, my Infantry platoons swept through the rest of the base camp. We soon discovered the complex covered an irregular oval more than six hundred meters across at the widest point. Reports of finding bodies, weapons, and equipment in the sweep came in over the radio in a steady stream.

Once I was satisfied that we knew the general outline of the camp, I assigned platoons sectors for security and a detailed search. Kim's tracks covered the most likely avenues of approach of any returning gooks.

Loeffke requested Engineer support to prepare an LZ and to destroy the bunkers. He also instructed Charlie Company and the recon platoon to link up at our location.

My RTOs were establishing our CP in the center of the complex when Schmalz radioed that his men had found a body that appeared to be a GI. Taking Coleman and his radio along, I quickly joined Brian.

Near a bunker on the western edge of the camp was a half-buried body. Dirt had been thrown hastily on the chest and legs, but the jungle boot-clad feet and head remained uncovered. No one had approached the body, as Brian had warned his troops that it might be booby-trapped.

Three days in the jungle heat, combined with a head wound now teeming with a huge ball of wiggling white maggots, made it impossible to recognize Bill as I had last seen him. However, we were missing only one American. The six-foot-long corpse, dressed in jungle fatigues splitting from the pressure of bloated flesh, could be no one but Bill.

I took a thin rope from Coleman's pack as I told him and the others to move back. After carefully tying the cord to one of Bill's legs, I retreated behind the nearby bunker and tried to pull the body toward me. I pulled a couple of times, but my last tug on the rope pulled the leg loose from the hip socket. I was afraid the rotting limb would come off completely if I increased the tension any more. Still, I made enough progress to satisfy me that the body was not booby-trapped.

I walked back to Bill to pull his body clear of the rest of the dirt. As I lifted the supine corpse, the gleam of something metal made me dive for cover before my mind registered the fact that the objects under the body were rifle magazines and not a booby-trapped grenade. On closer inspection I found eight empty magazines and six more still fully loaded with M-16 rounds.

Bill's West Point ring, which he had worn so proudly on his left hand, was gone as were all the patches and the name tag from his uniform. However, except for a bullet hole in his chest and the head wound, his body was unmarked other than by the elements of deterioration.

I had fully expected to find Bill in pieces. The gooks had not mutilated him at all but, instead, treated him as a fellow warrior. Empty and full magazines had been left in tribute to a man who had bravely died fighting.

The dirt which had been thrown on him had likely been an effort by the dinks to control the smell of rotting flesh while they defended their fire base. The valorous stink as much as any other dead.

Schmalz's platoon and my RTO left me alone with Bill. Brian asked if he could help, but I told him all he could do was to get me a poncho. When he returned a few minutes later, Loeffke was with him.

Loeffke made no comment as he dropped to his knees beside the body. I was untying the rope from Bill's leg when I noticed tears streaming down the battalion commander's face. He reached into his pack, took out a can of insect repellent and began spraying the maggots. The chemicals seemed only to make the creatures more active. Loeffke continued to spray until I said, "That won't do any good."

He responded, "Are you sure it's him?"

In answer I pulled Bill's shirt apart to better expose the bullet hole and the rest of his chest. Although the bloated flesh looked hardly human, I recognized the torso from having seen Bill go shirtless around the fire bases we had shared. "It's him," I said.

As we sat by the body, I showed Loeffke the magazines, remarking about how Bill must have gone down fighting. Loeffke said he was putting Little in for the Medal of Honor.

Loeffke and I wrapped the body in the poncho, tying it in place with the rope. Several troops joined us as we carried the body toward the LZ that LT Kim's troops had blown. About halfway to the clearing we stopped for a break. Without saying anything, I left the others to complete the task and returned to my CP. Bill had been taken care of; I had other responsibilities awaiting me.

I had felt little emotion during the recovery of the body. In some ways I envied Loeffke's tears. Perhaps he was mature enough to release his sorrow while still maintaining his composure. At twenty-three I was not so confident. The only way I could handle my feelings was just not to feel at all. I set my jaw, concentrated on my duties, and shed not a tear.

Later in the day Charlie Company joined in our search of the bunkers. Although everyone was subdued because of Little's death, it was good to see McGinnis and my old platoon. DeForrest, my former RTO, now carried the company radio, and Doc Bass, who had been my aid man, was the senior medic. I told McGinnis that it looked as if the old first platoon CP was now his.

McGinnis and I divided the complex between our companies and established a joint CP while our troops continued ferreting out the equipment and supplies left by the gooks.

Recon arrived a short time later to be extracted by helicopter from our LZ. I talked with several of my old NCOs, but they were able to add few details to the previous accounts of what had happened. Obviously saddened by the loss of their leader, they appeared all but humiliated at their failure to recover his body. As the choppers were coming in, SGT McHaffey told me that they had done their best to fight their way to where they could hear Little's M-16 blazing away on full automatic. He lowered his head and sighed, saying that there were just too damn many of the gooks and too few of recon.

Throughout the day Bravo and Charlie soldiers found weapons, food and equipment. By late afternoon the troops were tiring of their search, so McGinnis and I took an RTO apiece and wandered throughout the complex talking to our soldiers. On our way back to the CP, I noticed a wooden trap door obscured by trees blown down by the artillery. Coleman and I carefully removed the door, exposing a small spider hole. DeForrest, as the smallest of the four of us, volunteered to check it out. Seconds later he reappeared with a pistol and an RPG launcher, then with bags of rice and finally with more pistols.

Capturing one handgun was unusual—six was unbelievable. The guns included one US 45-caliber, three Chinese 7.62-millimeters, a Canadian-made 9-millimeter Browning and a Walter P-38 9-millimeter boldly stamped with the eagle and swastika of the Third Reich. Their varied backgrounds were just as mysterious as their numbers.

The American and Canadian pistols could not be kept as individual war trophies because of their origins, so we

sent them to Battalion with the other captured goods. Mc-
Ginnis, our RTOs, and I kept the others for ourselves.
Because I had been the one to discover the trap door, I
got first choice. The mystery of just how the P-38 had
gotten from Nazi Germany to an NVA bunker complex
fascinated me. How many hands had it passed through or
how many times had it been sold in the international gun
market, I could not imagine. Whatever its source, it was
mine now.

Loeffke later told me that Bill had been buried in the
West Point cemetery at the request of his parents. The
battalion commander had followed through with his promise of trying to get Bill the Medal of Honor. However,
because there were no living witnesses, at least on our
side, of Little's final fight, the medal had not been approved. Instead, Bill was posthumously awarded the Distinguished Service Cross, our country's second highest
valor award, along with a Purple Heart.

It was not until the winter of 1978—nine years later—
that I finally dealt honestly with the death of Bill Little.
During a tour of the historic grounds of the United States
Military Academy at West Point, my brother, who was
then on the Academy staff, asked if I would like to see the
cemetery.

My answer was yes, but my desire was not to see the
graves of famous generals and honored heroes. I felt com-
pelled to visit the plot of my old platoon-leader buddy.

Directions for finding his grave were on a simple card
in the cemetery chapel files. Once headed on the correct
course, I did not need to count rows or the numbers of
crosses and Stars of David. An inner force seemed to lead
me down the snow-covered gravel path to Bill's grave.

My brother and our wives were a few steps behind as I
reached and touched Bill's headstone. By the time I had

read his name, unit, and death date that I remembered so well, they quietly joined me.

Feeling as if they were intruding upon my grief, my brother asked if I would like to stay for a while. I could only choke out, "No, it doesn't take long to look at a grave." With these words, I hurried from the cemetery. By the time I reached our car, the tears had dried, but the emotions and complete sense of loss remained. The feelings that I had not confronted for all those years were no less powerful for the delay.

✈ 15 NOVEMBER 1969

> Continue search of base camp—More rice, food, etc. found
>
> Also NVA graves found—One of which appears to be an officer as it was buried deeper and better taken care of
>
> The stench of dead men does not wash off—I have an Engineer sqd to blow bunkers—Loeffke came back out— He says we are on top of a tunnel complex—I had Engineers blow shaped cratering charges—As we figured: no tunnels

Spread throughout the entire complex were enemy dead. Some were lying where they had fallen while others were buried in shallow graves. Some of the bodies appeared to have been dead for several days either from Little's bullets or Charlie Company's unsuccessful assaults while others had been ripped apart by the artillery and air strikes.

To confirm the body count, we dug up each of the graves and inspected the green plastic-wrapped bodies for cause of death so the correct units could be credited with the kills. We re-buried each corpse, often kicking in an additional unburied body—not out of any sense of respect other than for our own noses.

For the first few hours in the complex the stench had been overpowering, and although there were plenty of complaints, only the newest replacements seemed to be particularly bothered. After awhile, everyone got used to the rotten-sweet smell of decaying flesh.

The most interesting grave was one near the center of the camp. Dug much deeper and outlined with a two-foot high border of bamboo stakes, it contained the body of an older dink who had been hit by small arms fire in the chest.

We ended up exhuming and re-burying him three times—first for my initial inspection, later in the day when Loeffke returned, and then finally for the S-2 who wanted to take pictures. When the intelligence officer arrived to say that he wanted photographs, I told him he could dig the dink up himself. After he explained that the documents we had captured indicated the body was the commander of the 274th NVA Regiment, we complied. It was worth the effort, not because later reports confirmed the corpse's identity, but to watch the S-2 throw up between camera shots of the now thoroughly putrefied body.

Over the next few days I was surprised to hear that the ten bodies I had counted had grown to twenty-seven and then to thirty-three. My initial thoughts were that the count was inflated as it went up through higher headquarters, but that was not the case. Charlie Company moved out that afternoon following a heavy trail out of the camp. In the next few days they found single graves as well as a caved-in bunker containing twelve bodies.

Over the next weeks I continued to think about what had bothered me since the first word of Little's death. I had been troubled about why we had not made more of an effort to recover his body earlier and why the gooks had decided to make a stand, only to retreat before inflicting any more casualties on us. It all made more sense as the additional dead gooks were discovered.

The NVA had obviously thought we would mount continued ground attacks to reach Bill. Loeffke, with the 3 July fight well in mind, had decided to seal off the area and let the artillery and air strikes destroy the dinks. Only after being pounded for two days and hearing the approach of the tracks and Bravo did they realize their mistake. At least thirty-three, including their commander, had died for one of us. Although they had been able to evacuate much of their equipment, their losses were so heavy that they had to leave ten of their comrades behind and hastily bury the other twenty-three where they were easily discovered. Other signs—including blood trails and abandoned litters—indicated that their casualties were even greater than the final official body count of thirty-three.

From my study of the base camp I decided that the dinks had withdrawn down the stream bed we had had so much difficulty crossing just before our final assault. The number of bunkers indicated that over two hundred had originally occupied the camp.

Loeffke agreed in part with my synopsis but believed that some of the enemy might still be in tunnels under the camp. Using forty-pound shaped cratering charges, the Engineers blew over twenty holes down to depths of twenty-five feet in search of tunnels. My troops also went again over every foot of the complex looking for entrances, air holes, or any other evidence of tunnels. I was not surprised at our lack of findings, as I was sure the only dinks underground near us were in graves.

---

16 NOVEMBER 1969

> Lost the tracks today—Elements of 3rd plt found 300 lbs of rice, one 60-mm mortar round, 3 NVA uniforms, 50 AK rounds—Most gear and supplies were removed before we got here I feel
>
> Engineers blew a total of 74 bunkers
>
> Also in area painted on trees we found the following: (Near 6 graves of NVA) "This is something to think about." (Near a command bunker) "Opopse [sic] the agressive [sic] war in Vietnam. Demand immediate repatration [sic]."
>
> They must have an educated gook with them
>
> Call sign and push changes because gooks got them off LT Little's body—My call sign now Brash Trick Bravo 29

With the departure of the tracks and the attached platoons from Alpha Company and the Engineers, I was more than ready to get Bravo out of the bunker complex. The third platoon's discovery of more equipment led, however, to another day of searching and another night in the foul-smelling camp.

The English-speaking gook who had taunted us by radio

was the likely author of the neatly printed signs in black paint on areas of trees where the bark had been peeled away. Except for his misspellings, his grammar and vocabulary were at a much higher intellectual level than that of our normal grunt conversations. I wondered just how or when the dink had been able to prepare his messages in the midst of the bombardment. In view of the number of NVA dead, his warning, "This is something to think about," seemed more a self-prophesy than an effective message to us.

🖎 17 NOVEMBER 1969

Finally got word to depart the area—While moving northeast, point element engaged one enemy—Neg results—Night time in same area

I hear that by the time report got to the Bde, it was that we found 27 bodies—Also one grave was possibly 274th Reg CO—With a rotted body, this is a pretty good guess—We had to dig him up for S-2

One of my men showed me a letter today—Is from a doctor saying the soldier's girl is pregnant—I will grant him emergency leave to marry her

We had only moved a half a klick from the bunkers when a brief exchange of M-16 and AK47 fire sent us diving for cover. We pursued the enemy until losing any sign of his retreat a few hundred meters later. The point man reported that he had only seen a fleeting image of one dink and both he and the dink had fired at about the same instant. We found no blood trails or signs that any of our man's bullets had hit their mark. I thought it likely that the lone enemy soldier was watching his old camp to see when we would depart, indicating that the enemy might return, and when I reported this to Battalion, I requested that occasional artillery be fired into the complex for the next few days. Perhaps the camp would yield even more bodies before the enemy gave it up for good.

The nineteen-year-old with the doctor's letter verifying the girlfriend's pregnancy was not happy with the news of his impending fatherhood. I was not either as the man, who had been in-country only a month, had already proven to be a good soldier. I had gotten to know him fairly well because he had been on the detail that dug up the NVA commander's grave three times. When he asked for leave to return home to marry his girl, I reluctantly agreed. I did not like the idea of losing a rifleman for a month, but even considering the past week's events, I never doubted that he would return. The same feelings of responsibility that drew him to marry his pregnant girlfriend would bring him back to share the tribulations of his fellow soldiers.

Daylight ambushes in same area—Afternoon moved east for night positions—Raining again—Word to move to FB Crystal tomorrow

Very slow day—VN can be a damn boring place

7 months over here today—Seems as if I've been in VN all my life

I remember fire fights before R&R—Used to pray I would not get hit before R&R—Now, as always, praying that all my men and myself will get out of damn place alive

As I told Linda Ann on R&R, losing a limb etc. is bad—But to get home alive is a great accomplishment

We welcomed the cooling return of the rains—for the first minute or so. Then we again cursed it for adding to our discomforts.

Black scorpions, over three inches long, were as common as leeches in this part of the jungle, and they provided the day's only excitement. SSG English captured one of the ugly stingers and placed it in a plastic box meant to protect a pack of cigarettes. The platoon sergeant proudly showed me the scorpion while explaining that it would make a good lab specimen when he returned to college. I did not ask just how he planned to keep the creature alive nor how he was going to get it home.

It was better to be humping the boonies than sitting in an ambush all day. When moving, we had little time to think about anything except navigating and looking for the gooks. When in static positions—even though we remained alert—we had time to think of other things, proving that often one's mind can be far more dangerous an enemy than soldiers on the other side.

I did my best not to dwell on Bill Little. When my thoughts did drift back over the last seven months, I had little trouble dismissing any bad memories, as I could do nothing to change what had already occurred. While responsibilities for the continued welfare of my men and killing the enemy weighed heavily, I thought of my own vulnerabilities. The longer I stayed in the field, the more the odds stacked up against my remaining alive. I still prayed, but I had few promises left to negotiate with. All I now asked for was to make it out alive—it no longer seemed right to ask to survive with all the pieces still intact.

 19 NOVEMBER 1969

Moved out early for FB Crystal—Crystal is built triangular with one point extending out into jungle—This is so patrols can go out and come in unobserved—Also means gooks can almost walk in—Good bunkers etc. here—Are supposed to be here 3 days

CG Bennett was at this location today—I heard Bn CO tell him I was doing "outstanding job"—CG later told me he would try and see to it I could keep Co.—Was in doubt since we are getting new Bn CO and Bde CG

More reports that they think we got 274th CO

CPT Hartley, A Co CO dusted off 2 days ago with possible malaria

Call signs and frequencies changed again—My call sign now Fair Thieves Bravo 114

The more I thought about it, the more firmly I believed that being concerned for the soldiers' and my own well-being was a pretty sane way of looking at things. I certainly did not want to be anywhere in Nam other than in command of Bravo, and I was willing to take the risks that went with the assignment.

We approached Crystal with extreme caution. Surrounded by jungle ten to twenty kilometers in all directions, it had been built in one of the 200-meter-wide lanes cleared by the "Rome plow" operations. By using bulldozers and cutting and blasting trees, the Engineers had created brown strips that snaked through the thick vegetation in efforts to help us find the enemy or to at least deny him triple-canopied protection from airborne observation. My first impression of the "Rome plow" destruction of the jungle was to think that perhaps we were indeed finally going to clear the whole damn country and cover it with concrete as DeForrest had suggested months before.

We stayed on the radio with the fire base CP and popped smoke as soon as we reached the edge of the "Rome plow" strip five hundred meters south of the wire perimeter. As soon as the CP confirmed that everyone was aware that we were coming in, we proceeded.

Crystal was a vulnerable-looking place. Although we could see over a kilometer to the north and to the south, the tree line to the east was only two hundred meters away. However, the amazing characteristic of Crystal was that the western point of the triangle-shaped base extended fifty meters into the jungle on its western side. A small berm with a few rows of concertina wire was all that separated the tree-surrounded, sandbagged bunkers from the thickness of the jungle. The exchange factors of allowing our patrols to exit the base without being seen set against the apparent invitation for the gooks to approach in complete concealment did not compute as a good trade-off.

Some precautions had been made in that the artillery battery in the cleared eastern portion was in a complete perimeter within a perimeter. Small lanes existed in their thick concertina wire so that we could pull back to prepared bunkers if unable to hold the outer fortifications.

Alpha Company had been in Crystal since its beginnings nearly a month before. They had done an adequate job of establishing the defenses, so it looked as if we would have a fairly decent break over the next few days.

Keeping command was my main worry now. Loeffke and General Bennett were both due to rotate soon. New commanders, combined with the fact that many captains were waiting for companies, might mean my leaving the company. The reassurances from my bosses that I would stay in command were as welcome as the hot chow and clean uniforms that Beckles had waiting for us.

I hated to hear about the A Company commander's being evacuated. We did not need any new strains of malaria to add to the existing threats, but, at the same time, I could not help feeling glad that a new captain was getting a command and would not be waiting in line for Bravo.

Crystal

Visits today by Bn CO and XO—Also Bde DCO—DCO said he had heard some good things about me so I guess I'm doing my job—Have new FO that I got before last mission—2LT Gulbranson from South Dakota—I am not impressed at all with him as yet but maybe he will work out

C Co found what they thought to be a tunnel today—In checking it, some of the men passed out—First word was some type of mustard gas—Total of 16 dusted off—Final read out: lack of oxygen and carbon monoxide poisoning—None in bad shape

Also 6–8 dust-offs in Bn today—Food poisoning from sandwiches they sometimes drop in to us

My initial impressions of my new FO were somewhat unfair. Rick Gulbranson was only five months out of college and ROTC. Due to the shortage of artillery FOs throughout Vietnam, artillery officers were sent directly to the war zone. Rick's only shortcoming was a lack of experience; with the help of SGT Barnes, he showed promise of being an important asset to Bravo.

Alpha Battery, 2nd Battalion, 40th Field Artillery was positioned on the eastern side of the base. Their company commander, a mid-thirties captain, had a Greek name that was impossible to pronounce or spell accurately enough to record in my journal. This was no problem, as in direct dealings I called him "sir," but to anyone else I referred to him as "the Greek"—as did everyone, including his own troops.

Relationships between the artillery and their Infantry protectors were usually amiable but not particularly close. I decided that we should get to know each other better, if not because of proximity, then for an ulterior motive. If the redlegs saw Bravo as friends rather than just fellow soldiers, perhaps their already rapid response would be even faster when we needed their firepower.

As an introduction, I asked the Greek to have his gun crews show my grunts how the weapons operated. A few grunts at a time were allowed into the Fire Direction Center bunker to see how the missions were calculated to produce the proper range and deflection settings on each tube.

Rumors were infectious. It took much reassurance to convince the troops that the gooks were not using chemical warfare and that the C Company soldiers had merely been victims of a lack of oxygen in the tight tunnel.

Later the reports of dust-offs in other companies from stomach cramps added to the stories that were sweeping Crystal. Explanations that the illnesses had been caused by food poisoning from sandwiches left too long in the sun at the Black Horse helipad before delivery did little to quell the rumors. News of the spoiled-sandwich sickness was bad, not only in dust-offs but also in that it meant an end to the brief experiment of providing something other than C-rations to the field.

> Went to Black Horse by Huey this morning—Bn having a going away dinner for GEN Bennett
>
> While at BH I was asked to write a statement on LTC Loeffke's actions on last base camp, which I did
>
> Before dinner, at awards part, received my Bronze Star with Oak Leaf Cluster
>
> Saw LT Sassner
>
> LOH back to Company

Pomp and circumstance in the US Army continued even in the war zone. The departure of our brigade commander required a proper ceremony, regardless of other pressing missions. Although I resented the time away from the company, the occasion did provide an opportunity to see McGinnis, Lewis, and the other company commanders as well as enjoy a hot dinner.

The dinner was actually lunch, but my country upbringing had taught me that the noon meal was dinner while the final setting of the day was supper. My journal notations of dinner are another reflection of how I was not as far removed from the farm as I thought at the time.

A brief ceremony before we ate allowed Bennett to formally present several medals. My second Bronze Star still meant little, but I appreciated the brigade commander's commenting that he recalled pinning the first one on me back in August.

Shortly after the festivities, the battalion XO approached me and asked if I would write a statement supporting a recommendation for the Silver Star for LTC Loeffke's actions on 10–14 November. Loeffke had been all over the battle area and had far exceeded what was expected of a battalion commander in such circumstances, including his being with the point element during the final assault on the bunkers. I was not certain about any specific actions of his that merited such a high award, but I wrote a glowing account of his bravery nonetheless. Loeffke was the only man I had ever seen who never showed any sign of fear. He took chances that I would not have asked of any of my men, and his very presence seemed to have a calming effect on all around him. Maybe those things in themselves deserved valorous decorations.

My men shared my feelings about the battalion commander. He never seemed to sleep or remain at Black Horse, but rather, he ran the battalion from his helicopter or on the ground. It was not unusual for him to arrive at a fire base or on a jungle resupply bird and ask which soldier was doing an exceptionally good job. When a grunt was identified, he would shake the man's hand and tell him to fly back to Black Horse where a case of beer and the battalion commander's cot awaited him. Loeffke would then take the grunt's place in a squad and remain with the troops until the next day.

Loeffke's "Old Guard Soldier of the Day" program drove his staff crazy in their efforts to confer with him or at times know what company to call to reach him. Whatever his staff thought, the troops loved his actions and would have awarded him every medal possible.

> Spent a pretty easy day—Read a lot—Supervised laying
> of more barbed wire and fu gas around perimeter
> Had a good talk with SFC Ullum today—He is temp
> assigned to me for 3 weeks till his job at Bn opens up—
> I am using him as a field first sergeant—We drank beer
> and told war stories He is a Korea vet Pork Chop Hill
> etc.—Good bull stories

Chinook helicopters delivered a jellied petroleum prod-
uct similar to napalm for us to add to our arsenal around
the perimeter. We filled 55-gallon drums about one-third
full of the ''fu gas'' and placed them in holes at the far
edge of the concertina wire entanglements. A fuse connected by wire to our bunkers then allowed us to produce
a wall of flames thirty to fifty meters across in the event
of a ground attack.

After dark I decided to test one to see how it worked—
and the results were all but disastrous. The gas exploded
in a tremendous fireball exactly according to plan. However, sandbags we had placed around the drum and metal
pieces that were once the drum itself began to fall around
us. Fortunately, no one was hurt. We would have to be
sure everyone was in a covered bunker before we again
used the ''fu gas'' bombs.

SFC Ullum was a tall, lanky NCO who looked older
than his age—pushing 40. His infectious sense of humor
and total optimism, combined with his previous combat
experience in Korea and Vietnam, made him a memorable
character despite his short time with Bravo.

Although First Sergeant Beckles visited us on nearly every resupply, he could best handle the company's administrative and logistical support from Black Horse. Ullum's taking on the duties as "field first sergeant" greatly assisted me in the day-to-day routine of running the company in the fire base. The sergeant also provided excellent guidance to the young NCOs who, along with me, never tired of his stories of Pork Chop Hill and his many years of peacetime service.

23 NOVEMBER 1969

New CG Bond visited Crystal today—We gave him short tour of jungle in a driving rain—He and we got soaked—I was impressed with him

Big rain here this afternoon—Heard one man say, "If dinks come out, cut a hole in berm and drown them in flood, like Holland"

This seems a bit educated—However I have more college grads in this Co than any other Co I've seen in the Army

BG Bond told me today that I was highly thought of by the Bn CO—I am not surprised—We get body count

"I want to end the war to save the lives of those brave young men in Vietnam."

Pres. Richard M. Nixon
Nov 3 1969

red mud of Crystal. For days afterward the troops talked of the general who had gone into the jungle.

Since the monsoons were supposedly over, Crystal had been designed with little thought given to drainage. The afternoon rains left ankle-deep water over much of the base because the exterior berm held it in, making the entire triangle look like one of the farm ponds back home. The suggestion that we "cut a hole in the berm" was funny, but it did not get many laughs.

My writing that I had "more college graduates in this Co than I've seen in the Army" was accurate but somewhat misleading. Except for the officers, only two of the soldiers had degrees and only another half-dozen of the 110-strength of the company had some college credits. Infantrymen may not have been well-educated, but they learned a hell of a lot more during their one-year combat tours than did their draft-dodging counterparts back on the ivy-walled campuses in the World. The only problem was that little of their knowledge gained in Nam would be of any use to them upon their return home. Jobs for snipers, machine gunners, and riflemen were in short supply back "on the block."

 24 NOVEMBER 1969

Crystal
Bn Commo section came out to work on my commo

Our new brigade commander, Brigadier General \
Bond, was of medium height and strong build. Hi
pearance was youthful despite his graying hair. I ii
diately noticed that he wore the Ranger tab on his sl
and a smile on his face.

Bond not only looked friendly but was, in fact, ali
jovial in his efforts to meet as many of my soldier
possible. His outgoing manner had the troops warmin
him as I had seen them do with no other senior offi
Usually the men were intimidated by, hostile toward,
just flat scared by generals, but by the time Bond had be
at Crystal for an hour, even the most recalcitrant we
talking about the "cool old man."

General Bond's comments about my being highly thoug
of made me feel good, as I took it as reassurance that I wou
remain in command. It was not until Bond asked me abo
the jungle, however, that he totally won me over.

I told him that the surrounding jungle was as thick a
hell and a different world from that of the fire base. The
general nodded and said, "Let's go take a look."

Within minutes I assembled a squad and we headed out
to make a circle five hundred meters from the fire base
through the thickest of the vegetation. We were working
up a good sweat when a hard downpour further drenched
us. The general's face showed no signs of discomfort or
irritation, and he said nothing on the short recon until we
passed back through the wire.

By the time we returned to Crystal, Bond, his starched
fatigues and spit-shined jungle boots in shambles, was the
wettest, muddiest general I had ever seen. Yet, he was still
smiling when he said, "Thanks for the tour. Now I will
know better what you all are up against out there."

He shook a few more hands before boarding his chopper
and departing with a wave to those of us standing in the

setup—A very hectic and nerve-racking day—Was on
horns most of day—Getting messages for my Co—Also
relaying for other elements

Bn CO came out this afternoon to visit us

Also today got in 9 new men—I remember when I first
got to field—You think it's forever till DEROS—7 months
later I think the same thing

LPs tonight had movement—The leaders did a good
job—I got artillery and mortars firing—LP saw two at 20
meters—Blew Claymores and three frags—Are sure they
got the two—Element 3 klicks south had fast movement
a little later—I feel it was a sqd sapper team

One of our duties at the fire base was to act as a relay
station for units that were too far from the battalion tactical
operations center (TOC) at Black Horse to maintain direct
communications. The assistance of the commo team increased our capabilities, and I spent much of the day passing messages back and forth between the units and
Battalion. Except for a small contact by Delta Company,
most of the radio traffic was routine. Nevertheless, with
all the location reports and coordination involved, there
was ample work to keep me and my RTOs busy on the
horns.

While Coleman relayed the final reports to Battalion, I
wrote a letter to Linda, using a sandbag for a lap desk. I
acknowledged her last letter telling me that Gene Oates, a
friend at A&M, had been killed in action. Neither Linda
nor I had known Gene well, but both of us were close to
his parents. Gene's father, a retired colonel, was a student
counselor on campus who gave his best advice over a beer
glass rather than a desk. I felt sorry for Gene, but I felt
even more sympathy for his parents, as it is the living who
grieve, not the dead.

In the letter I also included a roster of the 112 men

assigned to Bravo Company. I had mentioned to Linda several times that many of the men received little mail. She had asked me to send a list, saying that she would see to it that each soldier received at least one Christmas card from someone who cared. Linda kept her promise. Over the next weeks, after each mail delivery, troops would seek me out, asking me to tell my wife thanks for the card.

Before I sealed my letter, Nesmith added the names of the nine replacements to the list. New soldiers were always welcomed, but this was a better group than usual. Four of the men had been in-country two to six months with the 3rd Brigade, 82d Airborne Division and had been transferred to the 199th when the 82d went home. The fact that only those soldiers with more than ten months in-country were eligible to accompany the Brigade's colors back to the States meant that many experienced replacements were available for the rest of us. The continuing unfounded rumors that the 199th was soon to go home meant little now that we understood the early-outs were for flags and not for grunts.

Around midnight Coleman woke me up from the poncho liner I had spread in the corner of the commo bunker. One of our LPs had broken radio silence to whisper that they had detected movement headed in their direction.

While SFC Ullum alerted our perimeter to one hundred percent manning of the bunkers, I told the LP to remain quiet and engage with Claymores and grenades to avoid revealing their exact position. Rick Gulbranson was instantly at my side preparing to call for his preplanned artillery concentrations. Minutes later I heard the loud explosion of the Claymores, followed by the burst of hand grenades.

Another whispered report from the LP said they had engaged a squad that had been slowly crawling through the jungle toward Crystal. From the screams and blurs in the brief light of their exploding Claymores, they were confident that they had killed at least two. Gulbranson now had artillery and mortars pounding the jungle in areas of likely escape.

The three-man LP was excited with the kills, but the men were scared that their position had been compromised. I denied their request to return to our perimeter, as they were safer remaining in place than risking being shot by the jumpy men on the bunker line.

For the rest of the night I remained on the radios, giving encouragement and insisting that the LP remain quiet and respond to my calls for situation reports only by breaking squelch twice.

25 NOVEMBER 1969

Sweep of last night's contact area yielded two blood trails and one Chicom grenade—I am satisfied
Got an LOH VR of area around here this morning
My 3rd plt had an airmobile and a long RIF
Much arty, 8-in 155 and 4.2 mortar, impact 1 klick from here tonight—TOT (Time on target)
The following is very accurate in my opinion:

"In thousands of years of our history, we have seen the Chinese and the French and the Japanese come and we have forgotten them all. In time we will

forget the Americans, too. Whether they did good
or ill, they will only be a footnote to our history.''
A young VN Army officer to
NEWSWEEK 24 Nov 69 p 33

At first light I accompanied a platoon through the wire
to the LP's position. We were greeted by a nervous but
proud trio of grunts. Twenty meters in front of them were
pools of blood and bits of human flesh were stuck to nearby
branches. At a grenade's impact area was frothy pink blood
that indicated a lung wound. Bloody drag marks led back
through the jungle for over a hundred meters where we
finally lost the trail—either because of the thick under-
growth or because men do not continue to bleed after they
die.

When we returned to the LP site, one of the men discovered the Chicom grenade with its pin still in place.
Whether it had been dropped by a fleeing dink or thrown
by one too scared to remember to pull the pin, we did not
know.

Since we had found no evidence of a large force, we
concluded that the enemy unit had likely been a recon
team checking us out to see how easy a target Crystal
might be. At least two had found out the hard way that we
were prepared.

Late that evening, in coordination with the Greek, we
fired artillery from other bases that would support us in
the event of an attack. By calculating times of flight for
each projectile, we could get all the rounds from different
firing points to land at the same time. The Greek added
his guns to the barrage by lowering the barrels and shooting in direct-fire mode. Rounds screaming from his tubes
only feet above the ground hit at the same time and place

as those from other batteries located many kilometers away.

Gulbranson helped in the TOT (time on target) and did a fine job. The new FO was gaining confidence with each new experience.

I thought at the time that the young unidentified ARVN officer quoted in *Newsweek* was somewhat contemptible, but later years have proven him more a prophet than a cynic.

 26 NOVEMBER 1969

Crystal
    Another pretty dull day—However base camp time beats the boonies any time
    Good talk with plt ldrs tonight
    For the first time I'm beginning to think I may have been on the line too long—I am short-tempered—Jumpy as hell—However I still feel I am doing a damn good job

Seven and a half months in the boonies, combined with the present monotony of fire base security, was wearing my nerves thin. My frustrations were compounded by my never having current information on the condition of Linda and our unborn child. Letters from San Francisco took at least a week to reach me, so any news was already seven days old before I read it.

Despite my anxieties, I was pleased with the progress of the company. Discipline and morale continued to improve, and I became more confident in my NCOs and officers.

The platoon leaders now had more than three months each in the boonies, and I had grown to respect their skills as well as appreciate them as individuals. Ron Coleman occasionally laughed as he said our combined names of Kidalowski, Bolenske, Schmalz, Gulbranson, and Lanning sounded like a European law firm. I appreciated the joke, not only for the diversity of surnames but also for the symbol of a strong partnership.

The daily resupply bird offered a diversion to our normal routine with the delivery of a package from my mother. The food and candy quickly disappeared in the proximity of my command group, but a small box tucked in one corner of her package was the greatest treat. As soon as I unwrapped it, I placed the contents under my shirt and ran from the commo bunker to a lone tree standing in the center of the base.

Nailed to the tree were pieces of ammo boxes that served as steps to an observation platform near the top of its 100-foot height. Most of the men in the base, particularly my platoon leaders, watched my climb up the tree as if I had gone out of my mind. Their concerned expressions changed to smiles as I reached the platform and pulled a 12-inch parachute, complete with a small rubber soldier, from underneath my shirt. The toy paratrooper was greeted with laughing cheers when I released the chute and it slowly floated to the earth. As soon as the chute collapsed on the ground a soldier scooped it up and quickly climbed to my side to repeat the airborne assault on Fire Base Crystal.

During the rest of the day, many of the men of Bravo

and a few redlegs retrieved and dropped the small parachute. I never could figure out just why my mother sent a child's toy to a combat zone, but whatever her reasons, it was a great idea.

---

27 NOVEMBER 1969

> Crystal—Thanksgiving Day
> Truly a day of Thanksgiving—We have so many things to be thankful for and we all feel it
> Actually we have poor food, poorer living conditions—We are thankful because we are alive
> After seeing people close to you killed, and not very prettily killed, your life becomes that much more precious
> In talks today we all agree—The GI is the most effective, blood-thirsty SOB in the world—I would have never thought this before my tour—I now know it as fact

With the exception of a fine turkey dinner delivered in mermite cans, Thanksgiving was just like all the other days. We had no celebration or religious services. Patrols, LPs, and preplanned artillery fire were conducted as usual.

War returns men's values to the basics. A good meal, a can of beer, a few hours sleep, a letter from home, and a toy parachute were ample reward for seeing another sunrise. The death we observed and inflicted made our own lives that much more precious, but from a "we" and ''they'' perspective rather than in any appreciation for mankind itself.

Perhaps it was the luxuries of the World which we exchanged for the harshness of the jungle that made us so violent against the enemy. Pilots killed from the air with napalm and bombs, and they returned to air-conditioned clubs to talk of flying rather than destruction. Artillerymen scrambled to man their guns on fire missions that rained death on an unseen enemy, and they returned to half-eaten meals to complain that their food had grown cold. Infantrymen removed gold teeth, and occasionally ears or more from bodies of young men and women who surely must have thought their cause at least as just as we thought ours.

Yet I, like the others, expressed no regret nor remorse except about not being able to kill and destroy even more. I do not know why we were the way we were. The standard justification, that we were fighting for the survival of our comrades and ourselves was true. But we went beyond the means of self-protection with a blood lust that no American mother would recognize nor acknowledge in her son. I never knew a man who admitted liking the war, yet none of us ever seemed to live as intensely as when we were trying to kill our fellows on this planet.

> Crystal
>> Another base camp day
>> Listened to tape of TU–Aggie game, 49–12, so a bad day

Despite my bad humor toward the war in general and the results of the football game in particular, I made a lengthy attempt that afternoon to persuade one of my NCOs to reenlist and consider the Army as a career.

SGT Buddy Fairchild was nearing the completion of his tour and his two-year, draft-induced time in uniform. Fairchild, a natural leader, had risen quickly from rifleman to squad leader, and occasionally acted as platoon sergeant. The slightly built, blond, baby-faced nineteen-year-old from Florida was one of the most respected NCOs in the company. He never seemed unhappy, and he tackled every duty with enthusiasm and a keen wit. One of the few soldiers who had a wife and child back home, he frequently showed me pictures of his young son.

I took a long time explaining to Fairchild the merits of a military career, pointing out his natural leadership abilities as well as his future difficulties in getting a job as a high-school dropout. When I finished what I thought was a rather convincing discourse, Fairchild looked at me, grinned, and said, "No way, sir, no fucking way. I've done my part and I'll do no more."

He detailed his objections by listing family separations, low pay, no respect from civilians, and the possibility of later being sent back to Nam. By the time he finished, I could only laugh and say, "Buddy, maybe you're right. You've damn near convinced me to get out, too."

✙ 29 NOVEMBER 1969

> Moved out with a light CP on a one-day mission—
> Later changed
> Took 50-cal fire in perimeter from Crystal tonight
> Thoroughly confused mission

Leaving Bolenske's platoon behind to secure Crystal, I moved out with the rest of the Company to check out a suspected enemy position to our southwest. The distance was not great, and I thought we would be able to return to the fire base long before dark. In order to maintain communications with Black Horse, I left Bill Nesmith behind to man the radio relay station. Coleman was at my side with my battalion radio, and I alternated using SP4s Barry Bos and Clarence Speck, who usually carried radios for the platoon leaders, as my company RTOs.

Orders from Battalion later in the day had us reconning a hill mass three klicks from the fire base as darkness fell. I ordered the men to dig in amid their usual complaints about the work involved. Our one-day mission was complete, but it would be ten days before we returned to Crystal.

Our night defensive position was quiet until midnight when red tracers ripped the trees just above our dug-in positions. As the sound of their sources reached us, I could tell the rounds were 50-caliber from Crystal. My frantic calls to Nesmith and Bolenske stopped the sporadic tracers but only after a frightening few minutes as the huge slugs whistled around us.

Bolenske was soon back on the horn with the explanation that a track platoon of Delta 17th Cavalry had arrived at the base that afternoon. The tracks' FNG platoon leader had ordered a recon by fire without checking the locations of surrounding units. Our hillside position, although three klicks away, was high enough to prevent the jungle from stopping the rounds.

Just after Bolenske signed off the net, Nesmith called on the company horn and asked to speak to me. Bill said, "Since you are already awake, let me ask you something. When am I going to get out of the field?"

I was still too mad about the 50-caliber fire incident to see the usual humor in his question. I answered, "You'd better get a job in the rear because if you are still there when I get back, your ass is mine." I signed off without giving him a chance to respond.

Over the next days I noticed I was not hearing Bill's voice on the horn. When I asked about him, I learned he had turned his commo bunker over to Bolenske the next morning and caught the first chopper to Black Horse. Upon arrival there he had told Beckles that I had finally okayed his release, and he had quickly found a job working for the S-4 breaking down and loading supplies at the helipad.

I was so damn mad I nearly went back with the next resupply bird just to get my hands on my "ex"-RTO. After awhile I calmed down and later—much later—saw the humor in Bill's "honest misinterpretation." His maneuvers were not without advantage to us, however, for on our next resupply were bags of onions and peppers that he had stolen from the mess hall to add to the palatability of C-rations. There was also a note thanking me for finally letting him out of the field.

We never knew what to expect in the way of pilfered items Nesmith might add to our resupplies. Those extra items, along with my admitting the RTO was overdue in getting out of the boonies, finally allowed me to view the incident as funny.

I have not maintained contact with Bill Nesmith since the war; however, I can imagine his returning to his job on the railroad in Florida, adding a few more pounds around his ample waist, and occasionally breaking out an old three-legged stool and sitting down to tell war stories about how he got out of the field by outsmarting a young lieutenant.

30 NOVEMBER 1969

> Worked in area of 11 Nov base camp—Have 1st plt of Delta OPCONed to me
> On signs on trees in base camp found one where my men wrote in response: "Gooks suck. B 2/3"
> Separate plt positions for night

Loeffke called me early with instructions for Bravo Company to link up with a platoon from Delta Company and move back to the bunker complex where Bill Little had been killed. It was not a mission I looked forward to, but it did seem like a good idea to see if the enemy had reoccupied their old position.

We moved carefully to the edge of the complex and, under the cover of artillery fire Gulbranson "walked" a few hundred meters to our front, soon discovered there was no evidence of any activity since our departure two weeks earlier. A check of the area around the graves revealed no signs that anyone had returned to move the bodies or pay last respects.

The only thing new in the camp that I had not seen during our last operation was the addition to the signs painted on the trees. My soldier writing "Gooks suck" may not have been as articulate as the enemy's English-language message, but his meaning was quite clear.

🚁 I DECEMBER 1969

Linked up with other plts to the north—While waiting for resupply gunships propping an LZ for another unit opened up too soon—We took rockets and 7.62 mm fire—By some miracle no one hurt—I raised hell—Higher investigating—They at first said it was only ricochets—I again raised hell—A very scary day

When rockets came in I grabbed radio to try to get it cut off—LT Schmalz and my RTO dove for same log as

I did—They were on my back so I had pretty good protection

Schmalz and I were standing in a small clearing discussing our afternoon's direction of movement while we waited for the birds. Coleman, who was never far from my side, had just leaned his radio against a tree and strolled over to join us when two Cobra gunships came in low over the trees.

Suddenly the Cobras opened fire. Rockets and minigun rounds exploded all around us.

I dove for Coleman's radio. As I reached for the handset, I felt the weight of first Coleman and then Schmalz hit my back, all but knocking the breath out of me.

"Check fire! Check fire!" I gasped into the radio. Rockets were landing less than fifty meters away, throwing clods of dirt and tree branches all over us.

"Check fire! Check fire!" I repeated as I struggled to breathe. I could hear Gulbranson yelling the same instructions into his artillery net.

"What the fuck is going on?" I shouted into the radio.

The Cobras rolled away to circle before coming in again. "Tell the Cobras it's us!"

"Roger, Bravo," a calm voice responded over the radio from the TOC. "The gunships were prepping an LZ near you. You must be getting some ricochets."

"Ricochets, my ass!" I yelled louder as Coleman and Schmalz rolled off my back and I could finally get my lungs full of air. "Those Cobras made a direct run at us. Who the fuck is responsible?" I demanded.

There was a long pause. I told my other RTO to check the company net for casualties. With all the fire poured on us, I feared the worst.

The platoons reported no one wounded. While I was

relieved by the news, I grew even angrier about the attack by our own gunships.

When it became obvious that the danger had passed, my RTO began telling me with a reasonably straight face that he and Schmalz had "unselfishly risked their lives" to protect me. To his request for a medal for their "heroic" efforts, I answered, "If anyone deserved a medal, it's me. It was a record five-meter dive that got me to the log first."

A few minutes later, the Operations Officer called back to inform me that the pilots had confirmed their error of prepping the wrong LZ. Their intended target was five klicks away.

The admission of a mistake on the pilots' part did nothing to alleviate my anger. I asked for call signs and frequencies so I could deliver my own reprimands, but I never received the information. By the time we got out of the jungle days later, too much else had happened for the incident to seem important. All that remained in my thoughts was that if I ever was to have any sympathy for the dinks, which I did not, it would be when they were under the fire of the Cobras.

🐌 2 DECEMBER 1969

Moved north—Delta's 1st plt on point—Found 5 bunkers with activity in last 30 minutes—Put in artillery Findings:

        mortar sight bracket and tools
        30 lbs rice
        7 uniforms
        I lb fish
        100 AK rounds
        misc base camp gear
    Today is supposed to be "baby news" day—No word

It seemed strange to have another company's element on point for Bravo, but the Delta platoon had not hesitated when I told their leader it was their turn.

We were sweating our way through the thick underbrush when the Delta RTO called, saying they had found the tops of mud-covered, camouflaged tree stumps cut low to the ground. A hint of a breeze blowing toward us contained the slight scent of wood smoke and human waste indicating a bunker complex.

When we moved in after the artillery fire, we found a small camp of five bunkers. One of the structures showed the accuracy of the artillery as a direct hit had caved in its roof. A pot of half-cooked rice and the drag marks of a wide bloody trail told us a squad of gooks had just withdrawn.

A canvas sack of saltwater fish was the most interesting item of abandoned food and equipment because the fish were fresh and must have been secured from the Xuan Luc markets within the last day. Whoever had made the more than 30-kilometer round trip for a fresh fish dinner must have been awfully disappointed that we arrived before he could enjoy it.

After a quick search, we were ready to saddle up and push on in the direction of the gooks' retreat. Our move out was delayed when one of the FNGs, who had joined Bravo at Crystal a few days before, saw something in a clump of bamboo. Seconds later he approached me carrying a heavy, cone-shaped object that I immediately recognized as a 105-mm artillery round. From its shiny exterior, I deduced that it was a dud from our fire before assaulting the bunkers.

The FNG, proud of his find, had no idea what he was cradling in his arms. As calmly as possible, I told the man to walk back into the jungle for at least 50 meters, gently place the object on the ground and return to my location. My tone of voice, combined with the fact that the other soldiers were scurrying for cover, definitely got the troop's attention.

Without a word, he followed my instructions. I braced for the expected explosion as he walked away toward the jungle. My apprehension turned to a smile when he returned empty-handed a few minutes later. Before I could say a word, Schmalz and English grabbed the FNG and sat him down for a brief refresher course in company SOPs. They ended the instruction by allowing the man to destroy his find with a charge of C-4.

According to Linda's doctor, 2 December was the due date for our child. Beckles had sent me a message confirming that the Red Cross was aware of my assignment to Bravo and assured me that I would be informed within twenty-four hours of the birth. All day I had been certain each crackle of an incoming radio message would be baby news.

✈ 3 DECEMBER 1969

    Finally got troops paid—Hot breakfast flown in—Then moved out

    After about 800 meters, 3rd plt element got signs of a base camp—While maneuvering was hit by snipers

    I held Delta's plt as a cover screen—Gave word to my 3rd plt to pull back—3rd plt pt man PFC Smith had AK rounds through both arms—We knocked several snipers out of trees

    While pulling back I began arty and gunships

    We pulled back by sqd bounds—Total ammo we used: most of our basic load, 418 rounds 105 arty, air strike of two 500 lb bombs, 2 runs of napalm, one gunship

    A scary day—Fortunate to only take 1 WIA

    A & D Companies also in contact nearby—Caught our runaways

    No word on baby

From what I had seen in movies, babies usually arrived in the middle of the night; however, I was not sure just what the time was in San Francisco, and regardless of my calculations, there was no news.

The baby was not the only thing not arriving on time. Although we were three days into the month, the troops had not been paid. Steve Beig was finally able to secure a chopper when we were near an LZ. Any complaints about late pay, even though we had nowhere to spend the money, were quieted by the hot breakfast that Beig brought in.

By early afternoon we were again moving with the third-herd on point. As usual, my CP followed directly behind the lead platoon. SP4 Clarence Speck was now carrying the Company radio. The tall RTO was from Ohio, where he had worked in a National Cash Register assembly plant before being drafted. With his glasses and dark moustache, Clary looked studious and he performed his duties with a calm, methodical approach that greatly aided my CP team.

We were an hour out from the breakfast LZ when Schmalz reported more cut trees. Minutes after he began to maneuver his platoon, a half dozen AKs and SKSs opened up, joined seconds later by several light machine guns. Brian shouted that the gooks were in the trees. His warning was too late.

Snipers high in the third canopy were popping rounds around my CP. Coleman and Speck each handed me their hand sets as they dropped their packs and began spraying the trees on full automatic. We knocked the gooks from their perches, including one who hung upside down from the rope with which he had tied himself to the tree.

The bunkers protected the dink machine guns that continued to rake our positions. I ordered Brian to pull back under the cover of the artillery that the FO was by then dropping closer and closer.

Brian announced that he had a man wounded whom he could not get to and that he needed a gunship to cover the retrieval.

A long five minutes later, a Cobra dove in with mini guns hosing down the bunkers. Within minutes the third platoon started pulling back through our position. In the lead, PFC Sammy Jackson was carrying the wounded PFC Smith.

Jackson was an unlikely hero, but he had already been decorated with the Silver Star for bravery when Bravo had been hit hard back in September. At five-foot-five and weighing not over 130 pounds soaking wet, the nineteen-year-old black man was certainly the smallest in the company. His retrieval of Smith would add a Bronze Star for Valor to his growing list of medals.

There would be time to recommend medals later. Right then the machine guns, which had resumed firing when the Cobra completed its run, had to be silenced. The solution was soon forthcoming when a new voice came over the battalion radio and said he was overhead with two "fast movers inbound hot." The Air Force jock in his small observer plane sounded less like a warrior than an airline pilot pointing out the sights to his passengers, but he meant business.

Pulling back another two hundred meters, I popped smoke and told the observer that the dinks were three hundred meters due west. He dived his small plane near treetop level and delivered two white-phosphorus rockets right on target. He barely had time to warn us to get our heads down before two F-4 jets screamed in delivering 500-pound bombs and napalm. The earth seemed to roll like a wave under us, raising our bodies from the ground and slapping us down with enough force to knock our breath away.

After the jets made their last run, the jungle was silent except for the loud ringing in my ears and the low moans of the wounded soldier. Smith had bullet holes through both arms, but the morphine had masked his pain. A dust-off was orbiting nearby and dropped a cable-held litter through the canopy.

Another chopper soon arrived, kicking out crates of ammunition.

Darkness closed around us before we reached the bunkers. Gulbranson had artillery sporadically dropping into the jungle that now dripped with burning globs of napalm.

The day had passed quickly, yet it had seemed to go on

forever. I dug in for another long night of listening to a radio that made no mention of a baby's being born in San Francisco.

✍ 4 DECEMBER 1969

> Moved back into base camp—Delta plt released—My 1st plt joined us at enemy base camp
>
> Findings today: two 82-mm mortar rounds with 6 fuses, two B40 rockets, 3 Claymores, one large firing device, misc ammo, blood, etc., some documents
>
> No baby news—If he doesn't hurry he may be an orphan before birth Things are getting tight

At first light we moved back into a bunker complex that now looked more like the surface of the moon than a jungle fortification. Bomb and artillery craters pocked the earth, and splintered trees still smoked from the napalm. Much of the enemy's equipment and dead had been blown to pieces. That fate included the sniper I had last seen swinging from his rope-secured platform. The tree itself was now lying in pieces near a bomb crater.

I estimated that we had been opposed by a reinforced platoon of about fifty gooks. Bodies, pieces of bodies, and blood trails indicated that at least half their number had died, but I claimed only four for Bravo and equal numbers of kills for the artillery and Air Force. The destruction of the complex was so complete that it was impossible to estimate a more accurate figure.

In appreciation for the redlegs and jet jocks, we gathered up several sacks of NVA pith helmets, canteens, and belts and sent them to those who had supported us but who had had to forego the satisfaction of searching the dead.

Bolenske's platoon had spent most of the day slowly moving from Crystal through the jungle to join us. The Delta platoon headed west to rejoin Lewis and the rest of his company, but not before their leader stopped at my CP and said with a grin, "It's been fun. Let's do it again sometime."

Baby news—or, rather, the lack of it—was, of course, still foremost in my mind. The journal entry reflected my increasing awareness of how I was pushing the odds of survival with every day in the field. The snipers in the trees had taken their precarious positions with one purpose in mind—to spot the radio antennas that accompanied commanders. Much of the sniper fire had been concentrated on the CP, and only the quick reactions of my RTOs, along with the withering fire of the third platoon, had saved us.

We remained in the camp that night amid the smell of rotting and burnt bodies. As the sun went down, I lay back on my rucksack and followed my usual practice, staring at a hole in the canopy of branches. Each night for nearly an hour I watched the sky change color from blue to yellow to red to black. I concentrated to detect the first twinkle of a star and then continued to watch and count how many stars filled the small gap in the trees. During the cloudy monsoon season, I had missed my nightly ritual, but the dry season had returned star light skies that rivaled those on the open Texas plains back home.

After sky gazing, I took a two-hour turn on radio watch before stretching out under a poncho liner to try to sleep. It was not a restful sleep as the slightest movement or noise snapped me awake. As time went by, it was harder to go to sleep and even more difficult to remain that way for any duration. This night I blamed my sleeplessness on the worry about Linda and the baby.

I had put it off for as long as I could. I could wait no longer. I whispered to my medic to hand me his aid bag, and I rummaged around in the dark until I found the bottle of pills intended to combat allergic reactions to insect bites. Not only did these pills work for the intended purpose, but they were also adequate sleeping pills. Doc Crowe said nothing as I swallowed the pill except to acknowledge my instructions for him to wake me in one hour.

Sixty minutes later I woke up clearheaded at Doc's gentle shake. I was now satisfied that I could finally get some rest and still be able to wake alert.

My visits to Doc's aid bag later became an almost nightly occurrence, though it never developed into a dependence. The rest that came from a capsule was worth the nightmares that accompanied any sleep of over an hour.

5 DECEMBER 1969

Finished blowing bunkers in base camp—Continue search of area—Moved out to the northeast

Have been hearing much about Song My—Once again
the damn civilians are out to cut down our Army—I think
2LT Calley was completely in right—Many times I have
had to use great restraint to keep myself from killing
"innocent" women and children

While Schmalz and his platoon took care of the bunkers, the rest of us spread hundreds of yellow three-by-five
cards that said in English and Vietnamese, "Compliments
of the Old Guard, 2nd Battalion 3d Infantry." Several of
the troops laughed at the cards, and I admitted that they
were a bit dramatic, as they were supposed to strike fear
into the superstitious enemy. I really did not care if we
left the cards or not; what the hell did I know about what
went through the dinks' minds?

Schmalz reported to me that with only one bunker left
he still had over fifty pounds of C-4; much more of the
plastic explosive had been delivered than was needed to
destroy the fortifications. As we were already carrying
enough extra weight, I told him to blow it up with the last
bunker.

Because of the large amount, I told Brian to use enough
fuse to give us at least ten minutes to get out of the area.
Fifteen minutes later, we were several hundred meters
from the bunkers, but there had been no explosion.

Twenty more minutes passed, and still the jungle was
silent.

I called Brian to my CP. I asked him if he had used two
separate blasting caps in accordance with our SOP. He
nodded his head. Then he suggested, "Maybe some gooks
came in behind us and defused the charges."

I did not think so. Besides, no matter what, I was not
going to leave fifty pounds of C-4 behind. So I said,

"Brian, go back and reset the charges. I don't think the dinks are there. It's got to be done."

Schmalz had proven to be a cool leader in past fire fights, and I was surprised at his reaction. His eyes became wide and then began to mist. He looked down and did not move. We stood wordlessly for several minutes. Then he began to shake his head.

Finally I said, "Brian, if you are scared to do it, I will. Give me your blasting caps."

Brian looked up at me, hesitated, and then muttered, "I can't let you do that." He turned and took a squad back to the bunkers. Brian and the squad soon returned and less than a minute later, we heard the huge blast we had been waiting for. Schmalz rather sheepishly reported that the fuses on the first charges were too wet to work properly. I never saw him hesitate again.

For over a week, magazines, newspapers, and letters from home had been arriving with the accounts of Song My, or My Lai as it would later be known. From our limited information on the incident, we were convinced it was just another effort by the media and war-protesting civilians to portray all of us in uniform as killers of women and babies.

Calley and his men had been much farther north, but we all understood the anguish that could lead to such an incident. In my own mind, I doubted if Calley had done anything unusual at all. It was not uncommon for civilians to die in battlefield crossfire. My letter to Linda reflected my overall feelings when I wrote, "I don't give a damn if he personally killed 1,000 children if he was looking out for the welfare of one GI. As I told you in Hawaii, we killed a pregnant woman during a fire fight back in June— after all, there is a war going on."

Looking back sixteen years later I am not proud of my emotional letter to my pregnant wife, but I—and every other Bravo grunt—was mad as hell. Our anger was based on our own experiences as much as anything else, but beyond our dismay was also the fear that we, too, might be labeled by our families and friends as murderers for doing only what we thought we had to do.

As the years went by and more of the details of My Lai were revealed, I eventually understood that what had occurred went beyond the fine line of what was necessary. It had been Calley's responsibility as the platoon leader to stop the killing when it ceased being for his men's safety and started being for revenge. I cannot condemn Calley; in the insane world of combat there were many times when, but for the sudden, miraculous return of my self-control, it could have been me.

🛩 6 DECEMBER 1969

> While moving today I received following message from Bn CO at 1555: "You're father of baby girl, 8 pounds, ½ ounce. Mother and daughter doing fine. Name, Reville Ann. Date, 5 December."
>
> Messages of congratulations came in on Bn and Co horns from many people—A very proud moment
>
> Quote from SSG English: "If it had been a boy he would have named it Charlie Oscar."

By the end of the day, when I made my journal entry, the only thoughts that I recorded were those about the

birth of my daughter. However, there had been other events
as well.

That morning we had followed the smell of rotting flesh
and clouds of flies to a body lying next to a small trail.
The dead gook had no weapon, although his pack and
carrying gear were intact. My initial assumption was that
the corpse was the result of our attack on the bunkers.
That notion was dispelled by the battalion TOC when I
reported our findings. Apparently recon had killed the dink
in an ambush the day before.

I was wondering why recon had left behind the dink's
pack when a voice giving no call sign came over the company net and repeated, "Don't touch him! Don't touch
him! Don't touch him! Do you roger?"

I quickly spread the word to my men not to disturb the
body and to move on, giving it a wide berth. One of recon's RTOs had obviously overheard my report to Battalion and had changed his radio frequency to our push to
give the warning.

Only our initial wariness and the radio warning prevented our becoming victims of the booby-trapped gook
that recon had left on the trail. I was angry about the
incident but only because it was we who had been near
disaster rather than the intended targets. Booby-trapping
enemy dead bothered me only from the aspect of what
could happen to us or other GIs rather than from any sense
of right or wrong, for in war there are no villains—only
the war itself is the villain.

By mid-afternoon, when we were all drenched in sweat
from our continual movement, Coleman whispered that
Loeffke was trying to call us. The transmission was barely
audible. We halted and formed a quick perimeter as Ron
changed from the short to the long antenna. We still could

not pick up the battalion commander clearly, so I asked the station at Crystal to relay. I could distinguish bits of Loeffke's transmission, but it was not until the relay repeated the words that I understood the full message of my daughter's birth.

The radio was immediately jammed with calls of congratulations from many call signs I recognized, including McGinnis's and Lewis's, as well as others I did not know were on the net. Speck circulated the word around the perimeter and many of the soldiers waved a silent thumbs-up or okay sign. Regardless of how good the news was, our celebration had to be a quiet one.

The platoon leaders and sergeants took turns coming to my CP to deliver handshakes and back slaps. Many asked with muted merriment if the name was really correct. SSG English's pun, using Charlie Oscar, the Army's phonetic abbreviation for Commanding Officer, added to the humor.

I had known that the company and many in the battalion were aware of Linda's pregnancy; however, I was amazed by the genuine joy that everyone expressed. I deeply appreciated their concern; the fact that we could all welcome a new life in the midst of so much death was nearly overwhelming. I was so ecstatic that I felt like crying, but it was as impossible to weep in happiness as it had been in despair.

In celebration I decided to halt the company for the rest of the day. Babies do not hold up wars, however, and Loeffke was on the horn a half hour later asking why we were not moving. Soon we were again sweating through the jungle.

Hours later I finally recorded the message in my journal. Then I wrote to my wife, "My feelings are fantastic—unbelievable—I didn't know how much I would want to see the baby. Send pictures as soon as possible." I continued, "I thought you wanted a boy. I thought I did, too, till I got news of our girl. Now I know I wanted a girl. I couldn't be happier.''

It was weeks before I knew the correct spelling of ''Reveilee'' and of Linda's anxiety when she signed the birth certificate about what we were doing to our daughter by giving her such a name. I made no corrections in my journal's misspelling. By that time, it was all part of the story we would some day tell our little girl.

Today we have yet to meet or hear of another Reveilee. She likes the name, and as we thought, enjoys the retelling of how she became who she is.

After Susan Hargrove, who took Linda to the hospital, the first visitor to the new mother and daughter was Pete Petrosilli, a fellow platoon leader who had been seriously injured when his helicopter had been shot down. After extensive treatment in a field hospital and in Japan, Pete had been evacuated to Letterman Army Hospital at the Presidio in San Francisco. Pete was by then an outpatient at Letterman but far from total recovery from his wounds. It seemed quite appropriate that the visitor-patient roles of Linda and Pete had been reversed.

7 DECEMBER 1969

Contact today—Recon plt working near us spotted 4—
Fired too soon—Gooks ran our way—We opened up at

30 meters—Killed 2, one probable—Captured documents which higher has been yelling for

Bn CO flew over and said B Co is doing an outstanding job

SSG Standard at the relay station summed it up—I quote: "You used to be on bottom. Now you are on top."

The war did not care that I was a father. It was business as usual. We were paralleling the southern bank of a small stream from west to east while the recon platoon was doing the same on the northern bank. About noon four gooks were caught between our two units. Recon opened fire too early, missing the gooks but sending them in wild flight in our direction. We concealed ourselves quickly and minutes later we could hear the dinks running toward us. Apparently concentrating on the threat of recon's pursuit, they were looking over their shoulders instead of in the direction of our ambush.

Our initial fire sent two flopping to the ground. The other two fired bursts of poorly aimed AK rounds as they changed their path of retreat. We knocked another down before they disappeared into the foliage.

After throwing grenades to ensure the two nearest us were dead, we searched for the other body but could find only a heavy trail of black blood that meant the man had suffered a gut wound. We followed the trail until we lost it in the streambed.

The entire fire fight lasted only minutes, but it produced important documents on enemy units as well as weapons and bodies. One of the most interesting documents was a small cardboard-bound journal similar to my own. We could not read the writing, but the enclosed black and white photograph of an attractive Vietnamese and her baby made it evident that the gook, like ourselves, had family back home. One of the men suggested, as he placed a yellow "two-thirds" card in the dink's mouth, that perhaps we should send a "Compliments of the Old Guard" card to the gook's widow.

Bravo was in high spirits with our recent success of body and booty—without any losses on our part. SSG Standard, now a Delta Company platoon leader who happened to be relaying messages between Battalion and the company, made the day especially memorable with his comments. In fact, Standard's words acknowledging just how far Bravo had come overshadowed the congratulations from Locffkc and others. In less than two months the unit had gone from the company known as "no contact Bravo" to the leader in Battalion body count. More importantly, we accomplished this while taking few casualties of our own.

---

8 DECEMBER 1969

> Contact again—We killed one—Recon plt killed 2 but took 1 US KIA
> Long fire fight—Much action
> Nerves going to hell
> Bn CO said once again we were doing outstanding job—We had to take 2 emergency ammo resupplies
> WE ARE GOOD!

We continued our sweep of the stream bank with recon paralleling us on the north. They made the first contact again, killing one member of a squad element. A short time later we caught the dinks, and a brief fire fight sent them back in the direction of my old platoon.

To keep the dinks between our two forces, I told Gulbranson to put in artillery in the stream bed to our east. When the rounds took longer than normal, I picked up a large stick from the jungle floor and began hitting my FO, screaming at him about the delay. Rick could only cover himself with one arm while urging the redlegs on the radio to hurry up. He looked at me as if I had gone out of my mind.

Seconds later the artillery began coming in. At the same time, recon reestablished contact, sending the gooks once more in our direction. As we sought cover to prepare a hasty ambush, Gulbranson tried to explain that the guns had been firing another mission when he called for our fire. I answered, "Fuck it, Rick, I don't want any goddamn explanation. Just do what I tell you."

My words were barely out of my mouth when the jungle again exploded in small arms fire. Schmalz reported that they had killed one and had sent the others in retreat, dropping packs as they went.

Almost immediately recon opened up anew with a quick report that they had dropped one and that the remaining gooks had fled to the west. I tried to shift the artillery to cut off their withdrawal, but despite throwing the stick at Gulbranson, who this time had smartly separated himself from arm's reach, failed to get it moved in time to trap the dinks.

We began to sweep the area again, finding one body, complete with AK47, as well as several packs full of ammo, food, and cooking utensils.

Recon called and said they had one body and weapon and were looking for the other they were sure they had killed. Before the transmission was over, a short burst of AK fire—followed by many M-16s—filled the air. The missing dink was only wounded and had taken a recon soldier with him before they finished him off.

By the time we linked up with recon, the resupply bird was hovering overhead, kicking out crates of ammo. We grabbed the boxes with the intent of reloading and pursuing the dinks to the west. SSGs English and Reed were cussing and kicking the crates when I approached them. I demanded to know what was causing the delay. Instead of answering, they pointed at the five crates to show me that they contained not M-16 rounds but 50-caliber machine gun ammo. The resupply was worthless.

My scathing radio message to Battalion informed them that the wrong crates had been loaded on the chopper. By the time the correct ammo was delivered an hour later, it was too late to catch the rest of the dinks.

The new recon platoon leader, LT Kelly, was trying to get a dust-off to evacuate his dead soldier with no luck. Medivacs were for those who had a chance to live, not those already wrapped in a poncho. I finally called the Battalion commander to tell him that we were nowhere near an LZ but that we needed to get the dead soldier out as soon as possible. Loeffke said he would take care of it, and a dust-off was soon hovering over us.

As we tied the body to the jungle penetrater, I noticed that a single AK round had struck the soldier horizontally across the throat, tearing the flesh away from ear to ear. The wound was so clean it resembled a knife cut more than a bullet wound.

Weeks later I would hear rumors about the man who died in hand-to-hand combat from a bayonet-wielding dink. I traced the stories to Crystal where the body, still hanging from the penetrater at the end of the chopper cable, had initially been taken. Apparently, the dust-off crew had been unable to winch the body on board and had had to set down at Crystal to remove the remains from the penetrater. The redlegs had seen the throat wound and the rumors had begun.

With the exception of the KIA and the ammo resupply foul-up, I was happy. Bravo had acted well. Seeing recon back to its old form after the 11 November devastation added to my pride. Kelly obviously knew his business and had won the respect of the "Death Before Dishonor" platoon.

Gulbranson continued to keep his distance from me although he knew I realized the slow artillery had not been his fault. I did not tell him I was sorry about hitting him with the stick because after nearly eight months in the field, I had not apologized for a damn thing. I did not intend to begin.

9 DECEMBER 1969

Moved from nighttime position to PZ for airmobile— As usual, assets cancelled so we got orders to hump to Crystal—Long march but we made it

I felt very proud when we humped in the gate—We left here 10 days ago—We came back in with only one WIA and an enemy body count of 11

My nerves are shot but I am still capable

We approached Crystal with our usual caution. After ten days of almost daily contact, we were not interested in having a bunker guard get trigger happy. The Greek met me at the gap in the wire and shook my hand while extending congratulations on the birth of my daughter and Bravo's body count. He added his thanks for the bodies we had attributed to his artillery support.

My journal entry about nerves was the result of my concern over my shortness of temper, inability to sleep, and overreaction to the slightest out-of-the-ordinary sound or movement. At the same time, I recognized that I was developing a total confidence that no one could do a better job in command than I—that neither Bravo nor I could do any wrong.

We were the best, and I would tolerate nothing less. Yet, at the same time, I felt that I had done all I could do. For the first time since arriving in the boonies, I began to think that it was time to get out of the field. McGinnis and Lewis had both recently given up their companies to take jobs on the battalion staff. Officers who had arrived months after I had were already out of the field.

My personal vulnerabilities were much in my mind; however, I felt no more or less fear in fighting the enemy than before. What was bringing me to the edge was not my own danger but the constant responsibilities of command. Everything that happened—or failed to happen—was on my shoulders, and the burden was wearing me down.

My thoughts extended into my letters to Linda. From Crystal I wrote, "One thing I hesitate to write about, but feel I should—please don't take it wrong or worry. As we both well know I have been out for eight months. In the last two months my nerves have really gotten screwed up. I am still calm and don't lose control in contact—Higher has said I'm the coolest on radio of any of the company commanders. However, I am aware, and so is Battalion, that a man can't stay out forever. I should be getting a job in the rear in a month or so. This doesn't make me unhappy at all as my job is complete. Bravo has come from the worst to the best. A man can just stay out so long and he gets a little screwy. Nothing to worry about—nothing permanent—you just get a little edgy. I still take no unnecessary chances. Please don't worry as I still have not changed—except a little more arrogant and conceited. Being a father has added to that some!''

✈ 10 DECEMBER 1969

A day in a fire base—Always a welcome break
Visit today by LTC Ivey—New Bn CO as of 15 Dec—Seemed outstanding and a man that will look after the troops
The opinion of Higher of Bravo Co is very high—I feel I have accomplished my duty—B Co has gone from last to first

Although we continued to run local patrols and to man the bunker line, Crystal was a good break from the jungle. One of the redlegs, who had learned I was a fellow Texan, invited me to his bunker for a meal of pinto beans he was slowly cooking over a heat-tab fire. The red beans smelled delicious. Unfortunately, the artillery soldier was not able to cook them sufficiently to get them soft enough to eat; it was the thought that counted, for their smell brought a piece of home to the middle of the concertina-wire clearing.

LTC Benjamin F. Ivey, Jr., was making his initial visits to the field before his assumption of command. The new commander was a quiet, confident, graying man. I appreciated his manner of asking questions and listening to the answers. After our conversation, I put aside many of my apprehensions about having a new commander. Loeffke would be difficult to replace, but Ivey was well prepared to take over the battalion.

🐎 11 DECEMBER 1969

> New Bn CO LTC Ivey came to Crystal again today—
> We had a very good talk about the Bn—He seemed to respect my opinion
> Bn sent us steaks and beer—Boy, kill a bunch of gooks and you are Number 1
> Delta Co took 1 KIA today

No one mentioned the food and drink being a reward for our recent body count, although we were well aware that longer, less successful missions had not resulted in such bounty as steaks. Also we received word that in a week we would have a three-day standdown, not as a reward but because it was our turn.

My conversation with Ivey focused on the details of past operations and future missions. I tried several times to tell the new commander that I was about ready for a rear job, but I could not bring myself actually to say it. Only weeks before I had worried that the new commanders might not allow me to stay in command. Now that I knew I would be left in my present position, I could not find the words to say that it was time for me to get out.

Ivey must have felt my hesitation, for he told me he knew I had been in the field for a long time and asked what I wanted to do. I did not answer immediately but finally said that I was happy where I was and would like to stay in command until after the first of the year.

Ivey asked if I had any recommendations for my eventual replacement. I answered honestly that I had had little contact with anyone in the rear and had no idea who should follow me. I added, "Bravo deserves someone who's good. I don't want to go anywhere until you can find the best."

Ivey nodded and said he was glad to hear I was willing to remain in place until he had a chance to look over the entire battalion. He reminded me, although he did not need to, that I had been in the field longer than any platoon leader and now was the company commander with more time in command than any other in the battalion.

As Ivey's bird lifted off, I mentally kicked myself for not telling him to replace me as soon as possible. Yet, I was pleased at the same time, for I was not entirely ready to leave Bravo. My head and feet kept telling me to go, but my heart and my guts kept telling me that the field was where I belonged. The latter won out by a wide margin.

Other units continued to have contact although I rarely

noted any news in my journal that did not directly involve Bravo or one of my former commands. The Delta KIA was recorded because the dead soldier had been a member of the platoon attached to me the week before.

🐂 12 DECEMBER 1969

> CG Bond picked me up in his chopper and we took VR of area we're going into—Bond seems all right
> Got ready to move out—PVT Taylor finally off profile Refused to move out with Co—I will jail him
> Moved to north for nighttime so as to have a PZ available

General Bond became more impressive with each encounter. The visual recon was beneficial because it provided a familiarization with our next area of operations. I also enjoyed the ride in the CG's personal helicopter with its leather-covered seats that were each equipped with headsets so that we could talk above the rotor noise. The difference between his chopper and the regular doorless, seatless choppers was like the difference between a luxury car and a jeep.

When I returned to the Crystal helipad, I was met by 1SGT Beckles who had arrived with the resupply bird. Top told me that he had brought PVT Taylor, who had finally been cleared by the battalion surgeon as fit for duty. Beckles noted that Taylor claimed his knee still hurt too much to allow him to hump the boonies, and the private had said he would refuse to do so.

Taylor, a tall, gangly black who had been in-country for a couple of months, had managed to hump the boonies only a few days without riding sick call. His resulting medical "profile" had kept him in the rear for most of his tour. One of the soldiers to whom I had given an Article 15 for disobeying an NCO at Verna, Taylor had gone from Private First Class to Private for his actions, making him the only one of that rank in the company, for everyone—regardless of their time in the Army—was promoted to PFC upon arrival in Vietnam.

Top had Taylor report to me immediately. I welcomed him back to the field and then asked him if he had any questions. He looked down and replied, "My leg still hurts. I'm not going back out, and no one can make me. Besides, it ain't my war anyway."

We continued to stand for several minutes beside a bunker with our rifles slung muzzle-down over our shoulders. I reminded Taylor that I asked no more of him than of the other men. He shook his head and said he was not going with us.

I could tell the soldier had made up his mind. I ordered him to attention and asked if he knew who I was and what job I held. He responded in the affirmative. I then said, "Private Taylor, as your commanding officer, I am giving you a direct order to retrieve your rucksack and move out with the company."

Until that time, the soldier had been calm, but my words brought a wild look to his eyes as he said, "No way, man. I ain't going." Before I could answer he added menacingly, "You don't want me out there. Anything could happen. You might even get shot accidentally or something."

I remained outwardly calm. Slowly, so as not to display my inner rage, I said, "Taylor, you have only been in the jungle for days. I've been here for eight months. If you think you can kill me, try it now and I'll leave you lying in the dirt."

My voice became louder as I continued, "Go ahead, mother fucker, we both have rifles. Just remember, if you reach for it, you will think before you try to kill me. The difference is, I'll kill you and think about it later."

Taylor made no response. Beckles stepped between us without a word and began—none too gently—to lead the soldier away. I told Top to halt, as I decided to offer Taylor one more option. "Taylor," I said, "I'll give you one more chance. You go to the field and you can walk right behind me. If you feel lucky, give it a shot."

I walked to the commo bunker and told my RTOs to tell the platoons to saddle up. Both Coleman and Speck, who had overheard part of my confrontation with Taylor, including his threats, made no mention of the incident. I did not need to tell them to watch my back, as I had no doubt they would blow Taylor away if he so much as raised his rifle.

As I walked to the gap in the wire to return to the jungle, I noticed that Taylor had dropped his rifle and was standing empty-handed. Beckles walked over and said, "He's not going."

I smiled and replied, "No sweat, Top. Take him back and put him in jail. Let him rot there in pretrial confinement until I get time to formalize the court-martial. Have him stand here so every man in the company sees him as we leave."

I was apprehensive about the reactions of the rest of the company. Everyone was aware of what had occurred, including Taylor's threat and my daring him to follow through. No one had ever refused to go to the field, although I was sure the thought had crossed everyone's mind at one time or another.

I had no need to worry. Every man picked up his rucksack and followed me through the wire. Most looked directly at Taylor, who was standing with this eyes downcast, as they passed. No color lines existed in the grunts' disgust with his actions. The only soldier who spoke at all was a black machine gunner who spat at Taylor's feet and said, "Fucking coward."

Two hours later we completed a reconaissance in force (RIF) and prepared our night position. No one had said anything about the incident within my hearing, except for one soldier who said to a buddy, "How would you like to write your mother that you were yellow and in Long Binh Jail?"

I was eating a can of Cs when SGT Barnes sat beside me and asked, "Would you have blown him away if he had tried anything?" Before I could answer, he continued, "It doesn't make any difference because he sure as hell thought you would."

I offered the FO sergeant a cigarette but no answer of my own. His had been sufficient.

> Conducted airmobile operation to south—Further briefing there from LTC Loeffke—Then began sweep—Thick, slow, hot, no signs of enemy—Typical fucked up mission
> Moved north for nighttime—Poor commo—This is always bad

The LZ had recently been burned off, and the clouds of soot stuck to our skin as we jumped from the chopper skids. Sweat soon had black rivulets of ash running down our faces.

Loeffke landed as soon as we had the area secured, then briefed me on the NVA company which Intelligence thought was in the area. As McGinnis was now the battalion's S-2, I put more stock than usual in the report.

Our movement was slowed by thicker than normal vegetation. At many places, the point man had to cut a path with a machete to penetrate the growth. The farther we went, the hotter and more impenetrable the jungle became. Whatever was supposed to be there never had been.

Moved farther north—At resupply LZ Gen Bond flew in—Mostly just to see what was going on—Changed mission slightly
Nighttime Company perimeter

"The woods are lovely, dark and deep,
But I have promises to keep
And miles to go before I sleep."

Robert Frost

I was surprised to see BG Bond again so soon. He explained that the Intel folks were sure that there were dinks in our AO and wanted my opinion. After I explained that for a day and a half we had found no signs of any activity—recent or old—he nodded and directed me to change the direction of our RIF. He said if we continued to find nothing, he would move us back to the area of our successes earlier in the month.

Bond stayed after our conversation and went around our perimeter talking to the soldiers. A major in a disgruntled mood called me to one side to tell me our position was not spread out enough to secure the area properly. Noticing the Military Intelligence branch insignia on his collar, I deduced that he was from Brigade Intelligence and our wild goose chase had been his idea rather than McGinnis's. As respectfully as possible I told him that I felt the perimeter was satisfactory. I could not resist adding that if there were any dinks around, and I assured him that there were not, that they would shoot at his and the general's nice clean helicopter before they messed with us dirty grunts. That ended our conversation.

🛩 15 DECEMBER 1969

> Moved to north—Airmobiled from PZ
> Went in on first lift to guide airmobile into our contact area of last week—No sweat—Nighttime here
> Standdown nearly here
> Mail with pictures of the beautiful Reveilee Ann Lanning

After more fruitless search in the morning, we were ordered to move to a PZ for an airmobile back to the north.

During the rest of the day, we moved through the area of the previous week's contact, which was now just as cold as it had been hot only a few days before.

A resupply bird brought in a mailbag which contained a letter from Linda with pictures of our daughter. The stack of 60-second Polaroids made the rounds so that Bravo could see the company commander's kid. I suppose the dim photos must have looked quite ordinary to the other men, but to me they were shots of the most beautiful baby I had ever seen.

Despite the inactivity everyone was in good spirits because standdown was only a day away. In many ways, I was glad we found no enemy, for if we had, our three-day break would have been postponed.

I was not surprised that Loeffke made no visit to us on his last day in command. Anything not directly related to eliminating the enemy he had no time for. By afternoon, LTC Ivey was on the radio using the call sign of the battalion commander.

Several days later I received a brief letter from Loeffke congratulating me on the birth of my daughter and saying he looked forward to our working together again. He offered accolades on the performance of Bravo Company, but his most memorable words were in a simple sentence that read, ''There is no greater satisfaction than leading men in combat.''

In the past sixteen years, my contact with Loeffke has been limited to an occasional Christmas card, infrequent phone calls, and two brief visits. His military service has continued to be exemplary, with duty as Brigade Commander, a White House Fellow, Army Attaché to the US Embassy in Moscow, and Defense Attaché to China. As of this writing, in 1986, he is a Brigadier General and the Chief of Staff of the XVIII Airborne Corps at Fort Bragg, North Carolina.

> Moved east—After raising hell about trucks being late, finally began move to BMB
>
> A very successful last 2 months—Talked to LTC Ivey again—He sounds good
>
> Night: NCO Club—The usual standdown

Battalion called shortly after daylight with instructions for us to move to the rubber plantation around Cam Tam to meet trucks that would take us to BMB. We were given a pick up time of noon, so we had to push hard for three hours without taking breaks to make it on time.

We arrived with only minutes to spare. When I called the battalion TOC, I was greeted with a long pause. Then a voice admitted that the trucks had not yet left Black Horse. It was a good thing that we were in a fairly secure area, for I could not keep my voice down. I yelled into the headset, in terms generously sprinkled with profanity, just what I thought about the typical REMF support.

The duty officer's apologies did little to quiet my rage. As I continued my tirade on the radio, the otherwise silent perimeter suddenly broke into shouts and cheers. "Right on, sir. Give 'em hell!" someone hollered. By the time I signed off—telling the TOC that my next call would be to the battalion commander if the trucks did not arrive within an hour—the entire company was yelling, whistling, and cheering. My anger faded as I realized that the men appreciated having someone stand up for them more than they resented the trucks being late.

Less than an hour later the trucks arrived, accompanied

by gun jeeps and LTC Ivey. I thought that the battalion commander would have something to say about my temper tantrum, but he spent most of his time meeting the men as they loaded onto the vehicles. Just before we pulled out, Ivey called me aside and said with a laugh that he had intended to counsel the duty officer about our late trucks; however, he had been listening on the radio and had heard me do so quite sufficiently. He added that he could hear the company shouting in the background over the horn and wondered what any nearby enemy thought about the crazy GIs.

It was nearly dark before we reached BMB, where Beckles and Beig met us and began the routine shakedown to lock up weapons, ammo, and explosives. Beig was going over the standdown schedule with the platoon leaders and me while the NCOs were inspecting their men when two MPs arrived, flanking one of my soldiers. My troop still had on his weapon, bandoleers of ammo, and web gear holding hand and smoke grenades. He, like the rest of us after days in the boonies, was filthy, unshaven, and long-haired.

The MPs explained that the soldier had sneaked away from our formation to get a carton of cigarettes for his squad. At the PX door a starched and spit-shined Finance clerk had seen the Bravo grunt and in amazement asked, "Where in the world are you from?"

The soldier had responded, "I'm from the fucking jungle." And with one punch, he had flattened the curious REMF.

One MP said he had been a grunt before re-enlisting for his present job and thought the situation could better be handled by the company commander than through police channels. I thanked the sergeant and told him I was sure my First Sergeant could take care of the man.

During my conversation with the MPs, the "jungle soldier" stood nervously to one side. He seemed more comfortable when he overheard that the MPs were not going to take him away. For the next couple of days, Top put him on shit-burning detail, as Beckles said, "For leaving my formation and not for decking a REMF." The rest of the company treated him as a hero.

That night, the officers and sergeants visited the NCO Club, where we sat around a huge table and told each other how damn good we all were. Empty cans and bottles mounted before us in testimony to ourselves. It never crossed my mind that of the twenty or so of us, less than a third were old enough to buy a beer legally back in the World.

Few, if any of us, had a realization of just how young we really were. It would be years before it became common knowledge that the average age of the Vietnam soldier was nineteen-and-a-half compared to twenty-six during World War II. As time has passed, I have often wondered if our youth compounded the adverse perceptions by the general public of the Vietnam veteran. America was used to its warriors being older in both fact and fiction. In the general mobilization for World War II and Korea, it was not unusual for draftees to be in their late twenties and early-to-mid thirties. Movies of the period and of today display those veterans of earlier wars as men who had long since put their boyhoods behind and who were led by men with a hint of gray in their hair and a cigar clenched between their teeth. Americans were just not ready to accept the teenage warriors they saw on their nightly news programs as the country's killers and destroyers who defended our freedoms and democratic way of life.

Perhaps the young age of the Vietnam veteran also influenced the inability of many to immediately assimilate back into the society that had sent them off to war. Not only were there no bands or parades to welcome the Viet vet home, but many were also still too young to enjoy the basic rights and privileges bestowed on ''adults'' such as the purchase of alcoholic beverages and the right to vote for or against the elected leadership that was running the war.

🐦 17 DECEMBER 1969

> Went to Saigon to USO to call Linda—By the time we finally found it, it was too late
> Saigon is interesting, but filthy
> Bought a watch
> Party tonight—Hell-raising, fights, etc.—One bad note: a CWO took a broken leg—Still a good party
> MPs came—Hard explaining to them that I was the CO, not XO
> Still a good time
> 3 1st SGTs (people who count) said I was best CO in Bn—I have a good Company

Bravo had a company formation so I could pin valor medals on soldiers who had displayed their bravery during the last month. At the end of the ceremony, I called SGT Barnes, the artillery FO NCO, forward and presented him with a letter of appreciation for his months with Bravo. Barnes, who would be returning to his unit for a rear job until his DEROS, was a young, hard sergeant and by all standards was as tough as any man I had met in Vietnam.

As I read his letter to the formation, I looked up at the stalwart soldier to see tears spilling from his eyes and running down his cheeks. In my surprise at his emotional reaction to recognition, I concluded the award as quickly as possible.

Barnes followed me into the orderly room after he had composed himself and said, "I'm not ashamed to cry. This is the greatest bunch in the world, and I'm proud to have been with them."

It has taken many years for me to understand thoroughly the pride of the soldiers who served in Vietnam. Many, like Barnes, had little to be proud of back home beyond winning a few street fights. As high school dropouts, adversaries in brushes with the law, and failures in so many respects, they experienced the sense of self-worth in Vietnam that comes with achievements and camaraderie. As the troops said about Nam, "The cowards never started; the weak found a way out."

By afternoon Top had trucks shuttling troops on "laundry runs" to the village outside the gates. The company medic was on hand with huge boxes of rubbers and terrifying tales of the result of failure to use them. One of the most widely repeated stories was about a new strain of VD so bad that it could not be cured. Soldiers infected with it could never go home and were quarantined to an island in the Saigon River. The story did not seem to reduce the numbers climbing aboard the trucks, however.

While waiting for my platoon leaders to be reissued their weapons for our trip to the Saigon USO, I asked Beckles about a letter from Linda that had thanked me for flowers I had not sent after Reveilee was born. Top smiled and tried to change the subject, but finally admitted that he had ordered the flowers. He refused my offer of repayment with a laugh and said, "You weren't near a telephone in the jungle. Besides, you young guys never think of things like that or the sweet card I told them to include.''

It was years before I told Linda the truth about the flowers. I may have been young, but I was not entirely stupid.

The Saigon USO had direct phone lines to the States and conversations did not require the ''overs'' of the MARS shortwave radio system. It took us awhile to find the USO, but my journal entry about being ''too late'' did not refer to the time of day. The USO clerk explained that priority calls to new mothers had to be made within 48 hours after the Red Cross telegram was received. She said that since I had waited eleven days to request the call I would have to place my name on the waiting list and that it was already full for the day. I remained fairly calm and asked to see her supervisor. I told him just where I had been for the last week and a half and that this was my first chance to place the call. Again, I received the same explanation about the rules, all the while becoming more and more angry. My anger did little good, though, because the regulation-quoting bureaucrat refused to give in beyond saying he might be able to work me in in a few hours. With that remark I shook my head and told the supervisor, ''You really don't understand a damn thing about this war, do you?'' I walked out, slamming the door.

After a brief tour of Saigon, we ended up at the Cholon PX and commissary complex. We tried to go into the commissary to buy some chow, but we were stopped by an MP. As he explained that we did not have the proper ration cards, we watched a constant stream of Vietnamese officers, American civilians and Saigon warriors go into the building.

We next tried the PX where we were allowed in only after leaving our rifles with the jeep driver. My platoon leaders pointed out that the PX had fur coats for sale while I quickly bought a watch and headed for the exit.

Outside the Exchange we encountered baby sans hawking their usual trinkets. One of them had a mobile pet shop composed of birds and puppies. For a few dollars I bought a cage of four sparrow-like birds and, to the amazement of the baby san, I laughed wildly as I opened the door and released the small winged creatures.

On the way back to BMB, we cursed and laughed at our experiences in Saigon. We talked about the possibility that we would have better fit the REMFs image of grunts if we had bought the puppies and thrown them against the sidewalk. I was not for certain about the puppies, but I knew that I no more belonged in Saigon than the birds belonged in cages.

We got back in time for the company party which provided more steaks and beer, a band, and a stripper. The three first sergeants whom I quoted in my journal joined our celebrations and while I appreciated their compliments about my ability to command, I also realized that our inviting them to the festivities might have had something to do with their praise.

Everyone was having a great time until about midnight when a brief fight erupted. The chaos of sorting out the details was compounded by the necessity of seeing that the chief warrant officer, who suffered a broken leg, was taken to the hospital. The MPs added more confusion to the situation by insisting upon talking to "the captain in charge." Beckles finally shouted above the roar for them to get the hell out of the area so "the lieutenant" could clear up the mess.

The battalion XO, Major Daniels, arrived shortly after, upset that a member of his staff had been injured. He was even more incensed when he learned that the warrant officer had been assaulted by enlisted men, and he demanded that I court-martial the guilty party. I informed him that the incident had been investigated and the stories sorted out. The fortyish, pot-bellied CWO, who had come to the party un-invited, had been ignored until he became drunk and began talking about "young punks" in today's Army who could not compare to those in his heyday. He had made a further mistake by pushing three of my men out of his way so that he could get a better look at the stripper.

MAJ Daniels was not satisfied with my explanations, demanding again that I take action against the three men. My patience was at an end, so I said, "Sir, when I go back to the jungle, I'm taking these men with me because I need every rifle I can get. The goddamn warrant got exactly what he deserved. He's lucky he's not dead. If my men had been trying to really hurt him, they would have done more than break his leg."

That was the end of the conversation. LTC Ivey never mentioned the incident except to once say laughingly that if Bravo kept breaking his staff officers' legs, we would get no more standdowns.

As I wrote in my journal, it was "still a good party."

18 DECEMBER 1969

Close out another book—8 months today
Back to field tomorrow
Lots to write but am rushed
Damn call to Linda never went through—Sure wanted to hear the baby

Throughout the day I tried to get through the MARS lines to Linda with no success. The failure to hear my daughter's voice for the first time added to my bitterness toward the USO's by-the-book supervisor.

Along with replacements, several soldiers arrived from R&R with fantastic stories that were at least partially true about Hong Kong and Bangkok. Along with them was the PFC who had gone on emergency leave a month before to marry his .pregnant girlfriend. He looked even younger than he had before he left.

That evening Bravo's officers headed to the club for what we promised each other would be a quiet dinner and a few beers. Our plan, which was not terribly sincere to begin with, went awry immediately when we kicked open the door of the club and discovered it was "dime night." Each of us threw a $5 MPC (military payment certificates— military scrip issued to servicemen in lieu of American money to prevent currency speculation) on the table and began ordering the ten-cent drinks by twos and threes. We behaved ourselves fairly well for the first few hours, until the cheap alcohol started to take its toll. Schmalz was soon wandering around the club asking captains why they were in a bar at BMB when his company commander was only a lieutenant. Our comments about REMFs and our experiment to see if beer bottles would break against the club's flimsy walls finally brought an invitation from the nervous club manager, a warrant officer, for us to leave. When one of the platoon leaders asked the manager if he had heard how Bravo liked to break warrant officers' legs, the fellow quickly retreated, mumbling about calling the MPs.

Since it was getting late and the pool of money on the table was nearly gone, we decided that it was time to go. As we reached the door, we were met by an MP lieutenant colonel demanding to know who was in charge of our group. When I stepped forward, he informed me that he, the Brigade Provost Marshal, did not appreciate being gotten out of bed to quiet down a bunch of drunken grunts.

We walked outside and the colonel called me aside, ordering me to attention and chewing me out. That was the MP's second mistake. The first had been to drive his own jeep, with its prominent Provost Marshal's decal, without a driver to secure it. I listened intently to the verbal lashing I was receiving. All the while, just over the colonel's shoulder, I was watching Bolenske and Kidalowski raise the jeep's hood so that Schmalz could reach in and, with a grin in my direction, pull out a handful of wires. These he waved in the air before tucking them into his shirt. By the time the PM was finished with his one-sided conversation, the platoon leaders were standing to one side with incredible looks of innocence.

We walked back to the company, laughing and stumbling. I do not know how the Provost Marshal got home.

Before climbing under my trusty old poncho liner, I recorded the day's events in my journal. The book was nearly full, so I planned to leave it behind in the company safe when we went back to the field. Of the three black journals Linda had given me on R&R, one was complete—two more to go.

✈ 19 DECEMBER 1969

Trucked out to Tan Lap—There found out it was a mix-up—No Tan Lap for us
Inserted southwest of village—Good briefing from Bn CO, S-3 and S-2—Moved south to ambush—So here I am in jungle again
Amazing how people feel after standdown—Morale, including my own, near zero—More in life of the combat Infantryman

Ivey met us at Tan Lap, changing our mission from village security to an RIF in the same area where we had made several contacts in early November. We moved slowly, readjusting ourselves to the steamy jungle after the excesses we had enjoyed at BMB. Jungle fatigues were soon sweat-soaked from the beers that had tasted so good the day before.

✈ 20 DECEMBER 1969

Sweep south on 3 axis to nighttime positions—About only findings today were signs of elephants—Have seen signs of elephants before but never seen one in flesh—

Kind of hope we don't—Understand they play hell with
a perimeter

We began our day with the usual stand to. After enjoying the first cigarette of the morning, I lay back on my
rucksack and fell asleep while the rest of the company ate
breakfast in shifts. A half hour later, I awoke and overheard a platoon leader whispering instructions to my
RTOs, telling them to pack up and move out quietly to a
spot a hundred meters away. I lay still listening to them
gather up the equipment, hardly able to contain their
laughter as they plotted to have all one hundred men slip
away, leaving me to wake up alone in the jungle. I remained motionless for the next twenty minutes while they
took precautions not to awaken me, though I could occasionally overhear their speculations about what I would do
when I found them gone.

As the last soldiers were just about out of sight, I raised up
and whispered, "Good try, but you guys know I never sleep."

No one minded that I had spoiled their joke. I thought it
much funnier the way it ended up than I would have found
the intended outcome. The night in the jungle and the morning's activities had put the gloomy feelings of poststanddown
behind us. We were soon spread out, covering as much area
as possible as though we had never left.

Stories about elephants in our AO, as well as rumors
that the NVA used the pachyderms to carry supplies, made
little sense to me. How in the hell could the dinks hide
elephants? However, the crushed foliage and huge footprints were difficult to argue with.

I still clearly remember seeing the tracks of elephants and
recall a radio transmission from one of the other companies
trying to get a helicopter to lift out the skull and tusks of a
skeleton they had found. Even with the personal visual and
audio evidence, I continue to doubt that they existed. Then

again, there were things I clearly saw with my own eyes in Vietnam that I have trouble believing as well.

This day also marked Linda's and my second anniversary. Since our marriage, our time together had been measured in weeks rather than in years. I tried with little success to focus on our future times together rather than how much we had been apart.

 ## 21 DECEMBER 1969

> Moved to link up and resupply by truck—Even got some beer—Bad resupply because no mail for me—Damn, I'm getting tired of the field—But would hate to leave my men
> Gunships hit some gooks south of here—We went into block—No results—Ambush night with 2nd plt in rubber (My position is usually center of sector)
> Also visit from Bn CO today—Just talk—He gets around

Our route took us through the jungle from south of Highway 1 to the northwest of Cam Tam. Although we had fought several battles in this area over the last three months, this mission proved fruitless. By the time we reached the rubber plantation at midday, a resupply brought by truck and gun jeep met us.

Beckles had managed to scrounge up some artillery ammo boxes and filled them with ice, beer, and soda to go along with the usual C-rations. The ice had mostly thawed, but the beverages were still fairly cool. My body, dehydrated from the sweaty march, soaked up the two-beer ration and left me with a pleasant buzz.

Until the gunships made contact with an estimated platoon of enemy, I had planned to stay close to the resupply area for the rest of the day. The contact brought orders for us to move as quickly as possible into a blocking position four kilometers to the west at a point where the rubber met the jungle. As there was little vegetation growing under the neat rows of rubber trees, we covered the two-and-a-half mile distance at a trot in slightly more than half an hour. The gunships were still firing a few klicks to our southwest, but I could barely hear them over my and the RTOs' labored breathing. The beer that had tasted so good an hour before no longer felt so pleasant.

Our haste was futile. The Cobras reported that the dinks had changed direction. Another night was passed monitoring the radios, listening to the jungle, counting stars, and trying to sleep.

🪖 22 DECEMBER 1969

> Australians in contact to our south so airmobile into a blocking position to assist
> Aussies Bn is new in country but seem professional
> Rode around about 45 minutes in C&C ship getting instructions, etc.

We airmobiled in as close as possible to the stream that marked the boundary with the Australians, then spread out to try to catch any fleeing enemy. Except for a half-dozen Aussie mortar rounds that landed near us before we could get them to adjust the impact area, we saw no action.

The Australians operated on a one-year system like us, but rather than replace individuals at the end of that time, they rotated entire battalions. This process allowed better unit cohesiveness and morale than our methods, but new battalions were totally inexperienced in Nam and learned many lessons the hard way. My evaluation of the Aussies as professionals was based primarily on monitoring their various radio nets rather than on much first-hand observation. They were confident, precise, and, if nothing else, fun to listen to with their ''down under'' accents.

Although the holiday season and winter were coming back in the World, the calendar and a few Christmas cards were all that marked the upcoming event in our unchanging jungle. For the grunts, the days of parties, family gatherings, and religious celebrations were just more days to cross off on short-timer calendars.

✈ 23 DECEMBER 1969

Move from block to nighttime to west
Resupply today had lots of mail

"For a living dog is better than a dead lion."
Eccles. 9:4

Just another day in the jungle—hot, exhausting, boring—tedious with the knowledge that every sense could turn into fright in an instant. The highlight of the day was that the monotony was *not* broken by terror. Ranking very nearly as important was the delivery of several sacks of mail.

In Vietnam, mail was the most critical aspect of my existence beyond survival itself. Before opening each letter, I noted the postmark and return address, not to see who the letters were from but to assure myself that somewhere outside the jungle places like San Francisco and Sylvester still existed. In an environment so foreign, the familiar handwriting of my wife, parents, and brother let me know that there was a life before the war and, with a little luck, that there would be again some day.

24 DECEMBER 1969

Christmas Eve—Moved north where we ran into 20 "rubber workers"—Was informed they were not to be there—I must be getting a little war weary—Could hardly keep the men from killing them—If we thought we could have gotten by with it we would have

Night—Heard voices and a truck—Could not fire arty because of truce—My request for arty went all the way through to CG—Then MACV before denied—A hell of a war—I think it was VC/NVA resuppliers

Christmas Eve morning found us on a long reconnaissance in force (RIF) toward the rubber plantations south of Cam Tam. As we reached the edge of the rubber, the point reported movement ahead. I quickly checked the plantation map provided by the ARVNs to confirm that this part of the plantation was inactive and considered a free fire zone. Battalion added their assurance that no friendlies were authorized to be in the area.

I crept to the edge of the jungle to a point where I could see several individuals standing near a truck. I saw no weapons, so I deployed a platoon to each flank. When everyone was in position, we began to inch forward.

As we got closer, I could distinguish about twenty or so women, children, and old men. A Kit Carson scout shouted for the group to remain still or we would shoot. The figures froze.

When we had them gathered in close, we searched them, finding no weapons nor supplies of any kind. An old woman who seemed to be their leader explained that they were rubber workers who had gotten on the wrong road. The "workers" exhibited signs of nervousness, and several of the GIs, including me, expressed suspicions that they had brought supplies to the NVA before our arrival.

One man said, "We should have shot first and checked later."

Another shouted, "Let's do it now."

My journal entry is somewhat incorrect in what happened next. I counted the group and had Bolenske guard them with two of his M-60 machine gunners. When I reported my head count to the battalion TOC and asked what I was to do with the detainees, a simple return message said, "Waste them."

A good way to pick up an easy twenty body count as well as a method of ridding the area of enemy suppliers, the instructions had appeal. I considered the order, turned to Bolenske, and said, "Waste them."

Bolenske started toward his machine gunners and then turned back to me. After a moment's hesitation, he walked over and said, "If you want me to do it, I will, but it's not right. I'll kill them if you tell me to, but I'll report the circumstances when we get back to the rear."

Then as an afterthought, he added, "There is no way we can get by with it."

I said nothing. Then I walked to the group of prisoners and considered killing them myself. When I looked at them, I saw the scenes of the dead and maimed GIs. I stood there, thinking not of right and wrong but of what Bill had said. We could not get away with it.

I walked back to my RTOs and called Battalion, saying, "Reference your last transmission on disposition of detainees, give me initials of authorizing officer." After a short pause, a voice I recognized as the TOC duty officer answered, "We have negative knowledge, I say again, negative knowledge of any transmission. If you have detainees, hold them until we can pick them up."

Logic and relief replaced my emotional reaction. I responded, "Roger, we will hold them here, but I'm claiming their goddamn truck as a war trophy and taking it home with me."

Several hours later an interrogation team from Brigade arrived and took our prisoners—and my truck—away. Of course, we saw neither again. Sometime later I heard that the group had convinced their questioners of their innocence and had been returned to their village, likely as not to continue resupplying the enemy.

Just who had come on the radio telling us to "waste them," I never found out. The identity did not make any difference because all I had wanted was an excuse to do what I thought was necessary.

Neither Bolenske nor anyone else ever mentioned my order to kill the prisoners. I wondered for a time why I had given an order that was obviously unlawful—and even more why the platoon leader had not carried it out. It was not until this book was in its initial draft that I discussed the incident with anyone besides Linda. Late one night while talking with my brother, I told him the story of that Christmas Eve in the jungle. I explained to Jim that I was not proud of what had happened; however, I had no regrets because my job had been to make decisions, right or wrong. When I added that I had been fortunate that Bolenske had not carried out my instructions and that I still wondered why he had not done so, Jim responded with a question. He asked, "How long had the platoon leader been in the field?"

When I answered that he had been there only about three or four months, Jim said, "The difference was you had been out over eight months. If he had been there as long as you, he would have killed them. The more war you experience, the less human you see the enemy. Killing replaces compassion directly proportional to what you have seen."

That afternoon we received word that there was a 48-hour cease-fire in effect for Christmas; we were to shoot if fired upon but not to initiate contact. The troops laughed, and shouted, "Bullshit." We knew there was about as much of a chance of the gooks honoring a cease-fire as there was of Santa Claus coming down the chimneys of our rucksacks.

We dug in beneath the rubber trees to spend our Christmas Eve as if it were any other night of living in the dirt. Before dark, a soldier approached my CP and set down his rucksack next to mine. He then fixed his bayonet onto his rifle and stuck the weapon upright into the ground. Methodically, from his pocket, he pulled out a bright red stocking and hung it from his rifle butt. Then from his rucksack he took a small box and wordlessly assembled a foot-high plastic Christmas tree. He stood up with a smile, extended his hand, and said, "Merry Christmas, sir."

I shook the soldier's hand and returned his greeting. Then again he went back to his pack and produced a five-pound canned ham which he had carried since standdown, explaining that his mother had sent the ham and decorations.

Over the next hour, one at a time, every man in the company left his position and came to the CP to exchange Christmas greetings and to sample the ham. A five-pound ham split over one hundred ways did not provide much nourishment, but we all had a taste. I have yet to attend a more appropriate celebration. Christmas had come to Vietnam.

Our circumstances, however, did not allow relaxation. Near midnight one of the platoon RTOs reported hearing what sounded like a truck coming our way along a road in the rubber. I could soon hear it myself, clearly making out its stopping and dropping its tailgate with a crash. I wondered if our "detainees" from earlier in the day had already returned and resumed their resupply activities.

Gulbranson and I, after a quickly whispered discussion, estimated the distance at fifteen hundred meters. For the next half an hour we argued with Battalion and the artillery fire center, trying to get them to shoot the guns. Their response countered that the cease-fire prevented our shooting first. I continued to badger Battalion until Ivey finally came on to say that he had pushed our request for artillery all the way to Saigon with no success.

All three platoon leaders volunteered to go check out the noise, but by the time I was convinced we were getting no artillery, the noise had ceased. Besides, I would be damned if I would risk any of my men when apparently no one else was interested in getting the gooks.

🖙 **25 DECEMBER 1969**

> Picked up by trucks and transported to Black Horse—
> Good dinner—Good booze
> A hell of a Christmas
> Linda and Reveilee Ann are now back in Texas
> Back to field tomorrow

With the exception of the small plastic tree still standing guard in the middle of our perimeter, Christmas morning dawned like any other day. C and D Companies had been transported to Black Horse the day before for their "holiday," and as they returned to the field, B and A Companies took the trucks in to get our day off.

As usual upon our arrival, Beckles took charge. Along with fresh uniforms, he issued each man a small Red Cross bag containing candy, writing materials, paperbacks, and such. In addition, each bag held a letter from junior and senior high school girls in Jacksonville, Florida, whose teacher had asked that they write servicemen to wish them a Merry Christmas.

Several of the GIs said that they intended to answer the letters in hopes of "getting something going" for when they returned to the States. When I pointed out to one of the starry-eyed grunts that his letter writer could not be more than fourteen years old, he smiled and said with a wink, "Yeah, but she will be nearly a year older by the time I get home."

Top made sure I had time alone to read the stack of letters he had placed on my bunk. Linda wrote that she and Reveilee had moved back to Texas because Susan Hargrove's brother was moving into the apartment, and their place could not accommodate two waiting wives, a new baby, and a college student. Since Susan's parents held the lease, Linda felt that she had no choice but to return to her parents' home.

When I finished the mail, Beckles reappeared with a bottle of bourbon. Although it was only 1000 hours, Top calculated that it must be after 1700 hours somewhere in the World. He unscrewed the cap and handed me the bottle, which we passed back and forth as we extended our personal Christmas greetings to each other.

The rest of the morning I spent wandering through the company billets, sampling the variety of Christmas goodies sent from back home. I was surprised to find the men in such good spirits despite being so far from home on the holiday. I supposed that a day off and cases of cold beer were cause enough for the cheer. We all missed our relatives and friends, but in its own way, Bravo was family, too.

At noon we headed for the mess hall where tables heaped with real roast turkeys—not from a can and not rehydrated—awaited us. Surrounding the birds we found mounds of green salad and even shrimp cocktail and pumpkin pie. As fine a Christmas dinner as was served anywhere that day, this meal exceeded our every expectation.

LTC Ivey stood at the end of the serving line and spoke to each soldier as he went by. After all the troops had piled their plates high, he and I heaped our trays and joined McGinnis, Lewis, and several other staff officers at a table adjacent to the one occupied by my platoon leaders. I exchanged handshakes and the season's greetings with my comrades. A captain across from me, obviously new because of his pale skin and bright green fatigues, introduced himself as the Artillery Liaison Officer.

McGinnis, Lewis, and I traded a few war stories and "remember whens" as we wolfed down the turkey and trimmings. Near the end of the meal, I asked the artillery captain about our failure to fire the mission at the truck noise the night before. He explained the procedures he had followed, including the cease-fire limitations. When he finished, he added rather sternly, "Lieutenant, you should have checked all that out yourself. The artillery can't always do your job for you."

The table fell silent. Then McGinnis dropped his fork onto his tray, and Lewis muttered, "Oh, shit."

I stared at the captain. I fought to control the anger I could feel rising inside me. Finally I swallowed hard and said icily, "Sir, you are new and maybe you don't know what goes on out there in the jungle."

I could feel my voice volume increasing as I continued, "Bravo's men are the best goddamn fighters in-country, and I don't appreciate your . . ."

At that point I decided the hell with controlling my rage. I said, "Fuck it," and lunged across the table at him, knocking over my tray and several glasses. As my hands were closing around his throat, Ivey and McGinnis grabbed me from both sides, slamming me back into my chair. My platoon leaders, hearing at least part of the exchange, had left their table, knocking over several chairs in their haste, and were standing alert behind me.

Ivey still had hold of my arm and firmly but quietly said,

"Lee, that's enough. It's Christmas." He then turned and told my lieutenants to return to their table. They did not move until I nodded my head as Ivey released my arm.

Lewis, deciding early to ignore the inevitable ruckus, had continued eating throughout the scene. In the silence that followed, he looked over my scattered food and speared a piece of turkey off the table. Then, as though nothing had happened, he resumed the conversation. Ivey refilled my water glass and said, "Don't worry about it, Lee. Take it out on the gooks later."

In the ensuing discussions at the table, we ignored the artillery captain until McGinnis, with a glint in his eye, asked in mock seriousness, "Damn, Lanning, remember when you tried to kill Sergeant Bender for just trespassing through your AO?"

Lewis picked up the spirit with, "Is it true you guys broke a warrant officer's leg for bad-mouthing Bravo?"

McGinnis was just getting warmed up, talking about what messes fragmentation grenades made of bodies, when the liaison officer excused himself and hurried from the mess hall. If Ivey noted the quick departure he did not acknowledge it; he suggested that we have seconds on the chow.

On the way back to the company my platoon leaders made a few comments about the FNG captain, but they cooled down as we passed the remainder of Top's bourbon around. I never saw the artillery captain again. Later I heard Ivey sent him back to his original battalion and requested a new liaison officer.

All in all, it was a memorable Christmas.

26 DECEMBER 1969

> Airmobiled from BH to northwest—Before we took
> off, plt ldrs and I all admitted we felt it was going to be
> a bad mission
> > 1st plt airmobiled in just south of 2nd, 3rd, and my CP
> > Moved out on two axis
> > Nighttime to west

We assembled at the air strip early in the morning to
await the helicopters. My troops were spread out, with
many leaning back on their heavy rucksacks and smoking
or just staring across the field. Others stood with weapons
slung over their backs in the casual manner that only men
who live with guns acquire.

I had stood on many a pick-up zone. This morning a
foreboding troubled me far more than ever before. I hoped
that my anticipation was just the after-Christmas letdown
and made no comments about my frame of mind when I
talked with the platoon leaders. As the other lieutenants
returned to their units, Schmalz paused and said, "I've got
bad vibes about this mission. It's going to be a bad one."

A few minutes later Bolenske returned for verification
of the spot where his platoon would be inserted separately
from the rest of the company. While we talked, Kidalowski walked over to listen, saying nothing but acting more
nervous than I had ever seen him.

The incoming *whop-whop* of the choppers as they flared
over the horizon ended our conversation and put us into
action. Soon we were in the air with our fatigue trousers

blowing in the wind as our legs dangled over the sides of the birds.

The senses of the human body are quite remarkable. The longer we stayed in the boonies, the sharper our senses became, for our lives depended on our awareness. Some soldiers possessed extremely keen eyesight, able to detect gooks and signs at great distances. Others could hear the slightest out-of-the-ordinary noises that most of us missed, while several soldiers swore they could smell gooks many meters away. A few, like point man Larry Morford back in my Charlie Company platoon, had their combination of natural and developed senses fine-tuned to a remarkable degree.

While all of us became more sensitive to the physical world, it was our "sixth sense" that guided us more often than not. Soldiers would tell buddies before a mission that they had the feeling that they would not return, or a man might report that he had seen death waiting at the end of a trail. Perhaps some of these premonitions were, in fact, self-fulfilling prophecies. Yet, all too often they were correct. While I never knew a soldier to use a "gut feeling" as an excuse not to do his duty, the real terror of the sixth sense was the feeling that nothing could be done to change the outcome.

As we neared the LZ, the crew chief shouted over the rotor noise that the gunships had killed two as they prepped the area for our landing. As we exited the choppers, a burst of AK fire raked the LZ without hitting anyone. The door gunners converged their fire on the third enemy soldier, ripping him to pieces.

We ran like hell to the tree line. The birds lifted off, leaving an eerie quiet.

We waited. We listened. Detecting no movement, we began to search the LZ area carefully. Trails showing recent activity led in all directions into the jungle. Except for the three dead dinks the choppers had killed, we found no enemy.

Bolenske's platoon deployed into an LZ a half a klick to our south. When his men were ready, our two units headed west in parallel, finding more signs of the enemy's presence in the vicinity. When darkness arrived, Schmalz's and Kidalowski's platoons, with which my CP was traveling, set up an ambush on a trail that was wide enough for three men to walk abreast.

---

27 DECEMBER 1969

Ambushes in area of our night position—Lots of trail activity

I decided the best course of action was to stay in our present location even though we were only a few hundred meters away from the LZ. We remained hidden throughout the day in hopes that the dinks would think we had moved on and begin to reuse their trails.

The only things that moved all day were the hands on my watch—and they moved so slowly that minutes seemed like hours.

My sixth sense kept telling me the enemy was near. My plan was to give them a day to expose themselves, and then if they did not come to us, we would go to them.

Crossed stream—Moved out—3rd platoon was ambushed—1 WIA—Put in gunships—Went back in—Got hit again—2 more badly wounded—Pulling back 6 more WIA—Hit by our gunship
All WIA from 3rd plt:
   1st contact—PFC Rahn, ambulatory
   2nd contact—PFC Bookout, litter
           SGT Piesel, litter
   Gunships—SGT Bishop, litter
           PFC Wright, ambulatory
           SP4 Ross, litter
           PFC Deffendlefor, ambulatory
           PFC Robbins, ambulatory

We moved out with the third platoon on point followed by my CP and then the second platoon. Bolenske's platoon was still about five hundred meters to our south, paralleling our route. The jungle was not quite as thick as usual, so we spread out more.

A half a klick from our starting point, we reached a swiftly moving stream about ten to fifteen meters across with water depth varying from waist to chest high. After securing the far side, we crossed the stream, refilling our canteens as we went.

Less than two hundred meters later the jungle exploded. AK47 automatic fire ripped the stillness. Instantly an M-16 and a grenade answered.

My RTOs and I had started crawling forward when we met Schmalz and his medic dragging PFC Rahn toward us. Brian whispered that a gook had appeared from a spider hole only feet to the flank of Rahn, who was on point, firing directly into his body. The "slack" man—the soldier behind the point man—had immediately greased the gook, knocking him back into his hole. The slack troop had then thrown a grenade in after the gook to finish him off.

As the medic examined Rahn, I requested gunships to support our advance. While waiting for them to arrive on station, I overheard Brian telling his point man that he was all right. To this, Rahn only groaned. Brian told him repeatedly that he was not bleeding.

Rahn had taken a full burst of AK fire at less than five feet and would not even require a dust-off. Seven bullet holes were in his rifle stock, rucksack, and canteen. One round had been stopped by a bandoleer of M-16 magazines hanging across his chest while another round had hit him in the buttocks only to be stopped by a thick, plastic-wrapped billfold full of family pictures. The spent AK bullet was still in the wallet. Except for an ugly bruise on the cheek of his ass, he was unmarked.

Once we pointed out the holes to Rahn, he stopped moaning, took another look, and began throwing up until dry heaves were mixed with an attempt to laugh. He finally gained control and said, "I'm sorry. I could feel the bullets hit me. I thought I was dead."

Schmalz patted Rahn on the back and said, "You should have been. Every man in the platoon will want to walk next to you now. You are one lucky son of a bitch."

Unfortunately in his miraculous escape from death, Rahn had used up all of the third platoon's luck for the day. Minutes later more AKs and machine guns blasted at us from bunkers just beyond the spider hole, which had served as an observation post.

Schmalz reported that he had two men down. He was

up against at least a platoon. From my CP, thirty meters or so to the rear of Brian's men, the FO called for artillery and I ordered Bolenske to move to our location from the south and Kidalowski to come up on our right. Coleman was on the horn requesting more gunships.

The fire fight increased in intensity. The gooks were throwing out enough fire power for me to decide that Schmalz's estimate of a platoon was conservative.

I was switching from one handset to another, talking to my platoons and bringing in gunships, when I saw a man rise up from near Schmalz's position and run. With bullets zinging all around him, he was at full speed when I reached up from my prone position and grabbed him. I threw him to the ground next to me. "Where the hell are you going, Ross?" I demanded.

The soldier recognized that I thought he was fleeing in panic. Tears welled in the eyes of SP4 Ross as he said in a halting voice, "The el-tee [lieutenant] sent me for more ammo. We're running low. I volunteered. I'm not scared, sir. Give me some ammo and I'll take it back."

Then Ross added, "I think SGT Riedell is dead. We've got to get him out."

Members of my CP and I stripped off bandoleers. Ross dashed away, and I returned to the radios to let Schmalz know Ross was on his way back, making a mental note to be sure Ross received a valor award for actions which I had initially misunderstood as cowardice rather than bravery.

Kidalowski was by now in position to return the gooks' fire, but he reported he was unable to advance farther. I called Schmalz for his situation report. He said he had one wounded with him and he could see "Three-one" but could not reach him. From Ross's earlier statement, I knew that "Three-one" was SGT Riedell.

"He's hit in the head," Schmalz said. "Appears to be dead. I can't reach him without taking more casualties."

An air strike was en route. I told Schmalz to pull back rather than lose more men trying to recover a body. After a long pause, the third platoon leader responded, "Roger."

Seconds later Schmalz's voice broke into the net. "Goddamn it!" he shouted. "He just opened his eyes! He's not moving but he's looking right at me. The gooks are firing right over the top of him. We've got to get him out!"

I responded, "Concentrate your M-79s [grenade launchers] on the heaviest points of fire. Pop as much smoke as you can. I'll bring the gunships in close."

I heard Schmalz say, "Roger." Then a minute later he said, "Here we go."

The Cobras roared in. The M-79s unleashed their grenades, and every man in the company fired on full automatic. For endless seconds the explosions were deafening. I could barely hear Schmalz's voice above the noise when he screamed, "We've got him! We've got him!"

I continued to work the gunships while ordering Kidalowski to withdraw to the stream and secure it for the rest of us to cross. Bolenske broke in and said that he was nearing our location. I diverted him back to our original LZ to receive the ammo resupply that was inbound.

Schmalz and his platoon reached my position minutes later. We began pulling back to dust-off the wounded.

The dinks were still firing sporadically although the gunships were keeping them fairly well pinned down. Schmalz continued to pop smoke as we moved so the Cobras could cover our withdrawal.

We reached the stream just as the gunships made a rocket run. I knew instantly that the rockets were too close.

The whistling sound they made before impact told me they were off target. Schmalz knew it, too. Near enough for me to hear him without the radio, he screamed, "Jesus Christ! Jesus Fucking Christ! They've killed us all! Mother of God, stop the rockets! Please stop the rockets!"

Before I could grab the handset, the Cobra pilot's voice came over the horn. "Something's wrong!" he shouted. "Something's wrong with the fucking rocket pod!"

"We're hit!" I shouted into the radio.

"God! I'm so sorry!" the pilot sobbed in near-hysteria. "I'm so sorry!" he said over and over as he flew away.

Even then I thought that the pilot had fucked up and fired on the wrong side of the smoke, but I had no time for words with him. There were soldiers blown all over the jungle who needed help.

A squad of the second platoon waded the stream to aid their comrades in the third. Together we went back toward the gooks. I found Schmalz covered in the blood of his injured men but unhurt himself. In addition to the two wounded by the dinks, we now had six more hit by the rockets. The first wounded man I saw was SP4 Ross who had miraculously traversed a battlefield filled with gook fire minutes before only to lie unconscious with a chest full of shrapnel from our own gunship.

Riedell was carried past me, and I could see the path of the bullet that had penetrated his helmet, grazed down his temple and cheek, and entered his body near the collarbone before disappearing deep inside his chest. He tried to smile and say something, but his raspy breath was shallow. Blood came up from his lungs and into his mouth.

We spent another half an hour dragging and carrying our wounded to the LZ. Bolenske met us there with one dust-off already on the ground and another orbiting above.

SGT Bishop, another of Schmalz's squad leaders, managed a morphine-induced laugh as we put him on the medivac, saying over and over, "Million-dollar wound, mother fuckers, million-dollar wound."

While the rest of the injured were being put on board the dust-offs, Bolenske's platoon was breaking down the ammo resupply, a task made faster because Beckles had had the M-16 rounds loaded into magazines. As the ammo was distributed I continued alternating artillery and gunship fire into the enemy position. The same Air Force forward air controller who had supported us in our last fight came on the net with his usual calm drawl, saying, "You guys in trouble again? Don't you know it's the Christmas season? Let's see if we can deliver the gooks a little present of napes and five-hundred-pounders."

An F-4 jet streaked in and the jungle exploded in orange and black flames. When the FAC completed guiding in the bomb runs, he flew away with a last transmission, "Happy New Year. By the way, thanks for those helmets and things you sent us. No one ever did that before. Keep your heads down."

It had now been over six hours since the initial contact with the gook in the spider hole. Darkness was closing around us as I reported to Battalion that we would continue to put in artillery all night and go back in the next morning.

✒ 29 DECEMBER 1969

> Moved back in after air strike—Blew bunkers—22—
> sent in documents
> Moved north—Was ambushed again—1 WIA: SSG Bly-
> man
> Night in same area

At daylight, a different Air Force FAC put in another sortie of F-4s on the enemy position. We followed right behind, finding the familiar bombed and burned bunkers now abandoned by the gooks.

The complex was not large, but the reason for the gooks' staunch defense became obvious as we swept through the fortification. Fresh dirt and logs told us the bunkers were only a week old. Our discovery of the new complex had apparently made the gooks mad enough to stand and fight. They had lost at least seven men in their efforts—and the evidence of blood trails along their paths of retreat indicated many more.

Bravo soldiers were soon gathering up the usual weapons, equipment, and documents. The most interesting find was a small thatched hooch equipped with a barber chair, hand clippers, scissors, and a small mirror. Hair littered the ground around the chair, and we were all amused to realize that the enemy soldiers also had to get military haircuts.

Among the captured food supplies were items we found in every bunker complex—discoveries that never failed to bring curses from the grunts. Nearly half of the foodstuffs were in containers marked with red, white, and blue letters reading, "Agency for International Development (AID)" and in still larger words, "Donated by the People of the United States of America." Their logo, "Hands Across the Sea," was on sacks of rice, huge cans of cooking oil, and cans of meat.

These goods from AID supposedly only reached the gooks through the black market, but they were so common among our finds that we wondered if AID worked for the dinks instead of for our country.

The documents were the cause of another sore spot. Later I received a copy of a Document Exploitation Report prepared by the Brigade Intelligence Detachment. It listed the documents we captured as containing receipts for food, pay vouchers, anti-American political poems, battle reports, maps showing US and ARVN positions, and an unfinished letter to the "XO of recon" stating they were under attack by US forces. The Intel analyst noted the documents were in poor shape without mentioning that they had gone through three air strikes. About the unit identification, the officer would only admit that it was a recon element of a main force, but he added, "The only identifiable number or name on these documents is Q5 which is a designator for the 275th VC Regiment. This seems highly unlikely, however, since the 275th VC Regiment is located far out of this AO."

After reading the report, I sent a message to McGinnis asking him, in his role as S-2, to pass along my instructions for the Brigade Intelligence Detachment to go fuck themselves because that unit sure as hell was in our AO, and they now numbered seven less and were without a barber shop.

While we were blowing the bunkers, I talked with Schmalz. All nine casualties, including the two squad leaders, were from his platoon. Brian did not ask any special considerations; however, I called LTC Ivey and requested the remainder of the third platoon be lifted out and returned to Black Horse to receive replacements and a few days to refit and retrain. Ivey agreed, and Schmalz and his men were soon airborne. Although it seemed a good decision at the time, over the next two days I would regret having sent the platoon back.

By midafternoon our search and destruction of the bunkers was complete, and we headed west following the blood trails of the enemy's retreat. We had only moved a few hundred meters when the jungle exploded again.

Bolenske reported his point man had been raked by machine gun fire. Above the noise of the exploding bullets, I told him to deploy his men in support of his point element.

I called Kidalowski, telling him to maneuver to the right. My RTO had gunships inbound and I brought them in close despite the incident with the rockets the day before. The Cobras had saved our asses too many times to let one accident deter their fire power.

Bolenske was on the horn again. He reported that he still had only the one wounded and said that his men could handle the dinks. Then he added in a troubled voice, "I got problems. I need your help."

I crawled forward as the dinks continued to shred the jungle above my head. I found Bolenske and his medic struggling to hold SSG Blyman to the ground. Screaming and thrashing around more than I had ever seen a wounded man do, Blyman was all but out of his mind. A bullet had gone through his knee cap, but the wound was not life-endangering.

Blyman was swinging his fists wildly, shouting at the top of his lungs, "Get me out of here! Get me the fuck out of here!" The medic had injected morphine into Blyman's thigh, but it was not calming the man. Many times soldiers did not know where nor how badly they had been hit, especially after the morphine got into their systems. Blyman was different, and I knew why.

When Blyman had arrived two months earlier, I had been pleased to get a mid-twenties NCO on his second tour. The oldest and most experienced sergeant in Bravo, he offered mature leadership that Bravo desperately needed.

I tried to help Bolenske and the medic control Blyman as he fought them off, remembering my surprise when I had seen how scared this combat veteran had become during his first fire fight with us weeks before. Only afterward had I learned just what all his experience entailed.

On his first tour with the 101st Airborne Division, Blyman had been hit in the guts by an AK47 round and had barely lived to be dusted off. After over a year and a half in stateside hospitals, he had finally recovered—only to be sent back to the war.

Now he lay wounded again. This time, instead of a bullet threatening his life, panic was threatening his sanity.

I told Bolenske to pull his men back while I continued to wrestle with the terror-stricken NCO, noting nervous looks from the withdrawing troops. In desperation, I slapped Blyman across the face. He quieted. Then he grasped me in his arms, nearly crushing my breath away. He began to sob, "Get me out of here. Please! Get me out of here."

With bullets still zinging all around, the medic and I dragged Blyman toward the rear. We halted at a bomb crater at the edge of the bunkers we had hit the day before.

By now the intensity of the fire fight was lessening. Only a few single shots and automatic bursts zipped around us, but we were not out of trouble. Blyman was again screaming and fighting.

Coleman reported that a dust-off was inbound, and I started to act on my plan to take the wounded sergeant back to the LZ. Then I stopped. I saw the looks of growing alarm on the faces of many of the men near Blyman as they watched their NCO in the throes of total panic. I knew I had to get him out fast or the panic would spread.

I held Blyman with one arm and reached for the handset to talk to the medivac pilot with the other. "Listen," I said, "I need a hook and cable."

"What's the situation?" he asked.

I told him we were still receiving sporadic fire, knowing ahead of time what his reaction would be.

"No way," he answered. "I can't hover that long under fire."

"Listen," I said again, "we've got a man hit in the knee. He's gone crazy. I've got to get him out of here now! We'll put down all the supporting fire we can."

The pilot must have heard the urgency in my voice because after a slight pause, he said, "Okay. Pop smoke. Let's give it a try."

I turned to Speck and told him to instruct the platoon leaders to hose down the jungle with everything they had.

When I saw the extraction cable coming down from the chopper, I grabbed the other radio and put it on my back. My RTO looked at me questioningly. "There's no use in all of us standing in the clearing," I said. "Cover our asses."

The medic and I dragged Blyman to a small opening in the canopy. We ignored the rule about letting the hook at the end of the cable hit the earth to ground out any static electricity, grabbing it as soon as we could reach it. We folded down the T-shaped seat and had just started to strap

Blyman in when a gook exposed himself to get a better shot at the chopper.

I saw several rounds penetrate the chopper's skin and the gook fall in a hail of bullets from Bolenske's men. Still working with the straps, I screamed into the radio to the pilot, "If you cut the cable or drag my man through the trees, we'll shoot you down ourselves!"

With unbelievable calm the pilot responded, "No sweat. They ain't hit anything important yet. But hurry!"

I signaled for the still hovering medivac to winch Blyman up through the trees, and the medic and I hit the ground. As I lay prone, I felt a strange sensation and looked up to see blood from the NCO's leg falling on us like hot rain. The medic and I dashed back to my RTOs.

The dust-off was nearly out of range before I had time to call the pilot to thank him and to confirm his call sign so I could later put him and his crew in for medals for hovering under fire to complete their mission.

The dinks abruptly broke off their fire as soon as the dust-off flew out of sight. We cautiously pursued until darkness overtook us a short time later.

In our perimeter, I watched the stars appear in the blackening sky and was not at all surprised that sleep evaded me.

> Received resupply
> Moved out—Within 200 m hit a bunker complex
> 1 WIA—1 KIA
>   Steward—SP4, medic, ambulatory
>   PFC Vaughn—KIA, AK47 in chest
> Crystal mortared
> Worst 3 days I've seen
> VR in Dep Bde Cmd's chopper

An ammo resupply accompanied by a scout dog and handler flew in shortly after daylight. We welcomed the black Labrador retriever and his master, who had worked with us before. More docile than the German shepherds, the lab had the reputation of being good at smelling out gooks. His handler, an old hand at pulling radio watch at night, added to my CP strength. Also, with only two platoons in the field, I was happy to have another rifle.

The black lab joined up with the second platoon's point. Our route took us back into the area of the contact the day before. When we reached that point, we changed azimuth to the northwest.

Less than two hundred meters after we adjusted our direction, an RTO relayed a report that the dog had just alerted. At the same time, three single AK shots rang out, followed instantly by machine guns, small arms fire, and grenades by both sides.

I dove for cover behind a good-sized mound of earth. When I looked up, I saw a black streak flash into sight. Behind it was a hunched-over GI in trail. Within a blink the black lab charged in at my side, sharing the protection of the embankment with my CP. Seconds later the dog's handler slid in beside us, reporting the point man and maybe others were hit.

Kidalowski was now on the horn confirming his point man was down and his medic hit while dragging him out of the kill zone.

"Goddamn it!" I yelled. "I thought I told the medics to stay in the rear." Only that morning I had given instructions for any wounded to be brought to the medics in the rear rather than have the medics expose themselves. My rationale had been simple. I only had two medics left, and I needed both of them. Now I only had one.

I turned to my senior company medic and said, "Doc, move forward to the second platoon."

Doc Crowe looked at me with tears streaming down his cheeks. He said, "Please, sir, don't make me go. I've got less than a month before I go home and . . ."

I cut him off, saying, "Doc, you've got to go. You are all that's left."

Doc sighed, "Oh, shit," as he grabbed his bag and crawled forward.

I grabbed my battalion net to request gunships and a dust-off. The TOC told me we had no gunships in the area. It would be at least twenty minutes before any could be on station. At least a dust-off was en route.

To the FO I hollered, "Where the hell's the artillery?" My demands got a marking round on target in seconds. We waited for the HE (high explosive) rounds to begin impacting, but nothing happened. Then I suddenly heard different sounds—ones I had never heard before during a fire fight but ones I recognized. Less than two hundred meters away I could hear the sounds of mortar rounds sliding down tubes. Then came the *bloop* of the mortar fire.

I was not the only one who heard the new sounds. Frightened shouts of "Mortars!" and "Incoming!" ricocheted through Bravo. I grabbed the radio and made a net call to all stations, telling them not to worry about the mortars because the high trajectory weapons could not drop rounds closer than four hundred meters from their firing points, and I knew we were closer than that. I assured them that we were not the target of the mortars.

Seconds later we heard reports over the artillery net that rounds were landing at Crystal. One gun and crew had been knocked out by the initial blasts. Then came the report in broken transmissions that the fire direction center had taken a direct hit and the battery commander had been wounded. Silence on the arty net followed.

We were now without artillery support.

Concern for the Greek fleeted through my mind, but I could not stop to dwell on him. We were up against a force at least equal in numbers to our own, and they were firing from the protection of bunkers. They had artillery support; we did not. Our gunships and Tac Air were not yet on station. I had no trouble deciding that we should break contact and withdraw. It was our only option.

Even though our gunships had not arrived, the air above us was filling with choppers. The battalion commander, the brigade commander, and the deputy brigade commander all orbited our position, offering advice and encouragement. Their communications to us and to each other, however well intended, along with the reports from the platoons so jammed the radio traffic that in frustration I got on the horn and said, "Everybody get the fuck off this net and let me fight the company!"

I was surprised to hear General Bond's voice saying,

"Do what he says. He's doing a good job. Leave him alone."

With the radios clear I gave instructions to withdraw. As my RTOs passed along my orders, I crawled forward to the second platoon CP to direct the withdrawal. Kidalowski had everything under control—at least as much as possible under the circumstances. Doc Crowe was working on PFC Bill Vaughn. Medic SP4 Steward, who himself had been wounded by a bullet passing completely through the calf of his leg, assisted Crowe. Both medics were crying as Crowe said, "He's not going to make it, sir."

Crowe had cut away Vaughn's fatigue shirt, exposing a hole in the center of his chest. His eyes were rolled back as he lay unconscious. Still he gasped for an occasional breath with Doc's mouth-to-mouth assistance.

Bullets were cracking around us as I raised Vaughn in my arms, trying to help him breathe. Less than a minute later he exhaled with a death rattle I had heard about but never believed happened. He died in my arms.

Steward was still checking for a pulse as he said, "He was still conscious when I got to him. All he said was 'They shot me.'"

I was filled with many emotions, but anger was the only one I could express. Doc Steward, whom I would later put in for a valor award for the same action, was the most convenient target. "Doc," I said, "I told you not to go after any wounded. I'll be goddamned if we're going to carry you. Keep up on your own. Maybe next time you'll listen to me."

Doc Crowe and I began crawling to the rear, dragging along the body of Vaughn. Steward tightened his own leg tourniquet and kept up with us although he was leaving a trail of blood behind.

The second platoon was right behind us, firing at the

dinks who by now had left their bunkers and were attempting to flank us. Bolenske's platoon was ready for the dink maneuvers and picked up the fight as we passed through their ranks.

Finally the gunships arrived. Their fire sent the dinks back into the shelter of their bunkers. We continued our withdrawal.

By the time we reached the stream, which we had crossed and recrossed for three days, we were no longer receiving fire. Yet we were literally far from being "out of the woods."

The mental and physical exhaustion resulting from the fight made it all but impossible for anyone to carry Vaughn more than a few meters. Taking turns, we brought the body to the streambed. One soldier volunteered to take him to the other side. However, in midstream, the soldier collapsed, losing Vaughn's body beneath the swift water. PFC Van Arsdale dove for the body, and in a Herculean display of strength retrieved him and carried him the remaining half klick to the LZ.

By the time we got back to the LZ, the artillery, with improvised communication, had its remaining guns operational and began pounding the jungle. From the first minutes of the fire fight, Ivey had assured me that Alpha Company was only a few kilometers to our north. They were moving in to help.

I ordered my men to dig in and redistribute ammo. I was on the horn asking Ivey where the hell Alpha Company was when I noticed Vaughn's body left unattended in the clearing. Following my instructions, Doc Crowe covered him with a poncho and sat with him until the dust-off arrived.

Steward, dizzy and weak from loss of blood, refused

any assistance. He limped over to me and said, "I'm sorry, sir. I only did what I thought I had to."

I put my arm around him, supporting his weight as the dust-off landed at the edge of the LZ. I did not know why I had targeted Steward with my anger. He had always been a good troop, but I suppose he happened to be in the wrong place at the wrong time that day. I walked him to the bird, coming as close to an apology as I could at the time when I said, "Doc, that's all any of us can do." I helped him into the chopper while several other soldiers lifted aboard the poncho-draped body of Vaughn.

After the medivac took off, the deputy brigade commander landed to pick me up for an aerial recon of the area. We wanted to pinpoint the bunkers, but we could see little through the thick vegetation. We requested Alpha Company to pop smoke. I was astounded to see that they were still over a kilometer away from our fire fight area. As the DCG's chopper returned me to Bravo, I wondered what had happened to the days when companies literally ran through the jungle to help fellow GIs.

When I was back on the ground, I found the NCOs breaking down another resupply of ammo that had been delivered to the clearing already littered with empty cases from our previous days of fighting. I walked through the company perimeter, watching the exhausted men refitting and reorganizing.

When I returned to my CP, Speck told me Ivey was on the horn. I took the handset and listened to Ivey tell me he wanted us to attack the bunkers again. My RTOs overheard the transmission with looks of utter disbelief.

I drew a long, deep breath. I said into the horn, "If you want us to, we will. But be advised, we have been fighting for three days. You know how many we've lost. We're outnumbered and outgunned. If we go back in, this will likely be the last transmission from us. I don't think we can survive another attack.''

There was no response for several minutes. Finally the battalion commander came back on and said that Alpha was nearing the contact area. He said we were to go into a blocking position near the stream.

We did as we were told. For the next several hours, I monitored the radio, listening as Alpha reported that they had reached the bunkers. They claimed they found bodies, which they credited to us, and some equipment. However, they said there were no live enemy around.

I called the A Company commander and asked him to search the initial contact point for Vaughn's M-16, which had been left behind. They never found it. I doubted if they looked and wondered if they ever reached the bunkers at all. Their reports just did not match what I knew about the area.

As darkness approached, several of the men with Vaughn's squad sought out the lab's handler to tell him they believed the dog's alert had saved their lives. His alerting had forced the dinks to fire before more men were in target range.

The damn dog, however, was still cowering and shaking. Amid the sorrow of the losses we had sustained, we chuckled, and, in fact, openly laughed about how fast and low the lab had run from the fight. Perhaps the dog was the smartest animal of us all.

The Greek recovered from his wounds and later rejoined his battery. SP4 Steward's wound was serious enough to get him a ticket home. PFC William O. Vaughn was returned to his family's burial plot in his home of Jamestown, Tennessee, I suppose. I did not ever know for sure.

I wrote no letters to families of casualties, leaving that

job to my XO. Writing them may have been my duty, but the dead were beyond help. I had many more troops alive, and I chose to devote my efforts to keeping them that way.

On 16 October 1985 I was in Washington, D.C. and revisited the Vietnam Memorial for the second time. There were many names—too many names—to find on the black marble walls. One I lingered at was Bill Vaughn's. That night in my hotel room I wrote the first draft of this account of 30 December 1969. This book was written day-to-day, just as it occurred, and it was only coincidence that I wrote about Vaughn on the same day as my visit to the memorial. Coincidence did not diminish the hurt or tears; it just happened that way. If I had been writing about any of many other days, the feelings would have been the same. Only the names would have been different.

🖎 31 DECEMBER 1969

> Finally airmobiled back to Black Horse
> New Year's Eve
> Got word I may be S-3 Air when CPT Lewis leaves last of January
> Don't feel like writing much any more

The night passed in constant anticipation of mortars crashing through the foliage into our position. Occasionally I was able to drop off to sleep, only to be awakened by an RTO reporting that one position or another said they could hear movement in the jungle.

Just before daybreak, Speck gently shook me. He said he had crawled over to wake up his radio relief and found the black lab curled up under the poncho liner with the other RTO. Each time he had tried to get close enough to wake the man, the lab growled to protect his newfound friend. Clary was looking to me for a solution to the problem. I did not have one. Finally, after much whispered discussion between us, Speck said that he was not sleepy anyway. He said he would rather remain on the radio than risk the wrath of the still-nervous scout dog.

The time remaining before sunup passed slowly. We were all on edge, and doubting our senses. Nothing happened—the source of our fears was in our heads, not in the jungle. The enemy was as tired of contact as we, and apparently had withdrawn.

The sun was barely over the horizon when a call from Battalion TOC directed us to move back to the LZ for extraction to Black Horse. Five days before we had landed at the same place where we would now be picked up. We had never moved more than eight hundred meters from our starting point.

In terms of enemy killed, equipment captured, and bunkers destroyed, I suppose the Saigon warriors could chalk our mission up as another win for the good guys. Bravo felt neither victory nor defeat. Those of us who moved back to the LZ had survived, and that was enough to feel. We knew that our reward would be the opportunity to do the same thing all over again—and again.

The choppers were due any minute when another call from Battalion told us that only three birds were available and that we would have to be extracted in three separate lifts. Turnaround time between each sortie would be about thirty minutes. That meant that before the last group could be picked up, any lingering dinks would have an hour to plan an attack on the remaining eighteen men.

I did not like the setup, but I had no options. I passed the word for the platoons to leave their machine gunners and best riflemen behind with me and my RTOs for the final pick up.

When the second sortie lifted off, I gathered my group of seventeen and moved to bomb craters in the center of the LZ. The machine gunners linked their hundred-round belts of ammo together, forming continuous chains of more than a thousand rounds each. Riflemen arranged extra bandoleers of M-16 magazines left behind by departing troops. If the dinks came, we were prepared to make it worth their trouble.

Not a man remaining uttered a word of complaint, and several soldiers who left in the earlier sorties had argued with their platoon leaders, insisting they be allowed to stay with the last group.

A half hour can seem forever. We felt a tremendous relief when the trio of choppers finally appeared over the trees. Their skids never touched the ground. We jumped and climbed into the birds with the help of door gunners who pulled us in. Mounting the skids of the middle chopper, I checked to make sure everyone was on board. I was still hanging outside the bird as we began to gain altitude. My RTOs hauled me in as we cleared the trees.

I expected the air strip at Black Horse to be vacant when we touched down, as it normally was when we returned from a mission. I knew Top would be shuttling the troops back to clean up. No one else would have reason to be there. A unit returning from a mission, bad or not, found that all others avoided them until they had had a chance to adjust to the nonthreatening environment of the fire base. Men who had been enjoying the relative comforts and safety behind the wires had no desire to look into the eyes of those who just returned from seeing death.

But the scene at the landing strip was not what I expected. Beckles was there, as usual. With him, however, stood all the troops from the earlier lifts, still in full battle dress. I noticed that the filthy fatigues of many were stained with blood. Some troops sported bloody bandages covering minor shrapnel wounds, cuts from bamboo thickets, and burns from touching hot weapons in the heat of battle. Along with the first and second platoons stood Schmalz and the surviving members of his third platoon. In clean fatigues, they stood reequipped and fully ready to return to the boonies.

Our reception committee was a grim but determined group of soldiers. When we touched the ground their expressions turned from solemn to grins of relief.

Beckles said he had had trucks available to take the troops back to the company area as they arrived, but to a man they had refused to leave the air strip until all of us made it back in. He said the platoon leaders had been on the battalion net trying to get more choppers in case they had to go back to help us.

I smiled at Beckles and asked him for a cigarette. He handed me a fresh pack and a new lighter, and said, "Keep 'em." He turned to supervise loading the company on the trucks.

As I lit a cigarette, I saw a figure I did not recognize peering over a tall wall of sandbags used to protect parked helicopters. He was watching me closely. I walked toward him, noting the gold bar of a second lieutenant and crossed flags of the Signal Corps on the collar of his brand new FNG fatigues.

When I reached him, he began talking. In halted

phrases, he said, "Sir, I'm the new assistant battalion signal officer. I've been listening to you all on the TOC radios for days. And, well, the RTOs said if I wanted to see real fighters I should come down here. Sir, I'm sorry, I know you guys don't like anyone to be here when you come in. But, well, I just had to see what you all looked like, sir. Everybody's saying Bravo is one hell of a bunch of fighters and . . ."

I finally cut off the FNG lieutenant since it seemed that he was not going to stop. I said curtly, "Don't call me, 'sir.' I'm a lieutenant, too. Now get the hell out of here."

Beckles took the troops back to the company area as I got into my jeep and headed for the TOC. I did not need to explain the results of our mission because the men in the TOC had been at the other end of my radio transmissions when I requested dust-offs, gunships, and ammo resupplies.

The S-3 briefed me, saying we should be prepared to move back out the next day. I wanted to ask him why no one had come to help, why Alpha Company was so damn slow, and why the hell they kept sending us back into the dinks' positions, but I did not. From the looks on their faces, those were questions the S-3 and his staff had already asked themselves.

CPT Lewis caught me as I was leaving the TOC and said he understood that I was to replace him as the S-3 Air when he went home at the end of January. Walking to my jeep, I told him I was not sure I was ready to leave the company.

Lewis followed me to the vehicle. He placed his foot on its side as he leaned over to me and said, in controlled anger, "You did a good job out there—better than anyone else could have done. You've done more than your part. Now get the hell out of the field."

Then he softened, pulled back, and said with a laugh, "Go get cleaned up. You smell like hell. By the way, happy New Year."

I headed for the company, hoping Top had a bottle of bourbon. I had forgotten it was New Year's Eve.

Back at Bravo the holiday cheer was flowing. The men, although somewhat more subdued than usual, were engaged in horseplay, joking and bragging as only teenage warriors can.

I was mentally and physically exhausted. My sense of loss was heavy. However, my pride in the courage and tenacity of the men in the company outweighed all other sensations. To Linda I wrote, "The last few days have been bad. I lost men out of every platoon. I asked one of my platoon leaders to put it into words. He said, 'The most violent contact the battalion has seen.' I agree. My company's actions were beyond belief. The battalion commander told his staff, 'Bravo has fought harder than anyone can be expected to.' For three days we slept little, ate nothing. Battalion and Brigade say we accomplished a great deal. I wonder. I dusted off men with wounds that will disable them the rest of their lives. I dusted off a dead man that was one of the best soldiers I ever have known. I am realizing the full burdens of being a company commander."

I continued, "Enough on what happened. Now for my actions and feelings. I've done my job and kept the men going. I've shown no emotion—no one but you knows my deep hurt. I feel I've lost a great deal and hardened a lot, but now this action is over. I read back on this and realize I have matured—as only a soldier can. My nerves are, if anything, steadier. I feel good—even happy. I am alive; more important, more of my men are alive than for any reason should be. Once again, we have proven Bravo is the best.''

Writing several more pages, I also told Linda about the possibility of the S-3 Air job, explaining I would be in charge of coordinating the battalion's air assets. I acknowledged receiving more pictures of our baby daughter.

Then my pen returned to the last week as I wrote, ''The more I look back, the better I feel. This entire letter I've been just talking to you—same as we used to. Some of it should probably be scratched out; however, I will leave it. I look back now at my letter of worry and frazzled nerves before Christmas and say disregard it. I did no heroics during any of the three days, only did my job. I am happy, for the first time in some months I am satisfied. I am in command of the best fighting unit in Vietnam.''

I completed my letter and joined Top and the lieutenants in toasting the New Year. None of us were at all sad to see 1969 pass. We were just damn glad to be able to see 1970 approaching over the lip of a bottle of bourbon.

✈ 1 JANUARY 1970

Truck Co to Cam Tam
I was on my first dust-off bird—Pilots gave me a ride after I wrote statements for them
Training and reorganization

A new day, a new month, a new year, and a new decade dawned with no fanfare, for in Vietnam it was just another day. Back home everyone was watching bowl games and enjoying the holiday while we packed our rucksacks and prepared to return to the boonies.

The troops were climbing on trucks when a call came from the TOC with instructions for me to remain at Black Horse to meet with some pilots who were inbound. The platoon leaders took charge of the company move to Cam Tam.

Beckles and I were going over some paperwork when two young aviators, neither over twenty years old, entered the orderly room. They introduced themselves, and one explained that they were the pilot and copilot of the dust-off that had hovered under fire to evacuate SSG Blyman. The pilot stated rather self-consciously that he understood I was putting them in for medals and asked if I would go ahead and write my statements.

I gave them a look that mirrored my thoughts about their being overanxious for recognition. However, before I said anything, the copilot interrupted, pointing at his comrade. "Sir, we are kind of embarrassed to be here asking your help, but the aircraft commander here is going home in five days. If we don't get your statements now, the medal probably won't ever get awarded."

I responded, "You mean you hovered in the middle of all that AK fire with only days left in-country?"

The pilot shuffled his feet and answered in a low voice, "Yeah, I guess so. It seemed like the thing to do at the time. You sounded as if you needed us."

I shook my head and said, "I'll be damned. Thanks." I sat down and wrote statements recommending both pilots for Distinguished Flying Crosses.

When I completed the statements, the pilots offered me

a ride to Cam Tam. The thought crossed my mind that if my luck held a bit longer, this would be my first and last ride in a helicopter marked with a red cross.

Beckles arrived in the late afternoon with hot chow. We set up the mess line near the old French mansions, and I was not surprised to see the one-armed Frenchman, whom I had met when I was a platoon leader, wander over. I told the men to invite him to join us for supper.

Bolenske, who had taken French in college, served as a passable interpreter with the old man. I had heard that the Frenchman had been caught in a remote part of the rubber plantation with his car full of bread and other foodstuffs several weeks earlier. It was also rumored that he provided our intelligence folks information on enemy movements. It seemed that he worked for both sides with varying degrees of dedication. I figured the one-armed gentleman must be fairly wise and crafty to have survived unmolested for over twenty years in the midst of the war. If nothing else, he provided a welcome break to my routine.

Following our meal, the Frenchman invited Bill and me to his house for a glass of wine. We took along a squad to secure the outside of the mansion, left our weapons at his front door, and were soon sitting on comfortable rattan chairs enjoying what even my youthful taste buds could tell was a vintage wine.

The Frenchman recognized me from my previous visit with McGinnis (described in *The Only War We Had*) but repeated his tales of army service nonetheless. As before, his wife remained out of sight although he did volunteer that his daughter had married an ARVN lieutenant and was now residing in Xuan Luc. The old man liked to talk and except for occasionally halting so Bolenske could translate, our conversation was rather one-sided. He reminded me of the old ranchers back home who spent so much time alone that when they finally found someone to listen to them they were difficult to shut up.

The gray-haired, barrel-chested Frenchman was talking about damages to the rubber trees when he suddenly changed the subject, telling us he had recently seen an NVA unit with Chinese advisors near the village. He added that he had heard that another nearby enemy unit was accompanied by two GIs—one black, the other white—who had "gone over" to the other side.

I nodded in acceptance but believed little of his stories. Rumors about Chinese advisors, as well as the story of the two GIs, better known as Salt and Pepper because of their color, were as common as the tales of the 199th's soon going home in a big pullout. I would believe them when someone produced a dead Chinese or ex-GI.

🚁 2 JANUARY 1970

> Training at Cam Tam—Zero of wpns—Safety SOP, etc
> Visits from Bn CO etc—1st Sgt out with us—1st Sgt a damn good one
> Saw some of my old boys from C Co today—Not many of them left
> Went into 24th Evac Hospital to see some of my men—A depressing place—Some of my men had talked to VP Agnew

We began the morning's training by teaching the new

men "quick kill" techniques. This method of firing the M-16 emphasized pointing the weapon from the hip in a lunge at the target rather than raising the weapon to the shoulder and aiming through the sights. Resembling more closely the firing of a pistol than a rifle, the technique allowed engaging the enemy an instant faster than the traditional method. It provided an edge that allowed many a point man to live to claim a body count rather than his own body bag.

At midmorning Charlie Company called on the radio asking us to check fire as it approached Cam Tam. Minutes later I spotted them approaching with a familiar figure on point. I went out to meet Larry Morford and walked with him as the rest of the company followed. Morford was leaner than when I had last seen him and his eyes reflected the six months of walking point and his mounting record of individual kills. He still spoke gently, however, having lost none of his sensitivity or concern. When I asked why he was still walking point, he smiled and simply said, "Because I'm good at it, sir."

I had paid little attention to the man walking slack behind Morford until he spoke to me, saying, "I guess you are surprised to see me, aren't you, One-six?"

In amazement I recognized PFC Johnson who had "fallen in the showers" with serious injuries back in August after the platoon had gotten fed up with his constant complaints and failure to carry his own load. Johnson continued, "After I got out of the hospital, I cleaned up my act. You probably won't believe it, but I'm known as a pretty good troop now. Even got promoted to Spec 4." Johnson moved on without waiting for my reply.

Charlie Company took a break before moving out. McGinnis's replacement, CPT John Delano, was back for his second tour with the Old Guard. I was glad to see the company in capable hands but was surprised at how few faces I recognized.

Delano introduced me to his platoon leaders, all of whom were new since I departed Charlie. The officers were rather cool, and Delano said without my asking, "The lieutenants think you have set a bad precedent by staying in the field so long. They all want out as soon as they can."

DeForrest was still carrying a radio and we both talked at once. Our stories about the birth of my daughter, fire fights, and "whatever happened tos" were not nearly complete before Charlie saddled up and moved out.

Later in the day, I took the jeep, along with a couple of GIs riding shotgun and headed for the 24th Evacuation Hospital in Long Binh to visit my men wounded the previous week. I did not like going to the hospital because it was a place where I could do nothing for my men. I did remember, though, that Ross had always complained that we never got enough Marlboro cigarettes in the field. Taking him a carton was something I could do, so I stopped at the hospital PX and bought him the red and white box.

When I reached the reception area, I was greeted by a clerk who gave me the same story I had received long before as a green platoon leader at 3rd Field Hospital in Saigon. This time I was less accepting of the story that he could not tell me where my men were. I laid my M-16 on the countertop, reached over to his file of patient information cards, and began going through them. Cards that had names I did not recognize I threw over my shoulder to the floor.

The clerk hurried away to return minutes later accompanied by two Medical Corps majors. They were not very pleasant in their questions about what I was doing but remained somewhat wary of the unfamiliar sight of fully armed, smelly grunts in their orderly room. After they had their say, I replied, "I came a long way to see my men. I'm not leaving until I do. If necessary, I'll go through every ward until I find them."

The major who seemed to be in charge shook his head and with a laugh said, "Let's see what we can do. Just don't fuck up the records anymore, okay?"

A list was soon provided showing several men had already been transferred to Japan. A captain arrived to escort me to the wards of the others. The men seemed to appreciate the visit and enthusiastically told me that Vice-President Spiro Agnew had visited them, awarding their Purple Hearts earlier the same day.

The *Stars and Stripes* reported two days later that Agnew had told the troops to "hang in there, we're going to get you out of here," to which SGT John Bishop was quoted as replying, "Roger that," as he shook the VP's hand. Bishop, whom I had last seen saying, "Million-dollar wound" as we put him on the dust-off did not mention his comment to Agnew but rather told me how the shrapnel scar on his cheek would drive the women wild when he got home. He said nothing about the leg wounds that would keep him in a hospital for some time to come.

I had seen all my men except SP4 Ross. The captain explained that Ross had just come out of the operating room and that the recovery room was off-limits.

From where we were standing, I could see the recovery room. To the captain I said, "Sir, I'm going to see Ross. You can't stop me so just walk on like you don't know anything about it."

The captain wordlessly walked in the other direction as I entered the Quonset hut recovery room that contained twenty or so occupied beds. An orderly directed me to Ross, who was fading in and out of consciousness. His chest was crisscrossed with hundreds of stitches so that it more resembled a huge baseball than a man's torso.

The young soldier finally recognized me and managed a smile. When I told him I had brought him a carton of Marlboros, tears welled in his eyes. I had to lean over him to hear him whisper, "Thanks, sir, you keep them. The doctor says I've lost part of my lung and can't smoke anymore."

With that he fell asleep. From a bunk across the room a soldier awoke realizing he no longer had legs. He rocked the room as he shouted, "You mother fuckers cut off my legs! Oh, God, no. No! Goddamn it, no! Why . . ."

Two large orderlies held the thrashing man to his bunk as another injected something into his arm. The man was still screaming as I left the room and the hospital. I was glad to be returning to the jungle.

The hospital scene haunted me the rest of my tour and beyond. I vowed to myself never to let them put me under anesthesia regardless of wounds. If the doctors wanted to take my limbs, they would have to fight for them. Today the smell of a hospital still brings back the 24th Evac recovery room.

✈ 3 JANUARY 1970

Finished training today
Moved south to NDP on two axis
VR of new AO—LOH

I was satisfied with the training conducted and the orderly infusion of the replacements who brought the company's field strength back to over one hundred men. One-half of the third platoon was now composed of new personnel, but Schmalz and English had the experience, know-how, and leadership abilities to keep the platoon functioning well.

Our movement out of Cam Tam took us through the rubber and across the valley where I had lain in ambush months before when man first landed on the moon. We also traversed the area near the first bunker complex we had overrun in June, shortly after our arrival in the new AO.

I felt good about what we had accomplished while wondering at the same time if the price we had paid was worth it. We still controlled only the areas we physically occupied at the time, for we abandoned hard-fought-for terrain soon after taking it. No matter how many times we kicked the dinks back to their refuges in Cambodia and War Zone D, they returned to fight more battles for jungle that was of little use except as a battlefield.

The dinks kept testing our desire to fight—losing men in the process and fleeing only to try at another time. Their news was that the Americans would soon be gone, allowing them to carry on a war with the less enthusiastic ARVN troops. The enemy would be patient and avoid decisive engagements. Time was on his side.

Still in 2 axis
Nighttime farther south
Area seems cold

Personal dangers and the burdensome responsibility for so many men bothered me more and more as the days passed. I continued to have extreme difficulty sleeping. One morning I awoke to find Bolenske beside me. When I asked him what he was doing there, he answered, "You wake up talking sometimes. The platoon leaders take turns sleeping next to you."

I looked at him in confusion. He saw my questioning frown and continued, "I'm sure you don't know you give orders and yell. We just thought it better for an officer to tell you to be quiet than one of the troops." He shrugged and added, "You look out after us, so we look out after you."

I was embarrassed to learn that I had been guilty of violating our noise discipline and even more chagrined that I was not aware of what I had been doing. That revelation, as much as anything else, convinced me it was time to get out of the field.

> Same, same type day
> Hot—Much moving
> Nighttime farther south
> My arty recon sgt has a small pet squirrel he carries with him

We were working once again without an artillery forward observer. Gulbranson had come down with a high fever and other symptoms closely resembling malaria. I was upset that he had become ill after only a couple of months in the field and had refused the medic's recommendation to dust him off for several days. I had tried to convince Doc he would make medical history if he could cure the redleg lieutenant of malaria. No matter how badly I resented bringing in a medivac that would expose our location, it had become necessary when the FO's temperature hit 105 degrees.

Gulbranson had developed into a fine FO, serving bravely in many a fight. My delay in evacuating him was as much a reminder to the men to take their daily and weekly malaria pills as it was in not wanting to reveal our position. Weeks later I would visit Rick in the hospital to find him less than pleased to see me. The only thing he had to say was that he had taken his pills and that the doctors said his fever was not from anything the daily and weekly dosages could have prevented. Keeping the fever-ridden FO in the field had been another of those burdens that went with the responsibility of command. I had made the decision in good faith and what was in the past could not be changed.

My acting FO was now the artillery NCO who, before SGT Barnes departed, had been the FO team RTO. Since our initial rocky relationship back at Fire Base Maureen, where he had wounded himself by improperly firing an M-79, he had performed well enough to earn sergeant stripes, though he was still a bit of a free spirit as indicated by the chipmunk-like squirrel he had caught in the jungle and carried in a plastic container in his rucksack. Bravo accepted the squirrel's company because he made no noise and ate C-ration crackers with a vengeance.

The squirrel was with us only for a few days. Either the heat in the closed rucksack or the damn C-rations killed him.

6 JANUARY 1970

> Moving on 3 axis—No sign of anything
> Commo very poor—I climbed about a 50 ft tree to get it better
> Without commo an Inf Co CANNOT operate

We were nearing the extreme southern edge of the battalion's AO. At one point commo was so weak and broken that I placed a radio on my back and climbed high into the foliage to achieve a better transmission. The height helped somewhat but I could only laugh when the TOC RTO advised me, as I sat on a branch fifty feet above the jungle floor, to "try moving around so we can hear you better."

When I climbed down from the tree, I redirected the platoon routes to reach higher ground that had been cleared by the Rome plow operations. If we couldn't talk to the TOC, we were greatly limited in accomplishing our mission.

✈ 7 JANUARY 1970

> Broke into opening so we could get commo
> Moved to west for nighttime
> Sure has been hot lately

Looking for new trails or any other signs of the enemy, we concentrated on the edges of cleared areas. Although the platoons were spread out in three areas covering a strip well over two klicks wide, we were finding nothing. From monitoring the battalion radio net, I could hear the other companies reporting a similar lack of success.

Just where the dinks were might be a mystery, but our situation was all too apparent. We were walking our asses off and sweating in the 100-degree-plus heat of the sauna-like jungle.

Another factor, minor as it may seem, also was reminding me that my boonie days were nearing an end. Although many sets of fatigues had literally rotted off my body, my original canvas-top jungle boots had made every step of my tour. The seams were splitting and the soles were worn smooth, but I would no more have replaced them with new footgear than secured a replacement for my poncho liner. Other than pride, I had few possessions, and those that were mine were important.

✈ 8 JANUARY 1970

> Moved to west for nighttime—Word for AO extension to south—Then changed—Go to BH tomorrow
> Also got word change of command on 15th—R&R in Taipei on 17th—Sounds good
> Moving in plt size

When I got the news of my change of command's being only a week away, I experienced little of the regret that I had expected. Many emotions flooded me, but the overwhelming feeling was one of relief. Although three months remained in my tour, the meatgrinder days in the boonies were nearing an end. If I could survive for seven more days, I just might have a future beyond Vietnam.

Confirmation that LTC Ivey had also approved a second R&R for me made the news all that much better. The opportunity to see Taiwan and have a week to adjust to no longer being in command was beyond comprehension.

I immediately sat down on my rucksack and wrote Linda about the good news. I told her the approximate date I would call her from Taipei so I "could finally hear Reveilee's voice." I closed the letter expressing how much I liked her idea about buying a home movie camera to record the months I was missing of my daughter's life.

✈ 9 JANUARY 1970

> 99 days till DEROS
> R&R not 17 Jan—17 Feb—Doubt if I will get it
> Airmobile to BH—3 hrs—Truck back out—Moved on
> 3 axis—Again to nighttime position

Little of significance was happening throughout the battalion. Personally, though, it was an important day. With only 99 days before DEROS (Date of Estimated Return from Overseas), I had finally joined the ranks of the "two-digit midgets." Reaching that milestone relieved some of the disappointment in learning the R&R to Taipei was scheduled for February rather than January. I was not too surprised at the news because I had been in the Army long enough to know that the only thing that was constant was change.

Moved southwest—No activity in area last 3 weeks

The new AO was just as cold as the last. From the position of company commander, I now had more access to the overall battalion operations, resulting in better understanding of how the company mission fit into the overall plan. I wondered, however, why we were beating the brush for the enemy, who had obviously withdrawn to sanctuaries farther north and across the border into Cambodia. It seemed to make more sense to go after them rather than to wait for their return. Such decisions, of course, were not in the purview of a company commander.

Evidently my thoughts about going after the gooks in the "safe areas" were shared by those in positions that did make the policy decisions. In late April, US and ARVN units would cross the Cambodian border, destroying the enemy supply bases and killing many of the gooks in their previously secure areas. Although the Old Guard would not participate in the operation, several other elements of the 199th, including one Infantry battalion, did play a major role in the operation. The decision to cross the Cambodian border was long overdue. Any grunt who had chased the gooks back to their "safe area" had no trouble being in complete agreement with the so-called "invasion."

> Moved farther southwest
> At resupply MAJ Humphrey, S-3, came in to talk to me—He said GEN Bond may not approve the one to be my replacement
> I am ready to get out of the field

There were finally enough of the freeze-dried LURPs (rations designed for use on Long Range Reconnaissance Patrols—pronounced LURP) in the supply system for issue to the line units rather than only to recon platoons and Rangers. I was eating one of the LURP rations when MAJ Humphrey landed in the battalion command-and-control (C&C) ship. The reconstituted chow tasted pretty good after weeks of Cs, so I continued to eat while the S-3 briefed me from his map. I offered the operations officer one of the LURPs and was surprised that he did not know what it was nor how to prepare it. Once again, I had forgotten the comparative luxuries of a fire base equipped with a mess hall.

Before the S-3 departed he told me that General Bond had not concurred with Ivey's selection for my replacement and it was unlikely that one would be okayed before the 15th. My response that I was in no hurry to leave Bravo was not completely honest but was all I could think of to say at the time. As I recorded in my journal, I was "ready to get out of the field" regardless of my response to the S-3.

> Moved south—Then airmobiled to southeast
> Have one plt with tracks
> Lots of air time in C&C ship—Supposed to be a 40-man NVA hospital to east—Delta Co took 4 POW, 1 weapon today in lambretta—Had a red cross on it—Ha

The area due south of Black Horse, covered with large rubber plantations and smaller orchards of cashew trees, held a village of farm workers connected to Xuan Luc by a gravel road. We had paid little attention to the region because the only jungle in the vicinity was a patch of dense foliage about two kilometers square that was intersected by a steep-banked stream. When we were ordered to airmobile to assist Delta in searching the small jungle patch, I thought it a useless mission.

After being briefed on arrival at the LZ that Delta had captured two wounded dinks and their two healthy companions in a lambretta sporting a red cross, I thought the story was a bunch of bullshit. We had been humping the boonies for days with no sign of the enemy. Now we were being told that Delta was finding them on a well-traveled road advertising their location with a large red cross.

After being shown the captured vehicle and an SKS carbine, I still found the arrogance of the gooks difficult to believe. I recalled all too well the enemy's enthusiasm in trying to shoot down our dust-offs marked with red crosses.

Whatever their rationale, there was more than enough evidence to lend credibility to the reports from the POW

198

interrogators that a hospital was located in the isolated patch of jungle. Sending one platoon with the tracks from the 17th Cav, I took two platoons to begin a sweep.

The stream divided the jungle fairly well in half, providing a good boundary between Bravo in the south and Delta Company to the north. We proceeded eastward. We had found many trails and a couple of shallow, abandoned caves dug into the steep stream banks that dropped fifty feet or so down to the water, but we found no enemy. By dark we were in the center of the sector, where we stopped and dug in for the night.

---

13 JANUARY 1970

> Delta had contact 100 meters to our north
> Moved out early—As we broke out of jungle we stopped 2 lambrettas—11 adults, 3 children—Had them escorted to Bn—2 ended up to be VC—3 of them suppliers
> Nighttime in same area

Two hours before sunrise, the roar of M-16s, machine guns, and Claymores erupted from Delta Company. Their fire cracked above our heads, ripping through the foliage. As suddenly as it started, the shooting stopped. I was immediately on the horn trying to find out what was happening. Delta reported that a single dink had approached their perimeter only to be cut down before he could get his rifle off his shoulder. They called back minutes later to tell me that the dink's pack contained medical supplies and manuals, lending more credence to the possibility of a hospital being nearby. I did not attempt to get any more sleep, staring instead into the darkness and waiting for another sunrise in the jungle.

We continued a slow, methodical search of the area at daybreak. Everyone was pumped up with the excitement of Delta's easy body count and sought the suspected hospital with enthusiasm. By noon we broke out of the jungle on the far side, frustrated at our lack of success.

We were taking a break and waiting for further instructions when two heavily laden lambrettas rounded a turn on the little used rubber perimeter road. There was no reason for traffic in the area as the road led to the patch of jungle we had just exited. The drivers readily stopped, encouraged by a few M-16 rounds fired over their heads.

We separated the fourteen passengers so they could not cook up a unified explanation for their presence on the remote road. The detainees were a mixed lot of children, women, and four men of military age. We tied and blindfolded the older males and, with assistance of the Kit Carson, began questioning them individually. A middle-aged man who appeared to be the leader claimed they had taken the wrong road to the village where they were transporting food to relatives.

I had a squad search the lambrettas, where they found several hundred pounds of rice, noodles, and cooking oil in the familiar "Hands Across the Sea" containers of the Agency for International Development. A large box held knives and meat saws that one driver claimed to be the tools of his trade as a butcher. He had no explanation, however, for the more than forty boxes of sanitary napkins, absorbents which worked well as field dressings. We had more than once found them used as bandages on dinks.

No doubt remained in my mind that we had caught a supply element. The women and children were good cover, if not actively involved themselves. Information from the men might still lead to finding the hospital.

I told the Kit Carson to tell the driver to reveal his destination or we would kill him. The detainee made no response except to shake his head. The scout again made his demand for information, emphasizing his words with kicks to the tied man's chest. I walked over to the prisoner and held my M-16 to his ear. I pulled back the charging handle, ejecting a shell. I then placed the muzzle to his temple and told the Kit Carson to repeat our questions. The gook began to shiver and whimper but still would not talk.

I wanted to pull the trigger. The Kit Carson was convinced enough of my desire to move back so he would not be splattered by blood and brains. I continued to hold the gun to the man's head. Then I lowered it and told the scout that we would turn the prisoner over to the ARVN interrogators. They would get the information we needed by using techniques we would be unable to "get by" with. The scout seemed disappointed.

I was correct in assuming the ARVNs would get results. All four of the men and one of the women were VC or VC suppliers. The rest were guilty by association. I can only imagine how the information was finally gotten out of the prisoner.

We had been looking for a hospital that did not yet exist. One was to be established in the abandoned caves we had discovered along the stream. Our prisoners and the dink killed by Delta had been on their way to establish the facility when we intervened. All we could do now was to wait and hope our interception of the lead elements had not been detected.

🛩 **14 JANUARY 1970**

> Continue to cover this area
> Word from Bn rear is no replacement tomorrow—6 CPTs in Bn who have never been to field—CG says none are qualified replacements—Good pat on back for me—But it leaves me in field—Am ready to get out

We continued operations around the isolated patch of jungle in hopes more of the hospital unit would show themselves. Apparently the word of our presence had reached the remainder of the unit. We spent another uneventful day.

I was not surprised to receive the official word that no replacement had been approved. My anticipation of the decision did little to quell the frustration nonetheless. I had no desire whatever to leave Bravo in the hands of someone who could not take care of the men, but it seemed as if at least one of the many captains who professed wanting a company could meet the qualifications.

I did my best to hide my frustrations from the men, saying nothing in response to the news. The company's morale closely followed their confidence in their commander, and I would not let them down regardless of my growing anxiety about when a replacement would arrive.

I did not need to let Ivey know my feeling; as usual, Beckles was taking care of things for me. When the battalion commander announced at a meeting of his staff and first sergeants that I was remaining in the field, Beckles stood up and angrily said, "Leaving the lieutenant out there is not right, and everyone damn well knows it. We keep using up the good ones until they are wounded or killed while others sit on their asses doing nothing."

After Top had had his say, he walked out of the meeting. He never told me about his outburst nor the subsequent chewing out he had received from Ivey for disturbing the meeting. McGinnis later related the incident to me concluding, "Beckles may be lacking in tact, but he makes up for it in honesty."

✈ 15 JANUARY 1970

Rode tracks to near BH—Damn track people have it easy—Also with all their fire power are not at all aggressive

Clean up at BH

Talked with Bn CO Ivey—Explained why I was not being replaced yet—Am not sure about LTC Ivey—At least I can say he is on my side—Also he has the troops in mind

Drank bourbon with CPT McGinnis and LT Sassner—Talked about old times

The tracks dropped us about a klick from Black Horse and proceeded on their mission.

As we topped a cleared hillside near the base, I could see the entire company spread out in a well-disciplined formation. Using the radio, as well as arm and hand signals, I halted the company and then moments later gave orders to move on. A few minutes later I again stopped the formation to watch the orders relayed through the chain of command.

My stopping and re-starting the company several times had no real purpose except that this was the first time the terrain had allowed me to see clearly the entire company's movements at once. To mere words on the radio, the 100 men possessing the fire power to accomplish tremendous feats responded like a finely tuned machine. The pride, power, and responsibility I felt brought a smile to my face and a lightness to my step that had long been absent.

During the passing years those few moments of observing the teamwork and might of Bravo have remained a vivid picture in my mind. The opportunity to understand the breadth of responsibility and power of company command was nearly always masked by the jungle, the routine actions, and the day-to-day immediacy of survival. That short time on the hillside gave me a clear perspective of where I was and who I had become. The climax of my own human drama was nearing an end and I could not have had a better role nor script. The play would run on but the scene on the hillside would be the one that I would recall as the time when the quality of my performance became a realization.

After we reached Black Horse, I made my usual stop by the battalion TOC. LTC Ivey met me there and somewhat apologetically explained that he was still looking for a replacement who would be approved by the brigade commander. The fact that he had been unsuccessful in his quest, combined with my lingering doubts about why we had not received more support the last day of December, had eroded my confidence in the battalion commander. Yet, I could not find fault with his sincere efforts to take care of the troops. At times I wondered if perhaps everything was still pretty much the same and it was only me who was seeing things differently.

I barely had time to clean up before McGinnis and Sassner arrived at the company with several bottles of bourbon. Norm explained they had bought the whiskey to celebrate my leaving the field before they heard about my replacement being disapproved. Deciding there was no reason to let good booze go to waste, they had brought it to drink to our days in Charlie Company.

Over the next hours we enjoyed the distinctive flavor of bourbon and warm cola drunk from a canteen cup. We drank too much, and then drank some more. We told stories, laughed, and could not recall a damn thing that was not funny.

✎ 16 JANUARY 1970

Trucked to near Tan Lap on Highway 1—Walked to link up with tracks to south—Tracks took us to western boundary of AO—Moved to nighttime position

Have one plt farther south—One plt at Crystal
My call sign Rickey Bobcat Bravo 39

I was not at all surprised to wake up with a king-sized hangover. Green powdered eggs at breakfast did nothing to improve my outlook on another day in Vietnam.

Trucks soon pulled up in front of the company orderly room and we began loading to return to the jungle. The troops were on the trucks, and I was reviewing the mission with the platoon leaders, when I heard Sassner yelling my name from the doorway of his orderly room down the street. I looked up to see Norm running toward me dressed only in fatigue trousers and shower shoes. As he neared me, he began to shout, "Don't go! Don't go! You're going to die!"

He continued running toward me, saying, "I had a dream last night. You're going to die if you go back out."

My old friend kept shouting, "Don't go! Don't go!" until he reached me and grabbed me in a bear hug. Tears were welling in his bloodshot eyes as he said, "Damn it, don't go. You've taken too many chances. I could see you lying dead in the jungle as clear as could be."

I could make no response. I thought about telling Norm to shut up or to go to hell. I was still trying to figure out what to say when he released his grip, began to chuckle and finally was laughing so hard he fell rolling to the ground in hysterical merriment over his "joke."

Rather than finding the outburst humorous, I was scared half to death. I forced a laugh before I looked down at Norm and said, "You son of a bitch. I've been out too long to get killed now. But just in case it does happen, I hope you feel guilty as hell."

Sassner was still laughing when I extended my hand to help him off the ground. He grabbed me in another hug and said, "Be careful out there. God, you should have seen your face." He began laughing again. This time I joined in and said, "I owe you one." I got in my jeep and led the convoy out of Black Horse.

Although many of the troops had heard Norm's prophecy, no one commented except my RTOs. Just loud enough for me to overhear, one said to the other, "I told you last night when they were drinking all that whiskey that those mother fuckers are crazy."

I do not know for sure if my actions when we reached the dismount point were to reassure myself or to pump up the morale of the soldiers. Noise discipline was not a factor since the trucks had let any enemy nearby know we were present. The troops were spreading out in our RIF formation when I climbed on the hood of a truck and fired a full magazine on automatic into the air. I then shouted at the top of my lungs, "Hey, Charlie, if you are out there, you had better run like hell or die where you stand. This is Bravo Company of the Old Guard and we're going to kick your ass all over the jungle!"

My words were followed by a silence, then shouts of "Right on!" and "Let's get those mother fuckers!" The whole company joined in. After a few minutes, the shouts turned to laughter. Then we grew silent and went back into the bush.

> Move to south for nighttime
> Old methods of codes are no more—Now everything coded using SOI straight line—Still using point of origin for platoon operations

Our radio transmissions followed certain procedures that varied from a designated substitution of letters for the numbered map grid line to the use of daily code words such as BLACK NIGHT when B would equate to zero, L to one, A to two, etc.

A common method in the Old Guard had been to designate various map gridline intersections as "points of origin" with code names such as Horse, Dog, etc. To call in a location, an RTO would count grid squares from a "point of origin" and report, "From Dog, right 2.8, up 1.2." To change a radio frequency, an order "to go up 5.25 from Jack Benny" would mean to add 5.25 to Jack Benny's claimed age of 39, or go to 44.25.

These "bandit" codes had become more and more common throughout the brigade. None of the procedures were authorized because they could be broken easily by a quick-thinking enemy.

The official base document for our communications' security was a four-by-six-inch booklet known as the Signal Operating Instructions (SOI). Each page of the SOI was headed by numbers zero through nine with a left margin column of twenty-six letters, A through Z. Each of the letters was followed by a jumbled sequence of the alphabet

208

allowing each of the numbers at the top to be recorded by two or three letters. To encode a six-digit grid coordinate, an RTO would transmit an eight-digit series of letters, such as ZENXLFPG. The receiver would then check the left column for the Z line and read to the right until he found E. The next letter in the jumbled sequence would be the base line for converting the last six letters to numbers. SOIs contained up to 31 of these letter/number pages, each marked Day 1, Day 2, etc., so that a different set could be used every twenty-four hours.

The middle of the SOI contained a listing of radio frequencies and call signs for each unit in the battalion. An alternate set was also included.

At the back of the book was a series of several hundred words with a three-letter code designation. For example, XAR might stand for ammunition while HBL meant water. An alphabetical series of the three-letter codes was cross-indexed for rapid translation.

These systems of codes were easy to learn and all of the RTOs and leaders were proficient in their use. The only time our radio transmissions were not encoded was when we were in contact. It was no violation of communications security to give the grid coordinates of a fire fight "in the clear" because the enemy obviously knew where we were by the direction of our fire.

Although I knew of no instance where the enemy had broken our old "bandit" codes, the possibility was certainly present. Close adherence to the SOI procedures could only help in keeping the gooks off balance and unaware of our plans.

Security of our copies of the SOI was critical. A strong string, or "dummy cord" as it was most often called, secured the document to our uniforms or allowed the SOI to be worn along with the dog tags around the neck.

We made frequent checks to be sure all SOIs were accounted for. Many of us still had clear memories of the confusion caused by the gooks after Bill Little's SOI had been captured on 11 November.

✈ 18 JANUARY 1970

> Continue to south
> Mission is to screen AO boundaries—Looks as if we have run most of enemy out of AO—Trying to catch them coming back in now

>> "Next to valor, the best qualities in a military man are vigilance and caution."
>> BG James Wolfe to his troops before Battle of Quebec, 1759 (Wolfe was killed in battle)

With few exceptions, my morale had remained high during the last month. The time had not been fun, yet the intensity of the lifestyle of the combat Infantrymen had made me feel even more alive and had given me a sense of purpose. Of course, it had been a long time since I had known any living conditions other than those in the jungle, so I had little with which to compare my environment.

Still heading south

Slow day

LT Bolenske returned from R&R on resupply—A man back from R&R is always useless, even officers, the first few days back

21 T Bochnevetch, New York, is now 2nd plt ldr Not too strong but I think he will develop—1st name Sherman, goes by Skip

The jungle and our routine changed little from day to day, yet nothing in Bravo remained the same for long. Ends of tour, arrival of replacements, and departures and returns from R&R constantly provided new players in the drama that seemed to go on forever.

Steve Beig had completed his tour and boarded a Freedom Bird for home. Jack Kidalowski left his platoon to assume the duties of Company Executive Officer. Bill Bolenske returned from R&R.

Bolenske was more subdued than his usual unassuming self and only smiled when I asked if he was glad to be back. He did not need to answer, for we both knew the letdown of returning to the boonies. Officers and troops alike were mostly worthless the first few days back. After months in the jungle, the filth, fatigue, boredom, and occasional terror became routine. A week of R&R—with its luxury hotels, clean sheets, good food and drink, and female companionship—brought back all the natural things ordinary people take for granted.

Sherman Bochnevetch arrived on the resupply chopper

with Bolenske. I had learned over the past months not to judge Infantrymen by their looks or initial impressions, but my first thought about the new lieutenant was that he would look more at home in a clerk's office back at BMB than in the jungle. Of medium build and height, he had somewhat pudgy cheeks topped by Army-issue black-rimmed glasses. Although Skip was roughly my age, he looked much younger. Perhaps it was because he looked so naive and enthusiastic in his clean, new jungle fatigues, or maybe it was again only my own eyes and the way I looked at things that had changed.

Bolenske had already talked to Skip about the company operations and told me that the new lieutenant was eager to assume the leadership of his platoon. My primary guidance to him was to learn from his NCOs and not to take any unnecessary chances. He seemed to hang on every word, reminding me of so many lieutenants, myself included, who brought with them a sense of being part of something important and wanting to help "win the war." He would lose much of that boy scout attitude after seeing just how horrible war really was—that is, if he lived long enough.

The thought of "if he lived long enough" did not leave my mind as we sweated along on the RIF. Yet, I knew I could do nothing beyond train and lead the new officer. His destiny was his own.

> 3rd time over this area—No activity
> Note from 1st Sgt Beckles in resupply—CPT Shaw, new cpt, to be out this week as my replacement—Hope this is not another "get your hopes up"
> Gave more statements on 28 Dec rocket injuries to gunship company investigating officer that came in on resupply

The lack of contact did not bother me. In fact, I had made up my mind that I would not be unhappy never to hear again the crack of an AK bullet. We accomplished the missions given us by the battalion, but I selected the safest possible routes. A new commander would soon be leading Bravo, and I intended to hand over every man on the company rolls in his present condition.

Not only was I taking no unnecessary chances on our RIFs, but also I was avoiding other risks as well. Brigade had recently instituted a policy that each platoon would emplace a mechanical ambush near their positions each night—a policy I chose to ignore.

A mechanical ambush was composed of four or five Claymore mines wired together in a series. They were detonated by a trip wire and battery rather than the usual hand-held "clacker" firing device. The trip wire detonator could be rigged in several ways. An interlocking, insulated copper wire between the power source and the mines was the most common. When the device was tripped, it caused the two wires to slide along their surface to a spot where the insulation had been stripped, completing the

213

circuit and instantaneously blowing the Claymores. Another technique used an ordinary clothespin. Bare wires from the battery's positive and negative terminals were wrapped around the pin's jaws. A plastic C-rations spoon tied to a trip wire was inserted between the jaws. When the trip wire was hit, the spoon was jerked from the clothespin, completing the circuit.

Mechanical ambushes were, of course, little different from the booby traps we so despised in the paddies. Our legal experts, however, concluded they violated no laws of land warfare because they were within sight of the troops who emplaced them and were dismantled when the unit moved on.

Although I trained my soldiers how to use the Claymore ambushes, I did not follow the brigade guidance of emplacing one per platoon each night. My decision was not based on any ethical concerns, as I cared little about what techniques we used to destroy the enemy. What I was worried about was safety. If a unit was hit during the night and had to withdraw, the mechanical ambushes would be left behind. Also, the jungle around an ambush set in late evening might look different in the morning light, resulting in our men wandering into its kill zone. Furthermore, no matter how many precautions were taken, mistakes could happen. We in the jungle made our own rules and followed those made by others only to the extent that it was to our advantage.

The resupply bird brought two pieces of business.

First, the aviation investigating officer, who was more than anxious for the bird to return and pick him up, said a technical inspection of the aircraft and rocket pods had revealed no mechanical deficiencies. Apparently, he added, the accident had been pilot error.

I outlined for him what had occurred from my viewpoint as the ground commander, including the information that Schmalz had continually popped smoke during our withdrawal. I concluded by stating, "We knew at the time the pilot just screwed up and fired on the wrong side of the smoke. If he hadn't made his earlier runs, we wouldn't have recovered our wounded men. You do whatever you think is fair. The punishment from his own head will far outweigh anything you do on paper."

The visit of the investigating officer was the last I was to hear of the misguided rockets. As I told the investigator, the incident already seemed far in the past.

The resupply also brought a note from Beckles which simply stated, "Replacement has been approved—CPT Shaw—One more week."

After reading the note I placed it between the pages of my journal, doing my best not to give it any more thought. If a replacement did, in fact, arrive, I would think about it then.

✎ 21 JANUARY 1970

CP picked up by Huey—Airmobiled to southwest with 2nd plt

Have a 292 antenna—Setting up a patrol base—With damn little support—Bn has us too far out in my opinion

Have been getting in more replacements—Getting strength up which is damn good

No way to put in words how you get to hating these damn C-rations

The helicopters carried us to a small, tree-dotted hilltop clearing. Waiting for us on the aircraft was a canvas bag weighing over 50 pounds containing a collapsible 30-foot RC 292 antenna. We assembled the antenna quickly after we landed, as our radios could not reach Black Horse without its assistance.

Orders soon came to cover as much of the boundary as possible with the platoons, including the one that had air-mobiled in from their security mission at Crystal. My CP would remain in place with the 292 antenna. Not having to hump the boonies for a while was the good news. The bad news was that the hilltop clearing was only the size of half a football field and we were sitting under a tall antenna spire announcing our location to any gook in the AO.

More bad news arrived on another chopper. A shotgun-carrying handler and his German shepherd scout dog jumped from the bird and joined my CP. The young handler, who modeled himself after characters in John Wayne's movies with tailored jungle fatigues and a throwing knife strapped to the calf of one leg, told me that this was the first mission for him and the dog.

I cringed at the sight of his weapon. Shotguns were useless in my opinion. They were difficult to maintain. The six or eight slugs in each buckshot round had little range and their plastic cases deteriorated rapidly. An M-16 fired more accurately and, on full automatic, put as much or more lead downrange. When I had assumed command of Bravo, one of my first actions had been to get rid of the shotguns carried in each platoon.

In less than half an hour, the dog began barking each

time one of my men moved. When the handler tried to quiet him, he tripped and accidentally discharged his shotgun inches from my head. As calmly as possible I called Battalion and said, "Send a chopper after the team you just delivered. If it's not here in one hour, I will kill the dog. If you wait much longer than that, I may kill the damn handler as well. Don't expect us to train them out here. You do it back there."

In much less than sixty minutes the bird returned and the dog team was gone.

The echoes of the dog's barks across the jungle was strike one; the discharge of the shotgun, strike two. I would be damned if they were going to get the opportunity for strike three.

✈ 22 JANUARY 1970

Getting set in our "home" for the next few days
Plts finding very little—Rough on nerves just to sit here
Call sign Knifer Bravo 17

LT Bochnevetch and his men ran recon patrols around our hilltop during the day, returning at dusk to add to our security. It was a good opportunity for the new officer to get to know his men and the terrain. Skip's infectious sense of humor and enthusiasm seemed to make up for his apparent lack of natural leadership ability.

Just sitting on the hilltop made the day awfully long. Remaining in one place added to the tension. Clary Speck said, half-seriously, that perhaps Battalion was now using the Company's CP and 292 antenna as bait. I much more than "half-seriously" hoped he was wrong.

✈ 23 JANUARY 1970

> Not much to do—Read a little
> Men bathe in stream near here—Including me—2 on security, 1 in stream

Sitting on the hilltop offered time to write. Opportunity was available; motivation was not. For ten days I had written no one. I had no news and to write that I was soon to get out of the field only served to get my and others' hopes up.

On this date I wrote the only letter of my last two weeks in the field. To Linda I penned, "Dearest, Still in the jungle—That's not a very original start to a letter, is it?"

✈ 24 JANUARY 1970

> Still here—Will move tomorrow—Hard moving 292
> One of men spotted a large ape—He said "gorilla"—
> Troop said "He's 5-foot and that's hunched over"—He's
> actually scared of the damned gorilla
> Night—Much moonlight—Even kind of pretty

The longer we stayed in the same position, the more vulnerable we became. After several calls to Battalion, we received permission to move the next day to another location.

A full moon with crystal clear skies almost made the night in Vietnam beautiful. Instead of being romantic or awesome, it created threatening shadows, reminding me of how insignificant our presence was on the barren hilltop.

I had finally dropped off to sleep a little after midnight when one of the men awoke me to report seeing an ape. If any gorilla were present, it would be accurately spelled g-u-e-r-r-i-l-l-a. I had seen enough monkeys in the trees to believe his report, except regarding the animal's size. The soldier's sighting of a gorilla may not have been real, but his fright was genuine. The only thing I could not figure out was why a soldier whom I had seen kill men—who were trying to kill him—was scared of a damn unarmed monkey that was likely just looking for discarded C-ration cans.

Moved CP to a different location—Not as shady, no
stream nearby, but a hell of a lot safer—Good commo
These last few days have about driven me crazy—Don't
see why they don't bring my replacement on out

Carrying the additional weight of the 292 antenna made
our move to the new CP site difficult. We took no breaks,
however, as commo during the one-klick move was weak
at best.

The new site was in a clearing made by a Rome plow
cut. Stacks of downed trees provided good concealment
and cover, making the lessened shade and loss of a stream
seem insignificant.

We had just re-erected the tall antenna when strange
noises began coming from a pile of dead tree limbs. Closer
investigation revealed a foot-long, orange and green fat-
bodied lizard in a fight with a brown centipede almost as
large. The lizard was faster and had strong jaws, but the
centipede jointed shell was too hard to be penetrated.
For over two hours, the creatures, both the largest of their
species I had ever seen, fought through the brush. Several
of the troops made bets on the final outcome of the battle
with the lizard the apparent favorite. No one had to pay
off, for the fight ended, like most conflicts in Vietnam,
with no winner. The lizard finally managed to swallow the
head and about a third of the centipede's body. At that
point, the centipede's spiny legs became stuck in the liz-

ard's throat and, after another half-hour of thrashing, the struggle killed them both.

Time seemed to stand still. It was a common belief among grunts that the first and last days in the field were the most dangerous. Of course, if a man got blown away, it was his last day. The logic or illogic of the matter did little to make me feel any better. I laughed with my RTOs that apparently I was never to get out of the field. However, my insides were churning with the knowledge that bullets had no respect for how long one had been out nor how soon he was to leave.

✈ 26 JANUARY 1970

> LT Stewart, Asst. S-2, came out and put in some sensors near our position
>
> Linked up with platoons—Airmobiled to Crystal where I very happily met my replacement CPT Shaw—He has the experience
>
> Hard to believe—After nearly 9¼ months I am "fini" field—I just realized today, I don't really think I figured I would make it in one piece—I know at some points I didn't—Of course, I'm not home yet

Our portion of the battalion AO had been so inactive it was no longer worth keeping troops there. Sensors would be placed to release Bravo Company to better hunting grounds.

LT Stewart, who had completed his time as platoon leader in Charlie Company and was now working for Mc-Ginnis as the Assistant S-2, leapfrogged to each of my platoons by helicopter, setting sensors. By the time he made his last stop at my CP, I had received orders to consolidate the company for an airmobile to Crystal.

Stew had news of the battalion; the only information I paid any attention to was that my replacement was supposedly waiting at Crystal.

The last of my platoons had barely reached my location when the flight of slicks appeared over the horizon. There was nothing unusual about the airmobile whatsoever except it was my last as company commander.

When we landed at the fire base, LTC Ivey introduced me to CPT Roy Shaw. The battalion commander was in a rush and said he would send a chopper for me the following morning so we could talk about my next job.

My initial impression of Shaw was positive. In his mid-thirties and on his second tour in-country, he was cool, quiet, and confident. His thirteen years' service would provide the leadership Bravo deserved.

Ivey had not said when our change of command was effective, so I informed my replacement that as long as I was at the fire base the command of Bravo was mine. The responsibilities would be his on my departure the next morning.

I spent the remainder of the afternoon talking to my soldiers. There were no formal good-byes beyond a few handshakes and wishes of "Good luck" and "Keep your head down." Near sundown, I gathered my officers and NCOs for a final meeting. My talk was brief. I told them of the pride I felt in their performance and reminded them of the reputation they had achieved over the last months.

I concluded by saying that I expected them to give CPT Shaw the same support they had provided me.

I spoke in a matter-of-fact manner. Only the occasional crack of my voice caused by the huge lump in my throat indicated my true feelings. There was little eye contact as most of the men were looking downward or across the fire base. I knew it was time for me to move on, yet at the same time I was aware I was leaving a position and men that had been the center of the most significant time of my life.

I was about to dismiss the meeting when SSG English stood up and said, "Sir, we hate to see you go, but we are happy you're finally getting out of the field. We couldn't have asked more of a commander. We will miss you."

English was embarrassed in his position as spokesman and his words were low and halting. As he spoke, each man raised his eyes to meet mine. The first platoon sergeant continued, "We've killed lots of gooks and done things we wouldn't have done if you hadn't been there."

English started to sit back down and then changed his mind. He asked, "Sir, what do we do if the new commander isn't any good? What do we do if he's going to get us killed?"

My answer was immediate. It was based on the affection and closeness I felt for the men of Bravo rather than on the oath I had taken as an officer or the teachings in my military schools. I looked at English and with no hesitation whatsoever said, "Kill him."

English sat back down. There was little reaction to my response by the others. We had all lived, fought, suffered, and killed together for so long that we were part of each other regardless of rank. Our mutual survival had been in the hands of each as individuals and in all of us as a group.

I gave them the only answer they would have accepted or believed from one of their own.

It should be no surprise that my last conversation with my officers and NCOs was not recorded in my journal. My answer of "Kill him" reflected that any code of personal ethics or loyalty to the Army had been far exceeded by the love, respect, and responsibility I felt for the men of Bravo. It also reflected the genuine confidence I had in their dedication to give the new commander every chance to lead them in the manner they deserved. I was not particularly proud of my answer then nor am I now, and would have rather English had never asked the question. But he did, and I answered honestly. I was not going to bullshit the troops with my final words.

27 JANUARY 1970

> Choppered into Black Horse—1st time I've been away from Bravo in 3½ months
> My new job is to be S-3 training officer—Am going to BMB and get a few things taken care of before I begin
> Took B Co jeep into BMB—Stayed up till 0500 drinking and telling war stories with some of my old men
> Hard not to call Bravo Company MY Company

The sun was barely up when my chopper hovered over the helipad. After a brief good-bye to my RTOs, I handed my SOI code book to CPT Shaw and shook his hand. Our change of command was complete.

I trotted to the helicopter. As we gained altitude, I watched Crystal become smaller and smaller. A feeling of tremendous responsibility lifting from my shoulders almost overcame the regret at leaving the greatest group of men I had ever encountered. I turned my eyes toward our direction of flight and did not look back.

LTC Ivey and the S-3 were waiting for me at Black Horse. Ivey congratulated me on a successful command and said he had been impressed with the training Bravo had conducted at Cam Tam. He asked if I could establish a similar program for the rest of the battalion. Before I could answer, he explained that he planned to bring each company into Black Horse every two months for a concentrated retraining session. My title, he said, would be Assistant S-3 Training Officer, and I would work directly for the operations officer. Ivey concluded, "Lee, you have achieved high body count with minimal friendly losses. The biggest contribution you can make to the battalion is to pass along your experience and skills."

I was not sure if I wanted the job or if I cared what I did at all. Anything would be downhill after company command.

Ivey told me to take a day off at BMB to close out any necessary paperwork and transfer my records to the Battalion Headquarters Company. Before departing, I went by Bravo Company to say thanks to Beckles. According to military tradition, a company commander is always referred to as "the old man" by the senior NCOs. Many times I had heard Beckles say, "The old man wants . . ." or "The old man says . . ." or, on occasion, "The old man will have your ass if you don't . . ." As we shook hands before I headed for BMB in a jeep borrowed from

Top, he said, "You are the youngest 'old man' I've worked for. I hope we can do it again sometime."

---

28 JANUARY 1970

> BMB
> Took care of finances, etc—Mostly just took it easy

> "I want you to remember that no bastard ever won a war by dying for his country. He won it by making the other poor dumb bastard die for his country."
> GEN George S. Patton

I was amazed just how relaxed I was only hours out of the jungle. My nerves and temper were no longer on edge, and sleep came much easier. Danger was never far away anywhere in Vietnam, but now that I was out of the field the odds for survival were much more in my favor.

The paperwork involved in my transfer from Bravo to Headquarters Company was quickly finished. My next stop was at Finance, to arrange to get more cash on payday. A catalogue from the Pacific Post Exchange System offered bronzeware and gold jewelry from Thailand, brass from Korea, and electronic gear from Japan at very reasonable prices. It was time to put aside living from day to day and fire fight to fire fight, and think about enjoying the future.

Later in the day I wrote Linda that I was finally out

of the field, saying, "This is the letter we've been waiting for."

═══════════════════════════════

✈ 29 JANUARY 1970

Black Horse
   Getting used to being a REMF
   Am living in BOQ hooch with CPT Rendon from New Mexico—Arty LNO—A good man—FO for 8 months— On 6 month extension

I began to settle in at Black Horse. An officers' hooch partitioned into small rooms for two captains or four lieutenants was located between the company orderly room and the battalion headquarters. The Headquarters Company commander told me to move into a two-man room, saying, "You've been doing the job of a captain. You deserve to be treated as one." It seemed fair to me.

My new hoochmate was easy to like, and we soon became good friends despite our differences in rank. He laughed when he told me he had heard of my encounter Christmas Day with his FNG predecessor, adding that maybe I had helped him get his present job.

Our room was only about eight by twelve feet in size, containing two metal-frame cots, a folding chair, a shelf, and nails in the wall for hanging extra gear. Sheets were available for us, but I preferred spreading a blanket over the thin mattress and using my poncho liner for cover. Some aspects of being an REMF I was just not yet ready for.

🚁 30 JANUARY 1970

Black Horse
   Visited E Recon training with MAJ Bloch from Bde at Cam Tam
   The MAJ has 3 Vn tours—Also tours in Dominican Republic, Congo and was an NCO in Korean War—An old time soldier

Major Humphrey, the Operations Officer, suggested I visit as many of the sites as possible, as well as check out other training programs in the brigade over the next few weeks before finalizing my program by the first of March. I was surprised at the amount of time I had been given. It would be a while before I learned things moved much slower in the rear than in the jungle.

Black Horse
Usually work between 0700 and 1800—Nightly briefing at 1700
Usually go to movie, outdoors, at night

By doing much of my work at a field table in the TOC and attending the daily briefings for the battalion commander, I was able to keep up with the movement and contacts of the various units. Familiar voices on the horn made it difficult at times to concentrate on preparing the battalion training program. My major accomplishment thus far had been to convince the operations officer to rename the program "Refresher Training" because I knew the grunts would resent any implication of their needing more training skills when they were already convinced they were masters. The real selling point, however, would be the several days at Black Horse with lots of time built into the schedule for cleanup and rest.

The routine at Black Horse was very different from the boonies. Three hot meals a day, a movie at night, and electric lights—which allowed me to read instead of count stars—were not difficult to get used to.

Other than the mess hall, my favorite of the amenities of the fire base was the nightly movie. The outdoor screen and benches were surrounded by a low sandbagged wall with large bunkers nearby. The screen, solidly built of white painted plywood, was frequently the target of beer and soda cans that the troops hurled against it when the villain appeared. Films were frequently reversed to re-show some portions, particularly nude scenes, at the crowd's request.

✈ I FEBRUARY 1970

> Rode into BMB with CPT Lanham the S-4—His damn
> jeep driver is more dangerous than the dinks
>   B Co will be in on standdown tomorrow
>   Wild party at O Club tonight—Too much booze

The purpose of my trip back to BMB was to attend the court-martial of PVT Taylor. There had been no time for the trial while I was in command, so Taylor had been held in confinement since his refusal to return to the field at Crystal.

That night Sassner, Kidalowski, and several others took me to the club to officially celebrate my getting out of the field. Before we left, I overheard Sassner reviewing alert procedures with his driver. At the club's closing, Norm would call the driver on the telephone. Green alert meant we would make it back on our own; yellow alert called for the jeep to pick us up; and red alert required the jeep and trailer to haul us home. This was a red alert night.

✈ 2 FEBRUARY 1970

BMB
> Met with lawyers on Taylor's court-martial
> Another night at O Club
> LT Schmalz back from hospital

I could not understand why Taylor was pleading not guilty when it was such an open-and-shut case. However, his right to do so was one of the principles we were fighting for.

A call from the Battalion Adjutant asked me to stop by his office to pick up my orders for assignment after DEROS. Although I had requested to be sent to Fort Lewis, Washington; Fort Ord, California; or Fort Bliss, Texas, I was not too surprised when the S-1 handed me orders to Fort Benning, Georgia. The sheer joy of being close enough to DEROS to have orders in hand far outweighed any geographical preferences.

Sassner convinced me to give the club a rematch. Schmalz, who had returned from several days in the hospital with severe infection from jungle rot, joined us, as did CPT Shaw and the other Bravo officers. It was only a yellow alert night.

> BMB
>
> Damn—BMB sure provides a hangover—Actually I guess it is the Officers' Club—Went to Bravo Co stand-down—A damn good Co—I have some doubts about CPT Shaw—Doesn't know how to really trust the men for the best results—Time will tell
>
> Attended court-martial of PVT Taylor today—Guilty: 3-3-1

My role in the trial of PVT Taylor was limited to testimony confirming that the soldier had, in fact, acknowledged that I was his commander and had refused a lawful order. Taylor's threat and my response did not come up. I did not stay to listen to the defense attorney's sob story about the soldier's injured leg.

The maximum punishment that the court-martial could adjudge was six months' confinement, six months' loss of pay, and reduction to Private E-1. Although the guilty verdict was no surprise, the punishment of only half the maximum (three months' confinement without pay and the reduction from Private E-2 to E-1) seemed too light. However, any sentence less than being shot at sunrise, or earlier if possible, would have seemed lenient to me. REMFs had judged a man for a crime they no better comprehended than I understood the legalities of the resulting punishment.

My journal comments concerning CPT Shaw were no less biased than those of a man commenting on how his ex-wife's new husband was raising *his* children. Shaw was establishing his personality and philosophy as commander of his company. Although I might not agree with some of his methods, I readily admitted Bravo was holding steadfast.

After my DEROS, I lost track of Shaw until I read his name in the *Army Times* list of those killed in Vietnam. Some time later I learned that after six months in successful command of Bravo, he had been transferred to another unit. I never completely believed he was dead until I found his name on the Vietnam Memorial, a few panels from another of my replacements—Bill Little.

🖎 4 FEBRUARY 1970

> Took ration truck from BMB to Black Horse—Guess we've done some good—When we first came north you had to have a convoy and sometimes air cover to move on road—Now single vehicle with no sweat
>
> Worked with a civilian training team on XM-191—Flame wpn replacing LAW—Teaching 2 men from each Co—Would have been a good wpn in paddies—Will prove useless in jungle

When I got back to the fire base, I worked with the civilian team demonstrating the XM-191, a flamethrower with a pod of 66-mm projectiles that had a range of three hundred meters and that produced a fireball thirty meters in diameter on impact. Its workings were similar to the

LAW (Light Antitank Weapon—a small handheld rocket fired from a tube looking like a half-size bazooka. In Vietnam the LAW was generally used as an antipersonnel weapon and in bunker suppression), and the troops had little trouble learning its operations. The flame round had a built-in safety preventing it from exploding until it had traveled fifteen meters from the tube's muzzle. If it happened to hit a tree or log after its 15-meter safety range but before traveling past the thirty meters of the fireball's diameter, the operators would be its victims.

I submitted my report on the weapon's inherent dangers to Battalion. Others must have agreed, as it was not adopted, and I never saw another XM-191.

5 FEBRUARY 1970

Black Horse
  Usual stuff—Not much to do today
  Night—Went to movie

  "Life is either a daring adventure or nothing."
                                        Helen Keller

  "Fortune favors the brave."

                                        Virgil

The light punishment of PVT Taylor, combined with my observations of the inequities of life in the field compared to those at BMB, left me depressed. After my initial relief at being out of the field, I found adjustment from the excitement and responsibilities of command to the unhurried lifestyle of Black Horse was not as easy as I had first thought. Now that I had more time to read I was understanding better how unpopular the war and we who were fighting it were becoming. This added to my sense of gloom.

For a brief time, I considered leaving the Army after completing my commitment. However, if the war continued as I thought it would, my services would be in demand. If the war was ever over, the rebuilding of a peacetime Army would provide a more than ample challenge.

Linda and I corresponded about these possibilities as well as more personal matters. Her pregnancy and our being thousands of miles apart had negated any problems with birth control for over a year. Reveilee's birth and my nearing DEROS made it a most welcome impending decision. We wrote about the first news stories concerning possible dangers from the Pill and recommended alternatives.

After several weeks of letters back and forth, I wrote Linda to use the method she thought best. I said, in no uncertain terms, "One method we are not going to use is abstinence."

Black Horse
    Took a Huey out to FB Crystal to check on A Co training—On way out helped CPT McGinnis parachute some sensor devices into the jungle
    Observed wpns zero—Sqd attack, etc—Crystal is to be torn down soon
    Spending night at Crystal—It has been mortared 3 times in last month—No activity tonight

Loaded aboard the chopper were ten or twelve metal cylinders four inches in diameter and three feet long. Each contained an audio sensor harnessed to a parachute that would allow it to float gently to the tree canopy where it would become entangled in the branches. A monitor station would then be able to listen for any strange noises over the sensor microphone transmitters. At least that was the way they were supposed to work.

In reality several of the parachutes never opened, sending the sensors crashing to the earth. Others that correctly reached the canopy did not work well or at all.

With a shrug of his shoulders, McGinnis explained that each sensor had cost the taxpayers about $10,000. We had kicked out over $100,000 worth of useless electronics. Neither of us was very concerned at the waste. We had learned to value life a great deal and money little.

My notation of the previous mortar attacks on Crystal is a good indication of how a person's worries about dangers are in relation to their present degree of safety rather than actual threat. Possibilities of mortar attacks had never bothered me in a fire base when I had been a field soldier. Now that I was out of the boonies, mortar attacks were much more threatening.

═══

🪖 7 FEBRUARY 1970

> Choppered back to Black Horse—The TOC has been moved back next to Hqs—This is much more convenient
> I have been looking back through old records during my time in field—Bn had nearly 50 killed, 350 wounded
> At no time has the Bn ever had over 450 men in the field
> I feel very fortunate—The units I commanded took far fewer casualties than average and rated near the top in enemy kills in 283 field days
> I also in my mind count the KIA—WIA I've been with, near or had mission to recover—I've seen all I ever care to—However, I feel it is my job and I can keep these numbers down

The statistics of those killed and wounded during my 283 days in the field speak for themselves. The figures were no surprise to me as I had been a witness to many of the casualties. I could not understand how so many had been struck down next to me while I escaped unscratched. My extended time in the field and the fact that at six-foot-five I offered the largest target on the battlefield added to my questions about why I had survived while others had not. At various times I had attributed it to luck, skill, or divine intervention. I finally quit worrying about it as there were no answers. Being alive with questions was much better than the alternative.

🖦 8 FEBRUARY 1970

Black Horse
   Moved over to S-3 Admin across from TOC
   Was officer of day tonight—Checked bunkers, guards, etc—No sweat
   Quite a bit of contact going on in AO—I kind of miss the fighting—But not the humping
   The dust here is constantly blowing—Much like a small West Texas dust storm—Was not bad in field but here is something else
   Received word that LT Lee Horton, an Aggie buddy, lost both legs—Land mine—This damn war

> "All of us I am sure ten years ago thought that the need for the man with the rifle would be passing away. . . . But the very size and magnitude of the new great weapons has placed a new emphasis upon what we call rather strangely conventional war, and they have made even more necessary than ever that we keep the man with the rifle."
>
> John F. Kennedy 1962

When I realized I was paying much more attention to the activities in the field than to the work at hand, I moved my field desk to a nearby building. The new location provided a better work environment as well as ending the frustration of wanting to get on the radios and lend advice to my old comrades. I still knew what was going on because Ron Coleman and Vito Lovecchio, both working their last months in-country as TOC RTOs, filled me in on contacts and operational changes.

Besides updates on the battalion, I got more news from the world. I had known Lee Horton for four years at A&M and often walked to classes with him discussing his home town, San Angelo, Texas, or wondering together what it would be like in the Infantry after graduation. It was difficult to accept that Lee would no longer be walking anywhere.

My journal entries became longer after I decided to take advantage of having fewer responsibilities and the luxury of electric lighting after dark. It was a wise decision since without the more detailed recordings of the day-to-day events of my time in the rear, the re-creation of those times in this book would have been extremely difficult. Memories of days in the field have dimmed little over the years, while the times as a staff officer at the end of my tour made little impression at all.

> Something interesting near the ⅔ area here at Black Horse today—At the old supply issue point of 11 ACR a bulldozer and a large MP investigating team showed up and started digging and taking pictures—Uncovered today: 1 jeep, 1 truck, cases upon cases of fatigues—Seems as if 11 ACR had stolen the vehicles—And no room to carry equipment when they moved out of here in Oct.—Some squirrel probably wrote his Congressman—Am sure quite a few will hang—Still supposed to be in the area: 2 APCs, 2 Hueys, much equipment
>
> The officers and troops here have a very low opinion of our VN "friends"—They are a very sorry people—My contempt for them is growing stronger

Property accountability was loose at best in the war zone. A helicopter crash or a building destroyed in a mortar attack was an excellent opportunity for a supply sergeant to write off any equipment that had been previously lost or stolen. Everyone laughed at the widespread story about all the losses reported on a supply chopper that had gone down. When the weight of all the "missing" items that had been "added" to the cargo was totaled, it came to over five times the chopper's lift capability.

Often excesses of equipment were as much a problem as shortages. The 11th ACR (Armored Cavalry Regiment) solved the dilemma of too many vehicles and uniforms by burying them before their departure.

Except for our small corner of the fire base and the area for a battery of eight-inch artillery, Black Horse was now totally occupied by the ARVNs. Their poor sanitation and discipline fueled the contempt that had been fostered by their lack of aggressiveness in seeking out the enemy.

Like most of the other GIs, I made little effort to understand the culture and motivations of our allies. The closest I came to trying to get to know the Vietnamese as individuals was when an ARVN major assisted in coordinating use of the space outside the fire base for refresher training ranges. The major had been fighting the VC and NVA for over ten years and had been decorated many times for bravery. When we completed our work, he asked if I could give him some C-rations, soap, toothpaste, and other toiletries for his wife and children in Xuan Luc. He explained that it was difficult to support a family on a major's salary. It seemed strange that a field grade officer in the army we were trying to help had to ask for handouts when we were burying our excesses.

🎗 10 FEBRUARY 1970

Black Horse

Things keep on rolling along—And I get closer to DEROS—Received my orders for Ft Benning, Ga. last week

The man I work directly under is MAJ Humphrey from Fla.—Graduate of Fla. State

Bn has had quite a few contacts in last week—One KIA was not recovered for 24 hours—My Co fought like hell to get KIA—WIA out—This is important in a good

Co—Fighting spirit—We never left a man behind—I remember 28 December—Took nearly 1 hour of hard
fighting to get WIA point man—He is alive in Japan

"Killing is better than drinking—you don't feel so
bad the next day."

Latrine graffito

I expressed my feelings about the company's apparently
not fighting hard enough to recover its dead and wounded
in my journal, but I made no mention of my thoughts to
anyone else. Now that I was one of those safely behind
the wire, I felt no right to publicly criticize those in the
boonies who were making life and death decisions.

I felt somewhat guilty that grunts were fighting while I
worked on refresher training plans. Only days out of the
field, I already missed the intensity and excitement of the
boonies.

---

11 FEBRUARY 1970

Another day—The way a man can get lonesome over
here—And then again never be able to be alone
I think of the many who are never away from families
for more than a few days—I agree with quote below:

"If we had no winter, the spring would not be so
pleasant. If we did not sometimes face adversity,
prosperity would not be so welcome."

Anne Bradstreet

You meet a lot of people here in rear who are always saying or telling how troops in field should be doing it— Most have never got shot at, never really known fear for you and your men's lives—Never eaten Cs for weeks, never slept on ground—Or didn't sleep at all— Never was a combat Infantryman

For ten months I had been constantly surrounded by people. Growing up in West Texas had allowed me to walk across range land and work in fields where the nearest human being was miles away. I ached with loneliness for Linda, our daughter, family, and friends as only a young man eleven thousand miles from home can. At the same time, I yearned to be alone in the company of my own thoughts and feelings with no humans in sight or hearing.

 ## 12 FEBRUARY 1970

Black Horse
Toured the 18th ARVN Div training center here at Black Horse—It is pretty interesting—Much like US Basic Training—All here are volunteers—This way they are with an outfit close to home—Some of the trainees don't wear boots—They have them but are unable to wear them— Have always gone barefoot or in sandals

1st plt C Co had two men KIA today—One was Larry Morford—One of my old men—The ballet-modern dance instructor—Morford probably had more individual kills than anyone in the Bn—Was to get out of the field soon—A damn fine man

I spent most of the day touring the ARVN training center. When I stopped by the TOC in the late afternoon, Ron Coleman told me that Larry Morford had been killed that morning. My first reaction was disbelief. Morford was the best soldier I had ever met—there could not be a gook good enough to kill him.

Coleman ignored my doubts, explaining that according to the radio reports, Morford had been caught in a crossfire while trying to rescue a wounded man. When I asked if they had gotten his body out, Coleman glanced down and nodded his head, saying, "An LOH was able to land and bring both bodies back here. They've already been flown to the morgue in Long Binh." He continued, "CPT McGinnis was listening to the fight on our radios. He met the LOH at the helipad and damn near went crazy. Several guys had to hold him back from jumping on the pilot."

I turned to leave as Ron said over my shoulder, "I'm sorry, I didn't want to be the one to tell you. Is there anything I can do?"

I did not answer as I hurried away to find McGinnis. I found him sitting at his desk staring with red eyes at a wall covered with maps. He said nothing as I sat down on a folding chair in a corner. Several minutes passed before he looked at me and said, "The goddamn pilot did not even cover him with a poncho."

I started to answer that it was not the pilot's fault and that he had taken a chance in landing to get the bodies out quickly, but instead I said nothing. I shared the anger and the helpless feeling of being able to do nothing to change what had occurred. The pilot had simply offered a target for releasing those emotions.

McGinnis and I continued to stare silently at the map. I do not know what was going on in his head, but it is likely his thoughts were very similar to mine. Larry Morford had arrived in Vietnam as a sensitive, compassionate individual who much preferred to help his fellow man rather than to destroy him. Through leadership and coaxing by McGinnis and me, we had molded his extraordinary physical talents into the battalion's leader in body count.

I had never met a more caring, loving person than Larry Morford. The Army had made him into a soldier. McGinnis and I had made him into as effective a killer as has ever been put on the battlefield. Morford was now dead. McGinnis and I stared at a wall unable to say anything to each other that might help it make sense.

Another quarter-hour passed silently. Finally I stood up and walked away. Later that night I learned that the wounded man Morford had been trying to rescue was his replacement as point man. As soon as the man had been properly trained, Morford was to get out of the field. The dancer's last performance had not varied from his unselfish dedication to others.

Late that night I made my journal entry for the day. I wrote a longer explanation about my visit to the ARVN training center than about the death of Larry Morford. Perhaps it was because I understood training much better than I did another filled body bag. More likely, it was just easier that way.

Black Horse
   Bravo Co was in for the night—Saw most of my old troops—A damn good bunch of men
   Bn got a couple of NVA KIAs today
   Was up late tonight—BS with Bn SGT MAJ Quick—Has a small flag on his desk—Has carried it since 1948
   Did lots of work today for once
   Talked quite awhile with D Co XO, LT Gary Ames—Was only in field few months—Was hit pretty bad—Good man—Whole family in service

The news media continued to portray the mounting opposition to the war by those back home. Reports painted us in Vietnam as dope-taking and undisciplined. If there was anyone who hated the war, it was those who were fighting it, yet our skills, dedication, and tenacity matched those of any other soldiers our country has ever sent into battle. From the teenage warriors of Bravo Company to the aging sergeant major with the small, faded flag he had carried twenty-two years, each man believed in his nation, himself, and his fellow soldiers. Larry Morford had died doing a job he did not want to do in a place he did not want to be because he believed his country to be more important than his personal desires.

🖝 14 FEBRUARY 1970

Black Horse

Attended Bde training conference at Xuan Luc today—Was briefed there by CG and DCG

Then choppered to FB Mace and Libbey for some very good demonstrations—Also by FB Nancy

Met quite a few people at Xuan Loc—Many said they had heard of me—I always notice that some LTs I meet are not too friendly—I believe that many are afraid I tried to set a precedent about LTs staying in the field

CG and DCG briefings were typical high ranking talk However, they did make some good points

Recon plt got a couple of kills today—And one weapon

The emphasis by Brigade on refresher training continued to build. Our visit to the fire bases of other battalions north of Xuan Luc revealed several training techniques I would incorporate into our program.

Letters to Linda and my parents on this Valentine's Day included crudely drawn hearts and the explanation that Black Horse was a long way from a store that sold more conventional cards. As I sealed the envelopes, I decided that I might be a fairly good soldier but definitely lacked talent as an artist.

Went into BMB to check training records and C Co standdown training—Everything in pretty good shape
Went to O Club tonight—Fair band—Good dink on the saxophone—Got to drinking wine—Need I say more—A bad night

"A good soldier doesn't try to remake himself . . . He simply does the best with what God gave him."
GEN Jonathan Wainwright

"It isn't life that is so important . . . It's what one does with it that really matters."
Lawrence of Arabia

When I arrived at BMB, I dropped my gear off and went in search of Norm Sassner. His clerk, who had his feet propped on a desk and the latest copy of *Playboy* in hand, said I would find Norm at the swimming pool. I found Norm with Gary Ames and a couple of XOs from another battalion playing bridge. All four were dressed only in cut-off fatigue trousers. Except for the wound scars on three of the four bodies, they would not have looked out of place at any country club pool back in the World.

The card game ended amid much profanity, and Norm and I headed for his orderly room. We drank a few beers as we talked about Larry Morford and the other news of the battalion. As he pointed out a four-inch jagged piece of metal above his desk, Sassner told me of a rocket attack a few nights before. A piece of a 122-mm rocket had come through the wall and stuck in a support post. Scrawled on the bare wood next to the piece of shrapnel was "Today is the first day of the rest of your life." It was the first time I had seen that bit of pop psychology. I still never see or hear the phrase without thinking of that jagged piece of metal.

We were about to leave for the club when Norm rummaged through his desk, producing a dog tag chain with a yellow potato chip-size object hanging from it. It was not the first "ear" necklace I had seen. I remarked that the black thread used to sew up the severed side detracted from the art work. However, I did grant him that the shriveled ear had indeed been well dried and preserved. With a laugh Norm said that he had found the necklace in the gear of a recon soldier while the man was waiting for his DEROS Freedom Bird. Norm added that he had confiscated the trophy because he did not think the customs agents would appreciate it very much.

I do not recall much of the rest of the evening at the club. As best I can remember, there were debates about whether a person could pick up a full bottle of wine with the teeth, tilt it back, and chug it without touching the bottle with the hands. I am not sure how or why we did it; however, from the hangover I had the next morning, we must have been successful.

BMB
    Went to C Co training—Training on dust-off techniques at Redcatcher training center
    Then to TFTA—The first team academy—1st Cav Div ranges at Binh Hoa for weapons zero
    Slow night—Everyone still kind of hungover

> "If a man is not inclined to risk his life for his own country, he should look elsewhere till he finds a country he will risk his life for."
> Admiral Raymond Spruance

The 1st Cavalry Division facilities were decorated everywhere with their big black and yellow patch that sported a horse's head. A senior NCO in charge of the range was a talker and helped make the day pass a little faster. His best story was how during Tet of 1968 a group of FNGs zeroing their rifles on this same range had been attacked by an NVA company. The FNGs had done quite well in shooting at live rather than paper targets.

> Ordered some more stuff out of PACEX catalogue
> Back to Black Horse
> LT Fallon to be recon plt ldr—Has already 6 mos. in field—They leave the good ones in field—Get the bad out—The US Army is scraping the bottom of the barrel for officers in many cases
> Also saw LT Bolenske—Also 6 mos. in field

> > "The head is the fighting man whose deeds light up the torch of inspiration in darkness of death . . . for lesser men to follow."
> >
> > Gen Douglas MacArthur

Officer replacements arriving in the battalion impressed me very little. Entrance requirements for Officer Candidate School continued to be less stringent or not as rigidly enforced as in the past. America's longest war and the lack of support of its people was causing the military to dig deep for leaders.

Despite my reservations concerning the new officers, the battalion continued to function well. In the last two and a half weeks the Old Guard had killed over twenty-five gooks and taken few friendly casualties. Perhaps the enemy was becoming depleted of good soldiers as well. However, it was more likely that neither side had changed appreciably, and it was once more my way of looking at things as an "old timer" than in any real difference. As far as I had been concerned, the best officers and troops ever put on a battlefield had been those like Fallon, Schmalz, Bolenske, Kidalowski, Sassner, Little, McGinnis, Lewis, and myself. Surely no one could replace such grand warriors—but, of course, they would, and did.

✈ 18 FEBRUARY 1970

> Black Horse
> Just not much excitement here at BH
> I believe the Bn needs a good AO change—Like say to War Zone D—Everyone needs a good scare—No one seems to be very interested in the war anymore

> "Major, I failed in my mission. . . . But I will not hang as a failure. I will go as a soldier who did his best . . . in which success or failure has no bearing. I regret I have but one life to give for my country."
> CPT Nathan Hale

Black Horse offered neither the excitement of the field nor the hangovers of BMB—and that was not really bad in either case. The days at the fire base were boring, yet mostly secure in knowing there was a good chance of seeing another day alive and with a reasonably clear head.

🛩 19 FEBRUARY 1970

Black Horse
  Still getting training area set up—Everyone was told today about appearance—Polished boots etc—Stateside in a combat zone
  Up again late tonight exchanging war stories with some of my old B Co men

> "There is one unalterable difference between civilian and a soldier; the civilian never does more than he is paid to do."
>
> Erwin Rommel

All too often I was reminded that although I understood combat, there was still much to learn about the Army. Those of us who had "come of age" in the bloody paddies and jungles could scarcely believe the emphasis on personal appearance by those senior officers who had developed their standards on parade fields and company areas of raked gravel and painted rocks. The efforts of the higher brass to infuse peacetime regulations into the war zone were often as not ignored by us who knew that starched fatigues and spit-shined boots might make a man look like a soldier but have little influence on his ability to fight.

The more of the life in the rear I experienced, the clearer my realization that too many of our midlevel and senior officers were trying to run the war "by the book" when there was not a printed page in existence on our "different kind of war." My convictions became stronger that the only way we would ever truly win in the conflict would be for it to last long enough for those who had fought as lieutenants and captains to be in charge of the overall war effort. We endured the hardships, shouldered the responsibilities, and suffered the casualties while having damn little or nothing to say in how the war should be run.

My feelings have changed little over the years. We who fought the war have made the adjustments from the reality of muddy-boot battlefields to the traditional spit-and-polish parade field peacetime Army with reasonable success. However, there remains one staunch difference: We who fought learned not to sweat the small things. After you have run out of ammunition in the middle of a fire fight against a far superior force, or when you have been virtually surrounded while your artillery is destroyed, or when you are cut off from your main force with no commo, it is difficult to get upset about a pair of shoes not shined or paperwork that is a bit late in getting to a warm office at a secure stateside post. My basic premise has remained that if no one is bleeding or in danger of dying, there is no reason to get excited.

20 FEBRUARY 1970

Building of ranges—Visit from DCO COL Shelton—
Seemed impressed with our work—Training is impor-

tant—But sometimes people need to realize there is a
war going on
 At least time goes faster when you are busy

The days of planning and building the refresher courses
worked as a good transition from the environment that had
been mine as a field soldier. Nightmares still had me wak-
ing in reach of my rifle or a radio. Sudden noises would
send me diving for cover. All in all, however, I was adjusting to a world of sanity where there was a future beyond the next fire fight.

Linda had hinted at and finally asked in her letters why
I almost never mentioned Reveilee in my correspondence.
I responded that with what had gone on before and after
her birth, it had been difficult to believe I had a child. It
had been hard to ask about someone I hardly acknowledged existed. That was fading now with most of the danger past and home, wife, and baby before me.

21 FEBRUARY 1970

Black Horse
 I've re-read some of my writings since getting off the
line—Not very important are the things I've done—Then
I think of all the worthless bastards that this is all they
do their entire tour

I now understood why those in the rear avoided the field
troops when they came in for brief breaks. Despite my

previous experiences, I no longer truly felt a part of the warrior society. I had no great desire to return to battle, yet I felt almost ashamed that I was no longer sharing the dangers with my former command.

---

22 FEBRUARY 1970

> More of the same—And time goes on and USA gets closer and closer
>
> Saw an excellent movie tonight, *Castle Keep*—Best I've seen in a long time—It shows much of the humor of war—That only those who "have seen blood" can appreciate

Of all the things that help get a man through the day-to-day terror and boredom of war, perhaps humor is the most important. With GIs there is far more laughter than tears. In an existence where death and blood were so common that they virtually became an accepted part of the lifestyle, there can be little surprise that the humor was as much morbid as truly funny.

A soldier frantically trying to rip his clothes off after lying down in an ant bed brought far more laughter than sympathy. "Borrowing" the platoon leader's air mattress for a tryst with a prostitute moved men to hysterical tears. No one but a combat veteran could see the humor in the answer to a naive, incensed news reporter's question of

"How could you kill a woman?" when the 18-year-old sniper innocently replied, "Women can't run as fast so you don't lead them as far with your sights."

Comedy at its best is ridiculous, and what could be more ridiculous than men who have never met and know nothing of each other's origins going out and trying to kill each other? What else could you do except laugh? We were not old enough to cry and still maintain our image to ourselves and each other. The satiric humor in the motion picture *Castle Keep* had all of us laughing wildly. A few days after I saw the movie, I was pleased to find the paperback book the film was based on. Several passages of Eastlake's work found their way into my journal.

✈ 23 FEBRUARY 1970

> More training—Bn has more people in for training than they do in field chasing Chuck
> Bn has another new cpt—CPT Kiper—A West Pointer—Has been in Germany for a couple of years— We have several like that
> I am very happy I arrived in RVN as a 2LT—Every officer should

LTC Ivey was pleased with the progress of my refresher training course and decided to bring a company in to try it out. I knew the troops would not be happy with the concept of refresher training, so I had included as many of the things they would like as possible. When the troops saw that they would have the opportunity to fire an almost unlimited amount of ammunition with their various weapons, their morale took a marked upswing.

The first morning's training began with everyone confirming the zero of his weapons. Then each man went through a round-robin series of ranges which allowed him to fire the M-60 machine gun and M-79 grenade launcher and to throw several M-26 fragmentation grenades. Next, each man received a refresher in quick-kill techniques, followed by his going through a course of ten pop-up targets in which he used the lunge-and-shoot method without delaying to line up the rifle sights.

In the afternoon the training graduated to squad operations, beginning with techniques of maneuver and culminating with squads assaulting a bunker complex with live fire.

As this was the first time my refresher course was being used, I was learning, too—with nearly disastrous results. To mark the squad objective, I had run a long wire, attached to an electric blasting cap, to a white phosphorous grenade. I was walking back to the detonator after I had set the first device when either a short in the wire or static electricity exploded the WP grenade prematurely. Pieces of white phosphorous, which could burn through flesh without any means of extinguishing it, landed all around me. If the grenade had gone off a second or two before, I would have become a victim of my own training range. I made a mental note to use only regular smoke grenades in the future.

> Same, same
> More training that the troops don't want
> Night firing nearly hit an ARVN ambush—Missed—
> Damn it

> > "A play about a soldier boy who, when he left home, was given a bullet by his mother to put in his breast pocket for protection. In the first German attack, a Kraut threw a Bible at the soldier boy and it hit him right here and the bullet saved his life."
> >
> > From *Castle Keep*
> > W. Eastlake

The second day of refresher training continued with platoon-size operations. The schedule also included time for instructions on ambush procedures and emplacement of the mechanical Claymore ambushes.

Although the ranges were under my control, I made sure that instructions to the troops were given through the company commander and his chain of command. I provided the facilities and ammunition but was careful not to infringe on the commander's turf. I had not forgotten my resentment toward anyone besides the battalion commander telling my troops what to do.

Our training was not limited to daytime procedures only. The first night training proved useful to us as well as teaching the local ARVN force a lesson. We had just begun our night fire when several flares and frantic radio calls came from five hundred meters downrange. It took nearly an hour to sort out that an ARVN platoon had set up its position nearly a klick short of the location that had been coordinated with our TOC. Their attempt to save a few steps and to stay near the protection of the fire base had very nearly cost them in blood.

My journal entry reflecting displeasure at not having inflicted casualties on the ARVNs was not recorded in jest. The ARVNs were always taking the easiest way out and continued to be happy to defend the fire base while the GIs went into the jungle.

═══════════════════

🚁 25 FEBRUARY 1970

Finally finished this training session
Back to slow days

> "War is not much fighting. War is drinking. War is trying to forget the killing and the hurt that happened. War is all of those drunken nights in technicolor. But most of all war is a Cinderella story where each man turns into a soldier."
>
> *Castle Keep*
> W. Eastlake

The final day of the training was unstructured and allowed the company commander to use the morning in any manner he desired. After a hot noon meal, the company returned to the real war while I went back to finalizing the training course.

I had mostly enjoyed the three-day refresher period because time had passed quickly.

═══════════════════════════════════════

✈ 26 FEBRUARY 1970

Time goes on—Everything very quiet in the AO

"There's only one proper end for a professional soldier, a quick death inflicted by the last bullet of the last battle."

GEN George S. Patton

"Actually, why I'm fighting over here is quite cut and dried—I'm trying to stay alive."

SGT Mike (cartoon)
Army Times

My journal entries became briefer as time passed at Black Horse. The days blended into each other with little of note to distinguish one from the other.

Although the amount of my recorded words of day-to-day events were not massive nor remotely related to literature, I was proud of my efforts. After reading several books based on diaries kept by World War II and Korean War veterans, I began to think that one day there might be interest in publishing my account of our war. I wrote those thoughts to Linda, saying that "maybe someday I will want to expand these journals and share them with others.'' I had no idea it would be sixteen years before that time would come.

✈ 27 FEBRUARY 1970

50 days and ''Homeward Bound''—WOW!

Many soldiers kept calendars, crossing off each day since their arrival in-country. Others waited until they were down to one hundred days and then marked off each day— sometimes on creative calendars. Posters of nude females with voluptuous breasts converted nicely into calendars when gridded in squares. The troops would number each block on the figure with remaining days, coloring each in as they passed. Numbers 3 and 2 were usually over the nipples and the final ''day'' between her legs. I had no calendar for myself beyond my journal. I did not need numbered blocks to remind me of how many days remained.

My written plans and schedules for the refresher training were now complete. Sergeant Major Quick provided me a typist to prepare the mimeograph masters for reproduction. The clerk had claimed to be an expert typist in order to leave his rifleman's job in the field during his last weeks in-country. His two-fingered, hunt-and-peck skills better testified to his proficiency as a fast talker than a fast typist; however, as he often said, ''All we have is time,'' and eventually we completed and won our battle with the paperwork.

✈ **28 FEBRUARY 1970**

> B Co's LT Bochnevetch was killed today—By a mechanical GI ambush—From his plt—His wife to have baby in about a month—When he came into Bravo I thought he would be good when he got his feet on the ground—Looks as if he didn't learn fast enough
>
> This damn war

I was sitting at my desk writing a letter home when a new RTO from the TOC ran into my office saying, "Bravo's got trouble." He did not wait for an acknowledgment before he hurried back to his post with me just behind him.

As I entered the sandbagged TOC, I saw the familiar, frantic, yet controlled multiple radio and telephone transmissions passing along reports and requests for support. Above the many voices over the radio amplifiers, I could hear one shouting between sobs, "Where the hell is the dust-off? He's hit in the chest—losing blood and air. We can't get it stopped. Hurry up, goddamn it, or he's not going to make it!"

The TOC duty officer calmly responded that the medivac was inbound and was "05" from arrival. As he talked, he leafed through a line number roster searching for the number he had written at the top of the paper. I watched over his shoulder as his finger went down the page, stopped at the appropriate line number and followed the line to the right. His finger stopped at the name of Bochnevetch, Sherman.

Minutes later I could hear the second platoon sergeant directing the lowering of the dust-off's jungle penetrater. The pilot requested a status report. The sergeant responded, "He's hit bad through the lungs. He's quit breathing. God! Please hurry!"

A minute later the pilot reported he had the patient aboard and was heading for the hospital. After a short pause, he came back on the net saying he was sorry to tell us he was changing his destination to the morgue.

I stayed in the TOC long enough to listen to the reports on what had happened. In a broken voice the platoon sergeant explained that a mechanical ambush had detonated while they were checking the electrical circuit. The ambush squad had followed the proper safety procedures and set up a safe distance from the mines. When the Claymores had unexpectedly exploded, they had thought no one had been injured until they heard groans. Apparently Skip had left the perimeter to check out a nearby trail. Although he had not been close to the mechanical ambush, a steel slug had managed to penetrate the thick jungle, striking him in the chest. Of hundreds of steel balls in the Claymores, all had missed except for one solitary bit of metal. It had been enough to leave Skip Bochnevetch dead and a young, pregnant woman a widow.

> Black Horse
>> Today I can say "next month"
>> Completed paperwork in preparation for training
>> Letter from Linda Ann today—Says I will be a Florida
> Ranger Instructor—Sounds damn good

My nimble, two-fingered clerk-typist had finally finished the mimeograph masters of the refresher training outlines and we were ready to go to press. We declared victory without counting up the pencils broken and draft copies wadded up and thrown in the trash basket.

The future after Vietnam was focusing more clearly. A letter from Linda brought news that although I would be assigned to Fort Benning, Georgia, my duty position would be as an instructor at the Florida Ranger Camp at Eglin Air Force Base. I was pleased with the news because my Ranger training before Vietnam had without a doubt offered the best preparation for the war. The idea of trading the jungle of Nam for the swamps of the Florida panhandle did not bother me at all, for no one would be shooting real bullets at me and a warm, occupied bed would be waiting after work.

Linda wrote that this would probably be the only time she would know about our next assignment before I did. Her information had come by phone from my brother, who had called the Benning personnel officer.

2 MARCH 1970

> Black Horse
> Long bull session with 1st SGT Ploeger—C Co Top—
> About old C Co days
> Tonight a couple of troops beat hell out of one they
> caught smoking pot—One of the guys that did the beating
> said, "Guys are cooling in the ground because of SOBs like
> that"—We need more of this—It is good military justice

Drug use, according to all reports, was increasing rapidly back at the BMB-Long Binh complex and all across the protected rear areas of the country. In the boring citadels of REMFs, the accounts of the abundance of marijuana, opium, and heroin were likely accurate. However, the black mark of drug abuse was just another of the unwarranted slanders heaped on the field soldiers. Combat troops continued to police themselves.

3 MARCH 1970

> Began B Co training—Not much going on around here
> Soldier in 1st plt of B Co received a "Dear John"

letter—He was crazy anyway—More so now
Kind of miss the CO job

"War is the supreme test of man, in which he rises
to heights never approached in any other activity."
GEN George S. Patton

The soldier's Dear John Letter was a reminder of how young the men were. Written on lined notebook paper, the letter from the now-former girlfriend noted that she was writing during her high school study hall. She explained that she could no longer keep her agreement not to date anyone else because she wanted to go out with the captain of the basketball team. The spurned boyfriend was not yet a year out of high school himself; however, he had received one valor award and was respected as a first class point man. He had probably killed nearly as many men as there were players on the girl's new boyfriend's basketball team.

4 MARCH 1970

Dr. Mathson, Bn Surgeon, told me today that B Co medics told him I was best CO they ever had—I told him I didn't doubt it

"The chief foundations of all states, new as well as old or composite, are good laws and good arms, and

> as there cannot be good laws where the state is not
> well armed, it follows that where they are well
> armed, they have good laws."
>
> Niccoló Machiavelli
> in *The Prince*

My visit to the battalion surgeon was for medical reasons rather than to receive praise, but I appreciated hearing what my medics had to say nonetheless. Despite the more sanitary living conditions of the fire base, several boils and patches of bamboo poisoning had not yet healed since leaving the field. MAJ Mathson examined the infected areas and administered several injections of antibiotics.

Doc explained that the multiple dosage was required because I had built up a resistance through the many penicillin tablets I had been taking. On his advice, I ceased taking all pills except malaria tablets. His treatment must have been correct because within a week the infections dried up and began to heal.

🚁 5 MARCH 1970

Received some fantastic pictures of Reveilee today—I can hardly wait to see her—Actually I try not to think "short"

Tonight CPT McGinnis and I were told the men had a whore on the bunker line—We checked on it—Found

the whore on a cot—A soldier under the cot hiding from
us—We turned her in to ARVN security

One of the few good things about boring days was that
everyone had time to look at baby pictures. I took full
advantage of the situation.

McGinnis and I were working late when an NCO in
charge of the bunker line reported there was an uninvited
visitor. We first checked the bunkers along the outer berm
and found nothing but soldiers staring into the darkness.
In an area behind the outer line was another series of
bunkers that served as a sleeping area for off-duty guards.
We thought it was vacant until we discovered a young girl
hiding under a poncho liner on a cot in a dark corner. She
had not been alone very long by the looks of the roll of
money in her hand.

As the hooker got up, I noticed a foot sticking out from
under the cot. My flashlight revealed one of my old soldiers from Bravo Company. The soldier explained that an
ARVN had delivered the whore and that only those off
duty had visited her. He obviously expected to be in trouble for being caught with her, but all I did was to tell him
not to let it happen again. I added the advice that he was
too near DEROS to be running the risk of taking a case
of VD home with him.

McGinnis and I turned the prostitute over to the ARVN
MPs. They seemed unconcerned, saying that she was
probably the wife or girlfriend of one of the training center
staff. From the looks on their faces, I doubt if she was
paid for further services the remainder of the night.

Continue B Co training—CPT Rendon, my roommate, has a TV—So we stay up later now
Damn—I'm ready to go home

> " 'I feel so grateful for being here,' I said. 'You see, I was on the line for six months, and I expected to be killed every minute of that time. . . . I never expected to come out alive. And now to be here between clean sheets, with everybody so nice to me.' "
>
> PVT Henry Demarest, after losing a leg.
> *Company K*
> William March

Due to an overabundance of aircraft, many soldiers were getting their tours reduced by two or three days. No one knew if the extra Freedom Birds had been a scheduling error or if someone had planned for enough seats to accommodate the number of men who had arrived a year before without figuring in the casualties. Whatever the reason, no one complained about the opportunity to go home a few days early.

Rumors were circulating that by next month the "drops," as they were called, could extend to ten days. I listened to the rumors but kept my mental count down in line with my original 18 April DEROS. Drops became so much a part of conversation that items difficult to secure through supply channels were referred to as "hard to get as a 30-day drop."

> B Co training produced 5 wounded today—Just slight
> frag wounds—New man on M-79—I never allowed a new
> man to carry an M-79—Should be one of your most ex-
> perienced, reliable men

I observed Bravo Company with a far more critical eye
than they deserved. My outlook was not limited to Bravo,
however, as I followed my old Charlie platoon and recon
with like convictions that no one could do as well as I had
in their leadership. If there was any saving grace to my
lack of humility, it was that I at least would admit to my
abundance of self-confidence.

The injury to the five men by an FNG M-79 gunner
rankled the hell out of me. Enough men were being
wounded and killed in the jungle without our doing it to
ourselves on training ranges.

> Went to services this morning—I recall when I was in
> C Co the BN Chaplain told the Bn CO that C Co only
> thought about killing—This is bad?

> We had a steak cook-out—I did the cooking—3 months ago I would have given a week's pay for what I take for granted now

No two branches of the Army could be more widely separated in their purposes than the Chaplain Corps and the Infantry. One is dedicated to saving souls and providing comfort while the other does its best to kill and destroy. I felt no more hostile toward the chaplain's remarks about our thinking only of killing than he would have felt if we said he prayed well.

✈ 9 MARCH 1970

> 40 days—WOW—It could start raining now and I would still beat the flood home—Hope I can get a few days' drop

Many of the soldiers became nearly paranoid as they got short. Stories of men killed their last week in-country by the enemy or accident were rampant. I listened and continued to be as careful as possible; however, I became more confident of making it home in one piece. If the gooks had not killed me in nearly ten months in the boonies, I was not going to worry about my mortality in a base camp. Acts of God did not bother me either. I was too short to drown in a biblical, 40-day flood. Besides, there was not a cloud in the sky.

Late that night I found that while I had been hoping for a drop, McGinnis was doing something about his going home early. My old company commander had had a seamstress in Xuan Luc make three NVA battle flags. When he arrived at Long Binh to out-process before boarding a Freedom Bird, he intended to be loaded with bribes of "genuine" NVA flags that would speed the usual delays.

After McGinnis showed me the flags, he decided they needed a little work to add to their authenticity. Using a small piece of C-4, we burned the flags' edges to make them appear as though they had been near napalm strikes. McGinnis was still not satisfied, so he reached into a wall locker and pulled out a small 22-caliber rifle which he said had been a gift from the Frenchman at Cam Tam.

We soon had killed several sparrow-like birds that nested in the eaves of our hooch. The birds' blood stained the flags' fabric so well we now felt sure McGinnis's stories about the hard-fought-for war trophies would be readily believed. We laughed as we wondered about the magnificent war story some clerk would someday tell of the flag.

---

10 MARCH 1970

Black Horse
    Charlie Co in for training—Bn AO is very quiet
    Boy, am I ready to go home

There were few familiar faces remaining in the ranks of Charlie Company. DeForrest had come through Black Horse a few days before on his way to BMB and a Freedom Bird. We shook hands and bid each other an unemotional good-bye, more overcome with our surprise that we had both made it a year than remembering the time that had gotten us there.

During Charlie Company's training, their commander, CPT Delano, gave me a copy of a Document Exploitation Report that was a result of my old platoon's actions in August. Delano said I was likely one of the last ones left who had participated in the capture of the documents.

The three-page typed report was a translation of the diary of Nguyen Van Nhiog, covering the time period of the first of January through mid-August, 1969. Nguyen's journal entries were briefer than mine in that he had recorded only a sentence or two marking each day. There were many similarities, however.

The NVA soldier wrote in January about training and making last visits to family and friends near Hanoi. On 30 January he wrote, "Received my equipment in preparation to go liberate my country." After a final visit home, Nguyen started south on 8 February. The route of his journey was marked in his journal by stops at numbered stations with no reference to map locations or nearby landmarks, so the journal had been of little use to our Intel analysts. February was filled with notes of travel by rail and boat before entering South Vietnam by foot on 1 March.

The next five months were filled with daily notations that infantrymen from any war or cause would recognize: "moved for six hours"; "many slopes to cross"; "very hot today."

Nguyen also noted without detail of "B-52 strike nearly

got us," and days later, "We feel pretty good today because didn't make any air strikes our way." His comments, "enjoyed a day off in rest camp," and "good supply of rice today," seemed very familiar as did his complaints about his heavy pack, the constant rain, and his coming down with a fever.

A week before his final entry in August, the NVA diary writer noted that he had to retrace a day's march because he did not have an "introduction paper." Bureaucracy apparently reigned on both sides of the jungle.

Nguyen's journal noted only one direct contact with his enemy other than air strikes and helicopter gunships. He made no mention of casualties received by nor inflicted on the ARVN force he faced. His first contact with Americans was also his last. "Everything is ready for running away when we see enemy coming" was his final diary entry.

I suppose that I should have felt a kinship with my fellow keeper of journals. I did not. Killing the NVA writer had been far more satisfying than reading his words. I would not have expected him to feel differently if our roles had been reversed and my journals were later translated into Vietnamese. The late Nguyen Van Nhiog and I were infantrymen first—writing in journals was just something to help pass the time.

Today I feel somewhat differently. I still have no regrets about the demise of the NVA diary keeper, yet rereading his journal has done more to humanize the enemy for me than all the passing years.

✈ 11 MARCH 1970

> Training with C Co—Not much going on
> Am going to Vung Tau as soon as possible—This damn
> place driving me crazy

My attempts to go on another R&R to either Taiwan or Australia never worked out. The few open dates conflicted with times companies were scheduled for refresher training, which required my presence at Black Horse.

I had about given up taking a leave from the fire base when LT Stewart told me about a couple of allocations for the in-country R&R Center at the old French coastal resort town of Vung Tau. The boredom of assisting training and counting days drove me quickly to see the battalion commander to secure permission for the break.

✈ 12 MARCH 1970

> Black Horse
> Finshed C Co training—Went to BMB
> Incoming rockets tonight—We didn't even stop our
> poker game

Stewart and I headed for BMB en route to our R&R in Vung Tau. Soon after our arrival we were sitting in a reasonably "friendly" poker game in the Echo Company orderly room with Norm Sassner and several other XOs.

About 2200 two large rockets impacted near enough to shake the building, knocking dust from the open rafters onto the Army blanket covering our card table. Seconds later the lights dimmed and then went out across most of the base. We could hear the shouts of men running to bunkers. After several candles were lit, one of the players matter-of-factly said, "Lanning, you and Sassner are the shortest—do we play or go to the bunkers?"

Before I could respond, Norm, with two weeks till DEROS, said, "Shut up and deal. I'm due to finally win a hand."

We continued by candlelight until the lights came back on and then played on until near sunup. I do not recall if Norm ever won a hand or not.

✈ 13 MARCH 1970

Vung Tau

   Rode to Vung Tau with D Co—We arrived at beach— In 60 seconds every one of troops disappeared

   South China Sea—Surrounded by mountains—Resembles Calif. coastline—R&R Center is very nice—Hotel—Free beer—Town has many very nice bars and

clubs—Coastline has many large concrete embank-
ments—Most likely installed by the Japanese

Delta Company had managed to gain permission for a
day and night in Vung Tau during their BMB standdown.
At the invitation of CPT Kiper, their new commander,
Stewart and I joined their convoy for the three-hour drive.

The Pacific Hotel was a former French accommodation
complete with louvered window shutters and covered ver-
andas. Operated for officers, each room of the hotel came
with an icebox full of cold San Miguel beer from the Phil-
ippines. The only irritant among the luxury was knowing
that the military operators who ran it received the same
combat pay as grunts in the boonies.

Rumors had it that Vung Tau was an R&R center for
the enemy as well as GIs, and, as a result, no attacks or
sabotage had ever occurred there. I do not know how accurate those stories were, but the city had no war damage.
Outdoor cafes dotted wide tree-lined streets where potted
flowers hung from balconies. Except for the now-vacant
concrete hillside bunkers built in a "more popular war,"
there was no sign of military operations. A large rusting
freighter on the beach looked like it was there of its own
accord rather than by influence of man or nature.

We ate well, drank more than too much, and marveled
at how the war seemed so far away.

✈ 14 MARCH 1970

Black Horse
   Rode back to BMB with D Co
   Had a fantastic time in Vung Tau—Very relaxing and enjoyable—The people there I doubt are aware there is a war going on
   Australian band at club tonight—Outstanding

We spent the morning on the beach letting the sun treat well-earned hangovers. Baby san vendors delivered fruit, bowls of noodles, and Vietnamese "33" brand beer. I tried it all except duck eggs incubated halfway to hatching, boiled, and eaten directly from the shell.

Numerous military-age men, as well as children, who were missing limbs or eyesight, begged along the beach. One young man whose arms ended at the wrist had a note written in English pinned to his shirt saying the VC had cut off his hands. Few of the soldiers offered any charity. As one troop stated, "I've given all I intend to this goddamn country."

Black Horse
  Rode out this morning with Bravo Co
  Fired my 9-mm today—Damn fine
  Up late talking and drinking with CPT Atkins about
carnivals—He plans to get out of Army—Take over his
father-in-law's show—Told me I could get a job with them
any time—Always wanted to be a carnie—Guess I had
better keep the job I've got, however

Before leaving BMB, I went by the MP station in order
to process paperwork to legally take home the 9-mm P-38
pistol captured in November. After completing the forms,
I reported to a major who was the approving authority.

The major was a beefy, pasty-faced man who by all
appearances had not been in the sun his entire tour. He
fondled the gun passionately. After several minutes he
commented on the fine German craftsmanship of the pistol
and said, "You know, of course, that you can't take this
home. We will have to keep it here." He opened a desk
drawer and dropped the pistol inside.

I stared at the MP for a while and coldly replied, "Sir,
I don't have the appreciation for weapons that you evidently do. To me they are just tools of the trade, but the
gun is mine. I earned it and I'm taking it home. Don't try
to bullshit me so you can keep it yourself. If you want
one, go out in the jungle and get your own."

The officer's knuckles turned white as he gripped the
edge of his desk. Finally he let out a forced laugh, saying,

"Ah, I was just joking, Lieutenant. Let me sign your forms so you can get out of here."

Back at Black Horse that night, I ended up talking to Tom Atkins. Tom's job was to provide medical and food supplies to nearby villages in hopes of winning their hearts and minds. It was a futile task that no one wanted to perform except Tom. He was one of the few GIs I met who had a genuine affection for the Vietnamese and did his best to help in every possible way.

I knew nothing about Tom's background until we talked of plans after DEROS. A few beers into the conversation, I joked that we should run away and join the circus. Tom replied that he could suggest something better. He retrieved a colored postcard from his gear that had a night view of a large carnival on the front. On the back, big bold letters spelled out THOMAS SHOWS, Winter Headquarters, Lennox, South Dakota. Several hours and many beers later I was ready to join the carnival.

In my next letter to Linda I wrote that maybe I would become a carnie. I closed, "Next month I will likely want to be a fireman." There was no need to tell my wife that these thoughts of other jobs were only dreams. We both already knew I intended to stay a soldier.

I stuck Tom's postcard in my journal and kept it. In 1977 while driving on a Texas interstate highway, I met a huge truck carrying a part of a Ferris wheel. On its side was painted THOMAS SHOWS. After illegally crossing the median and a speeding chase to catch the truck, I pulled it over and asked the driver if he knew Tom Atkins. He replied, "Sure, he's my boss. That's where I'm headed right now." An hour later I was sitting with Tom in his trailer headquarters. It was good to find the job offer still stood. Perhaps someday . . .

Black Horse
  Have been feeling lousy lately
  Assisted in interrogation of a Chieu Hoi we had here for questioning—Had walked to Cambodia for supplies before—Said he saw tanks, arty, and choppers (Red) there—He led another battalion to a cache site of weapons—About 50—He said they were left over from TET 68—Is worth about $5,000 US to him

  "Old soldiers never die,
  Only the young ones"

Latrine writing

The Chieu Hoi's stories were interesting but yielded little information of any value for operations in our AO. For three years as an NVA private he had primarily been responsible for moving supplies from one location to another before he had seen an air-dropped leaflet promising money if he "came over" to our side. Cash evidently outweighed his previous political convictions.

Black Horse
    Just another day closer to DEROS—Still no word on
a drop
    AO is still very quiet
    Time goes slowly on

Going home was constantly on my mind; however, there was more to do than just think about it. I wrote letters to Linda which included paperwork and instruction for transfer of household goods in storage at Fort Bragg to Eglin Air Force Base.

I received a letter from my mother reporting on the progress of the house my parents were building. They would be moved in before I arrived. I was happy for them rather than disappointed that I would not go ''home'' to the same house. My only hope was that Mom would not have to move her map of Vietnam to her new living room wall to follow any more of her sons' travels.

Black Horse
   Time goes on—Most exciting part of day is the night—
Usually just drink beer and tell war stories
   Army is often very discouraging—Especially near the
end or beginning of a tour or assignment

> "The morn will dawn that fatal day,
> I'll not be home, but far away,
> In the warm jungle growth,
> Live and green,
> When they tear through me—
> Angry and mean."

>   CPT Joe Bush
>   Written in 1966
>   KIA Laos 1969
>   Quoted in *Time*, 23 Mar 70

Joe Bush had been an upperclassman at A&M whom I
had greatly admired. I heard nothing of him after his graduation in 1966 until reading of his death in *Time* magazine.
The fact that another grunt had been killed in Southeast
Asia was not significant enough news for national media
coverage; however, the location of his death was. Supposedly we had no troops operating in Laos in any capacity.
The media, as usual, were far more concerned with a per-
ceived "escalation of the war" than with the fact that another young American would grow no older.

Information that we were conducting special operations
outside Vietnam was no surprise to me. In the past months
more than one friend had made reference to mutual ac-

quaintances assigned as special advisors in Laos and Cambodia. I also overheard strong hints of brief operations in North Vietnam.

I was not bothered by where we were fighting the enemy. I supported going after the gooks wherever they could be found. What did bother me was routinely learning about the deaths of friends.

🐎 19 MARCH 1970

Black Horse

One of B Co men hit a grenade booby trap today—SP4 Dalton—1st Platoon—Not too bad I understand. 2nd time for him to be wounded. Had a rear job with S-4, volunteered to go back out. I suspect booby trap set by GI or ARVN rather than enemy. I never allowed it—not because of any moral standard but because of instances such as this.

Each evening I attended the 1700 briefing for the battalion commander where the S-2 and S-3 summarized the day's events and announced plans for the next. The AO was so quiet that the booby trap incident was the major event of the day. Apparently it was true that the dinks were satisfied to lie low or abandon the area completely until the 199th departed, leaving the less aggressive ARVNs in charge. Yet, I was aware that everything could be calm for weeks only to explode instantly into violent contacts and bloodletting.

After the briefing, the battalion surgeon told me of another incident. One of the senior medics, newly arrived for a second tour, had shot himself in the hand with a 45-caliber pistol—twice. The soldier claimed the first shot to have been accidental and the second to have been caused by involuntary muscle contractions from the pain and shock of the first. No one questioned the cause of the second round; it was the first that was the problem. Several statements from other soldiers had revealed the medic had openly bragged that he would find a way out of the field. Evidently he had succeeded; however, the two large slugs had left him minus most of a hand. The incident reinforced my belief that the only practical use of the damn 45-caliber pistol was to shoot oneself.

20 MARCH 1970

Black Horse
    Went to a Med Cap at Xa Thai Gao—Team treated about 219 people—Few actually sick—Just wanted a little attention and some of the free drugs and candy
    Some very nice unoccupied French villas in the village—Really wish I could have visited here before the war

Tom Atkins had arranged for a team of medics to set up a one-day clinic in Thai Gao. Despite the fact that the village, located between Black Horse and Cam Tam, had been the source of sniper fire in my direction twice while I was in the field, I accepted Tom's invitation to go along. Maybe I hoped the change of pace would pass the day a little more quickly.

Using a bull horn, Atkins's interpreter quickly assembled the villagers with promises of food and candy. After the handouts, the groups queued up for medical checks. Other than a baby with an eye infection and a woman with a pus-filled, lacerated arm, they appeared to be in good shape. However, once the medics started prescribing pills for various complaints, everyone seemed to have some ailment.

I watched as the medics handed out capsules and liquid medicine in unmarked containers. The interpreters rapidly translated the medics' instructions to "take one of these four times a day," "two of these once a day," and "a capful of this as needed." I could hardly follow the instructions in English and saw no way that the "patients" could understand when to do what after the rapid conversion to Vietnamese.

I finally asked a medic if they were doing any good and if he thought the medical supplies might end up in the hands of the enemy. He answered the first part of my question by only responding to the second, saying, "It really doesn't make any difference. All we are giving them is aspirin, vitamin pills, and cough syrup."

I walked away, spending the rest of the day sitting in Tom's jeep with his driver listening to an AFN radio tape of the NIT basketball finals. I do not recall who played, or won, for I cared only to pass the time.

🚁 21 MARCH 1970

Black Horse
So short I "sleep in a match box"

> "Every man in this battalion is a man. Some are only 18. Some are old men—about 23."
>
> LTC B. F. Ivey, CO
> 2/3 199th LIB

It was difficult to think of going home without being reminded that a second tour was likely after a year in the States. Although Nixon was withdrawing units and reducing the number of men committed to the war zone, I could see no end to the conflict. Matter-of-factly, I wrote my wife, "I believe it will be quite awhile before the US Infantryman is not required to keep South Vietnam free."

LTC Ivey made his comment about the battalion to a group of twenty replacements. When he mentioned "old men—about 23," he caught my eye. We knew how much older these FNGs would be at the end of a year in-country. We also both realized that many of the young men would never reach 23—or 19, for that matter.

> Black Horse
>
> Went to services this morning—Religion is very important to a soldier—I remember checking the pockets of a badly wounded man—His clothes had been cut off so we could get to his wounds—In his front pocket was a blood-soaked, small Bible

During World War II a popular saying had it that "there are no atheists in foxholes." From my observations, I would say that men in uniform look to God on the battlefield for two reasons. First, every man wants to survive, and he feels a need to "cover all the bases." There has never been any evidence that prayer does any harm and—who knows for sure?—it might help when the bullets begin to fly. Second, and perhaps more important, a battlefield bears no similarity to home and the day-to-day routines. In a war zone, one of the few things that remains the same is religious ceremony. Chaplains quoted the same Bible verses that we had heard in Sunday School as children. Communion followed the same rituals as in the neighborhood parishes of our youth. If nothing else, religion offered familiar words and procedures in the midst of a world that seemed upside down.

For most men, religion offered stability and comfort in a setting of turbulence and terror. For others, including myself, the war brought the first doubts that any supreme or divine being was really in control or cared what mankind was doing to itself in our small corner of the world.

23 MARCH 1970

Black Horse
More of the same—Just watch the calendar

News reports said that Nixon had directed a reduction of 50,000 troops in Vietnam by 15 April. To meet the quotas, soldiers were receiving drops of up to two weeks ahead of their scheduled DEROS. My hopes of an early-out soared until stories began circulating that the drop did not apply to officers.

A letter from my mother mentioned a visit by three ARVN captains to their home in West Texas the week before. The three officers had been at Fort Benning for a year's training in the same class with my brother and had stopped at my parents' house at his invitation on their cross-country bus ride. I wondered if they had found my home as different as I found their native land.

24 MARCH 1970

Black Horse
Time must be going faster than I thought—Forgot to write for a few days

When I realized there had been no journal entries for a few days, I went back and filled in the pages the best I could recall. It was not difficult; little had happened.

✈ **25 MARCH 1970**

> Black Horse
>   Pretty slow days—But short enough not to be worried about it

Brian Schmalz, now working on the battalion staff, gave me several copies of pictures he had taken shortly before my departure from Bravo Company. One was of the platoon leaders, FO, and myself. Standing in the middle was Skip Bochnevitch.

It was not until writing this book that I dragged out the many slides and pictures sent home to Linda. While reviewing the several hundred scenes of Vietnam, I realized that nearly every one of the snapshots contained at least one man who had been killed or wounded.

✈ 26 MARCH 1970

Black Horse
   Good news today—5-day drop—DEROS 13 April—Go
to 90th Replacement on 10th
   LT Sassner's short-time party tonight—Fairly good
   Checked today on final things before I begin clearing—
BMB is not too good of a place—Too many damn REMFs
   Word from Ranger Dept today—I definitely will be
going to Florida

News of the five-day drop and the confirmation of my assignment to the Florida Ranger School made for an outstanding day. I was no longer short—now I was damn near next.

Norm Sassner had called to invite me to his going-home party at BMB. When I told him there might be a problem with transportation, he told me not to worry because he would take care of it. After coordinating a ride with the battalion mail courier, I stopped by the TOC to let the S-3 know where I was going. As Major Humphrey and I were talking, a helicopter pilot came over the radio saying he was inbound to pick up the Training Officer for urgent business at BMB. Hurriedly grabbing the handset, I responded that transportation had already been arranged and that he could return to his base.

To my boss's question about what was going on, I said that it was best he did not know. He shook his head, smiled, and said, ''Have a good time. See you tomorrow.''

A few hours later a young warrant officer, who had taken

on the additional duty as taxi helicopter pilot, and I were hoisting drinks in salute to our friend Norm.

---

27 MARCH 1970

> Black Horse
>   Back to BH—Rode with courier
>   Started getting training ready for Delta
>   E recon captured a large amount of documents to-day—Also one Chinese and one Russian flag

One more company to guide through refresher training and I would be BMB-bound to begin out-processing. There were a few improvements and adjustments I had to make; however, the basic procedures had been validated by the previous companies. With the schedules and written outlines now finalized, company commanders could conduct the training without assistance. My final job was done.

✹ 28 MARCH 1970

Black Horse
Began D Co training
Received Air Medal today
Have been playing a little basketball after chow—Anything to make the damn clock move a little faster
Heard that one of my better old C Co men deserted after reporting to Ft Hood, Tex—Guess he didn't like stateside Army

The orders accompanying the Air Medal stated that I received it for "meritorious achievement while participating in aerial flight." What this really meant was that I had made at least 25 airmobile assaults into unsecured LZs. It was just another "survivor" medal as far as I was concerned, but it would add more color to the ribbon rows on my dress uniform.

Basketball goals with crude wooden slat back boards had been set up at either end of an old concrete building slab. Most of the players were cooks and off-duty TOC radio operators who did not seem to mind my participating as long as I removed my shirt with its lieutenant bar. Those hard-fought games were probably the most dangerous activity on the fire base.

✈ 29 MARCH 1970

Black Horse   Easter Sunday
    About-all I can write is what I constantly think: Short!
Went to Easter services this morning

    "Perhaps someday these things will be a pleasure to
recall."

Aeneid
Virgil

   My last major holiday in Vietnam passed as slowly as
the hundreds of days that preceded it. At Easter services
I could only give a prayer of thanks for my survival and
ask for protection for those still in the jungle.

✈ 30 MARCH 1970

Black Horse
    I guess every man has a few set goals in his life—Mine
are
   1. To be a credit to my family and the Lanning name
   2. To not miss a minute of precious life
   3. To say or write something that will be remembered
      if only by one person

"You can tell when a division isn't fighting, when it isn't getting enough lieutenants killed."

GEN George Patton

As DEROS drew closer, it was time to formulate objectives for the future. Considering I was only 23 years old at the time, I suppose the goals were fairly reasonable—not so high that I could not achieve them.

All in all I felt no apprehension about what would follow Vietnam. I was sure that no challenge or problem would arise that could rival those of the past year. Whatever occurred I would face without self-doubt or a lack of confidence, for I had proven myself to myself and little else seemed important.

✈ 31 MARCH 1970

Black Horse
    Time goes on
    Damn mail strike has it so we are getting little or no mail—And mail means a hell of a lot

The postal workers' strike was just another reminder that many people back home were more interested in their own welfare than in the young men they had sent off to war. We felt no sympathy for their demands for pay raises and additional benefits. After all, we were virtually cut off from our only communications with family and friends. Not having my name called at mail call was bad enough— knowing that there were stacks of letters going undelivered made it worse.

I was now two weeks from going home. However, with the sporadic mail delivery and lack of specific flight time of my Freedom Bird, I had no way to let Linda know when I would arrive. The only arrangements we were sure of was that she and Reveilee would return to San Francisco on the first of the month to wait at Susan's for my arrival. Hopefully I would be able to call her from the Replacement Center or at some stop along the long flight east- ward.

✈ I APRIL 1970

BG William Bond, the 199th CG, was KIA today—He had gone in on ground to see D 17th Cav after a con- tact—He is the 5th general officer to be killed over here—He was one of two Ranger officers (generals) originally with Darby's Rangers—Vet of 3 wars

Found out today I only go to 90th 2 days prior—So no earlier than 11 April do I go home

General Bond had flown into the 17th Cav's location shortly after a major contact between the tracks and an NVA company. Both sides had taken heavy casualties, and the battlefield was littered with destroyed vehicles and dead enemy. A wounded gook playing dead fired a rifle-propelled grenade which exploded near Bond. A piece of shrapnel hit the general in the chest.

Vietnam was a war fought by platoon leaders and company commanders and the men they led. A lieutenant's being killed was routine. Captains died with regrettable frequency. The death of a major, lieutenant colonel, or colonel was rare because those ranks fought the war from base camps and in the air. A general's death was virtually unheard of.

Of the four generals killed before our brigade commander, all had died in aircraft crashes. Having the only general killed in ground combat during the war was a distinction no one coveted.

I had had nothing but the highest regard and respect for the general since our first encounter in the rain at Crystal. Although no one mentioned it, our sense of loss was also mixed with a striking reminder of our own mortality. Bond had survived the Germans in World War II and the North Koreans and Chinese in the Korean Conflict only to die at the hands of the North Vietnamese in his third war. Regardless of the number of wars men participate in, they only die once.

✈ 2 APRIL 1970

> Black Horse
>   Memorial Services for BG Bond today
>   Will go back to BMB day after tomorrow

Memorial services for General Bond were the same as those for other fallen Infantrymen. An M-16 with fixed bayonet was stuck in the ground with a steel pot sitting atop the rifle butt. Empty jungle boots stood alongside in a silent tribute to the departed commander.

✈ 3 APRIL THROUGH 11 APRIL 1970

> Black Horse—BMB
>   Did little but drink, raise hell, and think about home
>   DEROS, or going to 90th put off till one day prior
>   B Co had a man KIA—A man who had come in since
>   I'd left

After more than eleven and a half months of daily writing in my journal, I ceased. I can offer no explanation as to why I made no entry for the next nine days except that I had no desire to write. I did nothing in the final countdown of days that seemed to merit remembering. All I wanted was to go home.

I recall little of those last days, and there are no letters to help in their reconstruction. Several days earlier I had written everybody that the next time they heard from me, it would be in person. I sought no bunker to hide in to ensure my safety those last days—but I did retreat nevertheless, withdrawing into myself to count hours instead of days.

On the third of April, I made the rounds of the fire base to tell Ivey, Beckles, and others good-bye. My stops were brief; there was little to say that had not already been said or that could be put into words.

I looked for Bolenske and Schmalz, but their duties had them unavailable. I was sorry not to have the opportunity to say good-bye, for they were important characters in my year-long drama.

Early the morning of the fourth, I caught a ride with the battalion courier to BMB. Although we were in the middle of the dry season and no rain had fallen for months, I was not surprised that a downpour soaked us the entire drive. Somehow, it seemed appropriate, and it did not dampen my spirits. I had been wet many times prior in Vietnam, but I had never been on my way home.

The following days blended into a blur of waiting. I turned in equipment, updated records, and completed paperwork plodding my way through the usual Army bureaucratic maze. Somewhere along the line, I was awarded a third Bronze Star for Meritorious Service as a company commander and training officer. The only real impact of the newest decoration was that it and my recently presented Air Medal required that I stop by the uniform concession to update the rows of ribbons for my khakis.

The only memorable event in the whole process took

place when I turned in my rifle at the arms room. I went prepared to strip and clean the weapon, knowing the armorer in charge had the reputation of requiring each soldier—regardless of rank—to clean the rifle and pass his inspection. When I asked for the cleaning equipment, he surprised me by saying he would clean it for me. It was a tribute that meant even more than his sincere congratulation on completing my tour.

As I handed over my rifle, I found myself thinking about how noble I had felt when it was issued to me a year earlier. That time seemed so long ago. I felt strange leaving the weapon behind. It had served me well, and now it would be issued to another grunt. I hoped they would take good care of each other.

The out-processing procedures did not begin to fill the days. Between steps, I read stacks of paperback books, escaping into the pages as earnestly as possible in order to avoid looking at the clock. At night I headed for the club, drinking not to remember nor to forget but to have something to do.

I made no attempt to evaluate the year nor to put it in perspective. Hearing about the death of the Bravo soldier reminded me that the war was still going on and would continue to go on without me.

> 381st Co—90th Replacement Center
> Saw Ron Piper—Also several others I've met in Army
> Just sit and wait for bird

I was reversing my route of a year before as I returned to the replacement center where I had begun my tour. The instructions from the center's staff were simple: Find a bunk and check the manifest lists posted on the bulletin board several times daily. With no apology, we were also informed that the 24-hour waiting time had been extended to 72 hours.

After hearing the instructions and announcement, I secured my duffel bag and headed for the club, where I found Ron Piper seated at the bar. A year ago at this time, we were vying to see who would get to the war first—he on one plane, I on another. We resumed our conversation as though the interim time had never been, except that now we reflected on the war rather than anticipated it.

Ron and I were sitting at a table talking when I looked up to see Bolenske and Schmalz approaching. I felt surprise and affection at seeing them. As they pulled up chairs, Brian chuckled and asked, "What are you trying to do? Sneak out of country without buying us a beer?"

I tried to think of some witty comeback but only managed to mumble some feeble response. I was embarrassed at how much their gesture meant to me.

Bill and Brian stayed for only one beer because they had sandwiched their visit to me between other duties. Several times each of us tried to say something that befitted the occasion of a good-bye among soldiers who had shared so much. However, we mostly drank our beer in a silent camaraderie that was more meaningful than words.

When we finished our beers, I walked with the two to their jeep. After the handshakes and "Keep your heads down," they drove back to the war and I went back into the club. We never did say good-bye.

I spent the remainder of my time at the Replacement Center checking the manifests on the board, reading in my bunk, or exchanging war stories with other Infantrymen at the club. Except for an occasional aviator, nongrunts were not welcomed at our table, not that they seemed to want to join us anyway.

Late during my last night in Vietnam, I listened to a twenty-year old helicopter pilot drunkenly recount stories of hot LZs, shot-up aircraft, and lost friends. When the conversation changed to what trophies and souvenirs we had in our duffel bags, the young warrant officer said all he was taking home was memories.

After hearing his remarks, I made a quick trip back to my hooch to get the control panel clock that my Charlie platoon had stripped from the downed Huey on Butterfly Hill in July. I do not remember the aviator's name, nor did I ever see him again after that night. But I do recall how happy he was when I gave him the clock as a souvenir of the war.

In truth, giving him the gift was no real act of benevolence on my part. I was glad to be rid of any reminder of butterflies floating over rotting bodies. Now all I was taking home were my pistol, journals, and poncho liner. They were more than enough to provoke memories.

Before leaving the club, I gave Linda's San Francisco phone number to several officers manifested on planes that night. I hoped at least one would take the time to call her and let her know that I would soon be on my way.

14 APRIL 1970

1330 hours
    At last—Am manifested on Flight X2B4—Saturn Airways to the World
2128 hours
    Lift off from Binh Hoa—Thank you, Lord
    Exciting—Unbelievable on take-off—I think of every fire fight of importance, numbering about 30-40
    Stops at Yokota, Japan—Night—Anchorage, Alaska—Phoned Linda Ann—Alaska is just cold
2345 hours
    Arrived Travis Air Force Base

    I AM HOME!

Ron Piper woke me up shouting that he was manifested on the next plane and would be on his way within hours. Ron said he was sure I would be on the next list because he had arrived at the Replacement Center only shortly before I had. He added that to ensure that I was next he was giving me his "lucky rock." I thanked him for the small pebble, and, as an afterthought, I asked him how long he had carried the lucky piece. "Only a couple of days," he laughed. "I picked it up off the street when I got here. But it must work—I'm going home!"

Despite the newness of Ron's "charm," it must have indeed been lucky, for the next manifest had my name on it. By the time I changed into my khakis, the camp's loud-speakers were echoing orders for our flight to assemble. After various stops to change MPCs to greenbacks and to clear customs, we boarded buses to take us to Binh Hoa.

At the terminal, we spent more hours waiting. Finally we were herded out of the barn-like structure onto the floodlit runway apron. In the dim light, I could see the huge Saturn Airlines plane with faded paint, dirty win-dows, and a huge rust-colored spot on the fuselage. It was the most beautiful aircraft I had ever seen.

The plane filled rapidly and began to taxi as soon as the last troop took his seat. I glanced out a window for my final view of Vietnam. What I saw was the airman ground guide holding his two long, nose-coned flashlights above his head in the shape of a V. I closed my eyes and thought about the past year. My thoughts were disturbed only briefly when a deafening cheer marked our lift-off. My heart beat wildly with exuberance at reaching this time that had so often been in doubt and always had been far away.

The year flashed through my mind in scenes of death, blood, exhaustion, and boredom. As we gained altitude, my thoughts gave way to a single emotion—overwhelming pride.

By the time I again glanced out the bulkhead window, all I could see was moonlight glistening on the South China Sea.

I had been saving one last paperback for the flight home. The hours passed surprisingly fast as I escaped into the pages of Mario Puzo's *The Godfather*.

With a two-hour layover in Japan for refueling and the crossing of the International Date Line, we arrived in

Alaska at six o'clock in the evening of the same day we had left Vietnam. The pilot announced another two-hour stop, adding that the terminal bar was open. Two hundred GIs were soon racing across the snowdrift-lined tarmac in 30-degree weather, laughing and shivering in our short-sleeved khakis.

I found a phone booth, and within seconds I heard Linda's "Hello" in San Francisco. We both talked at once. She said that she had had a call earlier in the day from someone who only identified himself as a guy who "had bought Lee a beer in Long Binh" and who had said I should be on one of the next planes. She had not left the phone since. I told her I should be at Travis Air Force Base around midnight.

With so much to say to each other, we managed only a fragmented dialog: "It's cold as hell here after the jungle," "I'm leaving Reveilee with Susan," "See you in six hours," "I'll be there."

I ended the call by saying, "It's over, Honey. I'm coming home."

Much later Linda would tell me that after she hung up, she "cried a year's worth with happiness and relief."

Halfway to San Francisco, I finished Puzo's story about men who kill for money and power instead of for duty and patriotism. I closed the pages and, in the finest Infantry tradition, dozed off. The screech of tires on the runway and the simultaneous shouts of jubilation jolted me awake.

The midnight darkness shrouded the Travis terminal as the long line of passengers snaked from the plane to the main building. No bands played; no one made speeches. Only one person met the flight. Standing alone at the gate, Linda was the most beautiful woman at Travis that night by default; however, no one in the world could have rivaled her beauty at that moment.

Riding into San Francisco in a taxi whose driver Linda had coerced into making the 80-mile round trip, we stumbled over our own words. I was exhilarated but exhausted; Linda was excited but anxious.

When we arrived at the apartment, Linda led me to the bedroom. She reached into the bassinet and handed me a frilly white bundle topped with a pink hair bow. "Lee," she said, "meet your daughter, Reveilee."

Reveilee was not at all disturbed by her middle-of-the-night introduction to her father. As her eyes focused, she reached out, grabbing the colorful rows of ribbons on my chest. I was home.

POST-JOURNAL

Time passed quickly after my return home. For several years, I anticipated receiving orders for a second tour in Vietnam; however, the continued reduction of US combat forces and the increased turn-over of the war to the ARVNs drastically decreased the requirements for Infantrymen.

The Army continued to provide its promised fun, travel, and adventure. Linda and I moved frequently and adjusted fairly well to the peacetime Army. In 1972 our second daughter, Meridith, was born with her father present at the hospital rather than 11,000 miles away in the jungle.

For awhile after my return from the war, I had problems with those who did not go to Vietnam. I resented their shirking of duty and their emphasis on personal comforts. I no longer feel that way.

Those who did not go to Vietnam simply missed the greatest adventure of our age. They missed the opportunity to truly learn about themselves and what they are really made of. They missed a chance to live intensely— as intensely as ever in their lives.

We do not need to glorify war. Yet war can be glorious. Those who have not been there can never realize the exhilaration of combat, the satisfaction of walking the battlefield and counting the bodies of the enemy dead, nor the greatest pleasure of all—the camaraderie of serving with fellow American soldiers.

A non-Viet vet will never know the thrill of returning from the war to a beautiful wife and holding a never-before-seen daughter.

The non-vet will never know how you can live a lifetime in a two-minute fire fight or on a six-day R&R.

The passing of more than a decade since the war has finally brought some of the recognition so justly deserved by the Vietnam veterans. Memorials have been dedicated, speeches made, and parades marched. All over our country, patriotism is once again raising its red, white, and blue head. It seems that many of my generation who protested, questioned, and avoided the war are now reexamining their former beliefs and, more importantly, themselves.

On Veteran's Day, 1984, over 150,000 citizens, including the President, gathered for the formal dedication of the Vietnam Veterans Memorial in Washington, D.C. A few weeks before, I had made my first trek to the monument. I am glad I did not share that emotional time with a crowd.

Walking down to the south end of the Mall I felt no presentiments nor even pride in the monument itself. A feeling of obligation was my only motivation for the visit.

It was a cool, cloudy day with occasional misting rain. Autumn leaves blowing in the wind covered the pathway.

I studied the memorial at a distance and tried to get an overall feel for its panels with the 58,000 names of the dead and missing. I felt nothing. I was unimpressed and wondered about all the notoriety it had received.

Few people were at the memorial that day and the only sound was the echo of footsteps.

To achieve a better perspective, I started pacing off the

thirteen panels containing the names of the more than 8,500 killed during my year's tour. The impact began to hit home.

It was not, however, until I took a closer look and found names of friends and fellow soldiers that the memorial became very personal.

The polished black marble of the memorial is mirrorlike in appearance. As I looked into it, I saw my reflection as well as the names. As I read and touched the inscriptions, the wall became a screen, and images I thought I did not recall, or had done my best not to, were vivid and clear. The sights, sounds, and emotions of every day my fellow soldiers died were as intense as if happening yesterday— or today.

At each panel, I paused and stared at the names in my own reflection. Why them and not me? I looked for my own name and was relieved and perhaps a bit ashamed it was not etched alongside my comrades'.

The first name I found was Delmer Reed, a high school friend who was killed before I went to Vietnam. As I traced his name, I finally knew how to say a long-promised good-bye.

I then found the name of Dave Smith. Dave had been a close friend during college. In Ranger school we had shared even more. One does not make many friends who will allow icy feet next to their body under their field jacket to prevent frostbite or who will share their last candy bar on a 12-day patrol. Dave was dead for nearly a month before I found out. I had not shed a tear for him until I touched his name on the wall.

Then I came to the name that hurt the worst, William F. Little III, my best friend in Vietnam, whom even the enemy respected as a brave soldier.

I found other names: Larry Morford, the professional

stage dancer and the best point man I ever had; Skip Boch-
nevetch, the good-hearted, sensitive lieutenant who joined
Bravo just before I gave up command; Robert Vaughn, the
Tennessee soldier who died in my arms.

There were other names I intended to find. Those were
enough for one visit.

I stayed until darkness surrounded the memorial, revis-
iting the names again and again.

The memorial and memories stayed on my mind for
days afterward, convincing me finally that I had to write
about my experiences in the war. It was time for my second tour in Vietnam—through the pages of my journal and
through the memories that do not fade.

ABOUT THE AUTHOR

Michael Lee Lanning was born in Sweetwater, Texas, and is a graduate of Texas A&M University with a Bachelor of Science in Education. He also holds a Master of Science in Journalism from East Texas State University.

Lanning entered the United States Army in 1968. He is a career officer and has served throughout the United States as well as in Europe and Vietnam. Past assignments include infantry, armor, airborne, and Ranger assignments as platoon leader, company commander, and battalion executive officer. He is presently assigned to the American Forces Information Service in Alexandria, VA, after being transferred from Fort Lewis, Washington, where he was the I Corps and Fort Lewis Public Affairs Officer.

Lieutenant Colonel Lanning is Ranger qualified, is a senior parachutist, and has been awarded the Combat Infantryman Badge, the Bronze Star for Valor with two oak leaf clusters, the Meritorious Service Medal with two oak leaf clusters, the Air Medal, the Army Commendation Medal, and other U.S. and foreign decorations.

He is married and has two teenage daughters. The Lannings now consider the Pacific Northwest home.